Not Your Momma's Feminism
INTRODUCTION TO WOMEN'S & GENDER STUDIES

Courtney Jarrett

Kendall Hunt
publishing company

CONTENTS

ACKNOWLEDGEMENTS

First, a huge thanks to the love of my life, Jayson Jarrett. He was a tremendous help during this whole process. He supports and loves me unconditionally.

A huge shout-out to my Double A Batteries, my A Team—Alexander & Abel. They make every day great and I'm so lucky to be their mom.

Thanks also to my Sturgeon family and my Jarrett family. I wouldn't be the woman I am today if it weren't for all of you.

In addition, a huge thanks to my co-workers, Larry Markle & Sharon Harper. They put up with my nonsense every day and make it fun to go to work.

Finally, this book is for my BSU WGS colleagues and all of my WGS students—past, present, and future. I never dreamed I'd get to teach and write about my passions, but you all make it possible.

Thank you all from the bottom of my heart!

INTRODUCTION

Not Your Momma's Feminism: Introduction to Women's & Gender Studies is a textbook designed primarily for use in the introductory course in the field of Women's & Gender Studies (WGS) with the intent of providing both a skills- and concept-based foundation in the field. The text is driven by a single key question: "What are the ways of thinking, seeing, and knowing that characterize our field & the importance of those in feminism?" Through extensive review of the published literature, conversations with several Ball State Women's & Gender Studies faculty, and my own informal research and assessment of student learning needs, I have identified several critical concepts for Women's & Gender Studies:

> History of feminism
>
> Privilege & Oppression
>
> Pop Culture & Media
>
> Body Image & Sexuality
>
> Reproductive Justice
>
> Family identities
>
> Definitions of Work
>
> Religion and Spirituality
>
> Intersectionality & Feminism in the Future

This textbook aims to introduce students to how these concepts provide a feminist lens across the disciplines and outside the classroom.

Distinctive Characteristics of This Book

I decided to create this textbook to create a more focused look at the topics I want to cover in my introductory to women's and gender studies classes. Readers of this text will see the same format for each chapter and find accessible writing and definitions in which they can learn and explore with throughout the semester. This book is specifically focused on feminist issues in the United States, but other international feminist ideas will be included where necessary.

My hope is that students who read this text will discover the key concepts and ways of thinking throughout each chapter, that they can, in turn, use to develop a deeper understanding and to approach the material like feminist scholars do, in an interdisciplinary fashion. With this format, students continually learn and gain more knowledge on how the concepts are utilized across multiple contexts, thus supporting their understanding in more applicable ways. Additionally, the chapters will have learning activities, feminist profiles, and other sidebars to further illustrate the main concepts. These additional learning spaces should help students move more quickly past the common misconceptions that keep students from progressing in their understanding of Women's & Gender Studies.

In *Not Your Momma's Feminism: Introduction to Women's & Gender Studies*, it is my assumption that learning will be done most effectively if students understand the course goals, the pedagogical approach, and the potential roadblocks to understanding right from the beginning. The work happening by the instructor and the work happening by students should not be independent, but part of the larger classroom dynamic, in the teaching and learning conversation itself, happening in and about the content, as part of the work of the classroom. Students will know from the beginning of the course what to expect and instructors can facilitate mindful, co-learning conversations to create a classroom community.

Features

Not Your Momma's Feminism: Introduction to Women's & Gender Studies is organized strategically and conceptually, with as much historical information included to set the scene. The main concepts are introduced at a broad level as the key ideas of the chapter, while ensuing chapter sections add levels of detail and complexity. Each chapter will be set up in the following way:

Opening: The opening engages readers in the topic—typically these are drawn from historical, cultural, biological, and/or current events topics.

Main Topic Discussion: To further develop students' understanding of the key idea, each chapter includes a discussion about a group of three main topics. Students will develop a multifaceted, nuanced, and complex understanding of the main topics through this part of each chapter.

Breakout Boxes and Related Concepts: More specificity is offered by one breakout box in each chapter that highlights real-life, related concepts. These concepts may also include other descriptive terminology and definitions that help students see how the main topics are illustrated by related terms.

Discussion Questions: Consistent with the historical feminist pedagogies of Women's & Gender Studies classrooms that focus on collaboration, interconnectedness, and creating a community of learners (Blake & Ooten, 2008; Brown, 1992; hooks, 2000; Shrewsbury, 1993), this book provides discussion questions for each chapter.

Additional Readings and References: Each chapter includes an additional reading along with a list of suggested readings. The references for each chapter are combined with suggested readings. Because the text is intended to serve as a wide-spanning introduction to main feminist concepts and not a reader, I have provided a list of optional, relevant readings that faculty can use to continue students' learning on the main topics. In this way, the book can be a part of a customized course in which the faculty can structure the curriculum around textbook, and then incorporate primary documents, essays, or online materials for a deeper learning experience that reflect learning goals and area of expertise for individual faculty members.

Goals of the Book

My goals for this book have been to provide a text that encourages student learning in introductory Women's & Gender Studies courses, based on what I have learned throughout my of teaching in the field as well as current feminist thinking in and out of higher education. I hope that this text will speak to students where they are in relation to feminism. I also hope that the information included in this book will spark students into productive dialogue about women's studies issues and encourage them to develop personal connections with feminism in their daily lives.

Ultimately, my intent is to help students learn the basic tenets of women's studies and feminism; then to be able to apply them to new subjects and the real world. I have tried to incorporate as much up-to-date data and research as possible, along with current news/issues. The tone underscores that conversations about sex and gender (and plenty of other issues within feminism) are unanswered, continuing, and divisive. The textbook provides historical context for a feminist perspective about these important issues.

While each of the critical concepts has its own chapter, which in one sense suggests their distinction and ability to be separated, they are absolutely interconnected. I strive to make those connections explicit within each chapter, which sometimes means returning to the same topic across chapters and emphasizing different parts of it. For example, I have attempted to include an intersectional viewpoint and intersectional exploration *all the way through* the book, focusing on the connectedness of systems of privilege and oppression as part of an intersectional analysis within topics and themes.

Adapting the Text to Your Class

While individual classes and pedagogical methods may vary, the critical concepts I have included are central to the learning outcomes of a large number of Women's & Gender Studies programs nationally (Berger & Radeloff, 2011; Levin, 2007). With those ideas in mind, using a text like this one can be helpful in making your learning outcomes clear and specific, while also making assessment easier along the way.

An approach to using this book in an introductory WGS course would be to spread the reading of the 10 chapters across the course of the entire semester, using additional articles, readings, or films in between. This approach would allow for in-depth time with each critical concept before moving on to the next. It also allows faculty to build in their own areas of expertise and current events.

More specifically, I wrote this text from the mindset of teaching an Introduction to Women's & Gender Studies solely online for the last few years. Based on my research in online learning, I wanted to create a book that would make the transition from on campus to online learning seamless (Chick & Hassel, 2009; Crawley et al., 2008; Kirkup, et al., 2010). I hope that faculty teaching WGS online will agree.

Faculty can find more materials to develop their course using *Not Your Momma's Feminism: Introduction to Women's & Gender Studies* at the textbook website (link). Materials accessible online include:

Sample syllabi

Additional suggested readings

Assignment examples

Additionally, my contact information is also available on the textbook's website. I'd love to receive feedback from other WGS faculty on their use of the book. Let's connect!

References

Berger, T., & Radeloff, C. (2011). *Transforming scholarship: Why women's and gender studies students are changing themselves and the world*. New York: Routledge.

Blake, H., & Ooten, M. (2008). "Bridging the divide: Connecting feminist histories and activism in the classroom." *Radical History Review,* 102, 63–72. Web.

Brown, J. (1992).Theory or practice—What exactly is feminist pedagogy? *The Journal of General Education*, 41, 51–63. Retrieved June 1, 2015, from http://www.jstor.org/stable/27797152

Chick, N., & Hassel, H. (2009). "Don't hate me because I'm virtual: Feminist pedagogy in the online classroom." *Feminist Teacher,* 19.3, 195–215. Print.

Crawley, S., Lewis, J. & Mayberry, M.(2008). "Introduction: Feminist pedagogies in action: Teaching beyond disciplines." *Feminist Teacher,* 19.1, 1–12. Web.

hooks, b. (2000). *Feminism is for everybody: Passionate politics.* Cambridge, MA: South End Press.

Kirkup, G., Schmitz, S., Kotkamp, E., Rommes, E., & Hiltunen, A.-M. (2010). "Towards a feminist manifesto for e-learning: Principles to inform practices." In S. Booth, S. Goodman, & G. Kirkup (Eds), *Gender issues in learning and working with information technology: Social constructs and cultural contexts.* Hershey, PA: Information Science Reference.

Levin, A. K. (2007). "Questions for a new century: Women's studies and integrative learning." College Park, MD: National Women's Studies Association.

Shrewsbury, C. (1993). "What is feminist pedagogy?" *Women's Studies Quarterly, 3,* 8–16.

CHAPTER 1

What Is Women's & Gender Studies?

Women's & Gender Studies has its beginnings in the civil rights & women's movements of the 1960s and 1970s. In its early years, faculty and researchers in the field specifically asked, "Where are the women?" That question may seem too simple today, but, during that time period, few scholars considered gender as a lens of analysis. The voices of women were not represented on campus or in any curriculum.

Today, Women's & Gender Studies goes beyond just looking for women. The field's examination of identity, power, and privilege go far beyond the idea of "woman." Drawing on the feminist scholarship of women of color from all over the world, Women's & Gender Studies has made theoretical statements and critical practices of intersectionality, which examines how categories of identity (e.g., sexuality, race, class, gender, age, and ability) and structures of inequality are connected. The field has also focused on transnationalism, which studies cultures, organizations, and relationships that are formed as a result of the flows of people and resources geographically. These two main topics are the foundations of the discipline.

Eras in Feminist History

We could spend hours debating who started feminism. There have been books written just about that subject. For this book, the first person to specifically influence feminism in the United States is Mary Wollstonecraft (1792) and her *Vindication of the Rights of Woman*, published in her native England. Her text is one of the first in the Anglo-American tradition that attempts to theorize the position of women within the dominant political and social discourses of its moment. Other authors came before who brought up concerns about women's issues, including Sor Juana Ines de la Cruz (Paz, 1988). Yet, Wollstonecraft's work is significant as a starting point because many other writers were influenced by her work.

The next major era for feminism in the United States is the time period where women's suffrage was at the forefront. Prior to this, the demand for female enfranchisement in politics and other areas, such as education, dominated much of the thinking about women, even by those who thought that focusing on suffrage as the center of the women's movement was wrong. Nancy Cott (1987) emphasized the difference between modern feminism and its past history, particularly the fight for suffrage. She placed the turning point as the time period before and after women obtained the vote, which can be defined as the first wave of the women's movement. She made the case that the beginning women's movement was primarily about woman as a total person. Then, in the early 1900s, the suffrage cause brought feminist concerns to the front in our cultural dialogue. The movement transformed into one above all interested in social differentiation, including individuality and diversity. New questions asked more about women as a social construct. These ideas included gender identity and relationships within and between genders. This symbolized a political shift from an ideological position at ease with the right, to one more radically related to the left.

Kent (1993) wrote that the rise of patriarchy was responsible for the diminished profile of feminism in the inter-war years all over the world. Some feminist scholarship shifted away from the need to establish the origins of family and toward analyzing the process of patriarchy (Stocking, 1995). In the immediate post-World War II period, Simone de Beauvoir stood in opposition to an image of the homemaker. She provided an existentialist dimension to feminism with the publication of *The Second Sex* (Beauvoir, 1949). As the title implies, the starting point is the implicit inferiority of women.

De Beauvoir thought that a woman defines herself through the way in which she makes something of what the world makes of her (Moi, 1999). Therefore, woman must regain her own definitions, to escape her defined role as "other" (Bergoffen, 1997). In her examination of myth, she appeared as one who does not accept any special privileges for women. Ironically, feminist philosophers have had to extract de Beauvoir from out of the shadow of Jean-Paul Sartre to fully appreciate her contributions (Sullivan, 2000). De Beauvoir brought forth new ideas that were later expanded in the United States.

Betty Friedan (1963) and *The Feminine Mystique* next influenced American feminism, and women all over the world. This is the text that most historians identify as starting the second wave of the women's movement. For her 15th college reunion in 1957, Friedan conducted a survey of Smith College graduates, focusing on their education, their subsequent experiences, and satisfaction with their current lives. She started publishing articles about what she called "the problem with no name" and got passionate responses from many homemakers grateful that they were not alone in experiencing this problem.

The reappearance of feminist activism in the late 1960s was complemented by new debates over what might be considered feminine issues, such as concerns for the earth, spirituality, and environmental activism. This created an atmosphere favorable to restarting the study of mothering as a central focus on women and their roles in their societies. Some saw this as a denial of determinism (French, 1985; Rich, 1976b). For socialist feminists, patriarchy held the assets of capitalism (Reed, 1975). The activism of the second wave allowed women to focus on different aspects of feminism, instead of fighting for one main cause as the first wave did.

The theory written after 1963 is not so much defined by historical events or dates of publication, but really by shifts in the discourse and concerns that arose from feminist theory. The shifts are gradual. They evolve over many years through the impact of both conversations and challenges. In a timeline format, the changes can roughly be recognized between 1975 and 1985 (Boxer, 1982).

The period from 1963 to 1975 showed feminist theory as part of the activism of the women's movement. Contrastingly, during the period from 1975 to 1985, writing about feminist theory was produced by academic women that associated with the new field of women's studies. This new field brought forth many new concepts and ideas (Conway, Bourque, & Scott, 1989; Ginsberg, 2008).

Before this time, feminists worked primarily from grassroots organizations. The shift gradually moved into academia. Women's studies was first conceived academically apart from other departments in the late 1970s. It gained momentum as the second wave of feminism gained political influence in the academy through student and faculty activism. As an academic discipline, it was modeled on the American studies and ethnic studies programs that had arisen before it (Ginsberg, 2008).

In 1977, a decade after the first women's studies course appeared across the United States, the National Women's Studies Association (NWSA) was founded to promote and sustain "the educational strategy of a breakthrough in consciousness and knowledge" that would "transform" individuals, institutions, relationships, and, ultimately the whole society (NWSA, 1977, pp. 6–8). Insisting that the academic is political and the cognitive is affective, the NWSA's constitution clearly reflected the influence of the women's liberation movement on women's studies. Research and teaching at all educational levels and in all academic and community settings would be not only about but for all women, guided by "a vision of a world free not only from sexism, but also racism, classism, age-ism, heterosexual bias-from all the ideologies and institutions that have consciously or unconsciously oppressed and exploited some for the advantage of others" (pp. 6–8). Women's studies challenged its practitioners to think beyond the boundaries of traditional sex roles, of traditional disciplines, and of established institutions. By breaking down the divisions that limit perceptions and deny opportunities and by revising pedagogical processes as well as courses and curricula, this educational reform has itself become a social environment.

Forty years after the first women's studies program was established, there are more than 900 programs in the United States, boasting well over 10,000 courses and an enrollment larger than that of any other interdisciplinary field (NWSA, n.d.). There are around 40 scholarly journals (Association of College & Research Libraries, n.d.) as well as countless newsletters. There are numerous community groups and centers, along with conferences and programs all over the world (Banaszak, 2005).

The literature about women's studies as a field in higher education has many aspects: its history (Kennedy & Beins, 2005), political issues (Martinez-Alemán & Renn, 2002), theories (Bowles & Duelli-Klein, 1983), and structures (DiGeorgio-Lutz, 2002). Because of the nature of women's studies itself, these categories often overlap, and some literature will be mentioned more than once. Much of the writing done about women's studies first appeared in periodicals, but now books and monographs are more prevalent and are included in this review.

History of Women's Studies

Women's studies first appeared in the last half of the 1960s when women faculty in higher education, stronger in number than ever before, began to create new courses that would facilitate more reflection on female experiences and feminist aspirations (Evans, 1980). Supported and sometimes led by feminist students, staff, or community women, these innovators were often political activists who sought to understand and to confront the sexism they had experienced in movements for the liberation of other oppressed groups. The free-university movements and the civil rights movement inspired their efforts at organization and course development (Rossi & Calderwood, 1973). A "passion for women's history" represented "more than just a desire for female heritage" (Trecker, 1971, p. 86). It also was a "search for ways in which a successful female revolution might be constructed" (p. 86).

In the mid-1970s, in one of the first essays to discuss the neglect and distortion of women in university courses and curricula, Sheila Tobias called for a new program of "Female Studies" at Cornell University, justifying her stand with an analogy to Black studies. At the same time, courses on women appeared at a number of universities, including a program of five at San Diego State. That fall, *Female Studies I* was published. It was the first of a 10-volume series through which practitioners of the new classes shared their syllabi, reading lists, and experiences. Compiled by Tobias (1970), it featured outlines of 16 courses taught or proposed during 1969 and 1970, as well as a 10-course curriculum from San Diego State, which in September 1970 became the first officially established integrated women's studies program in the nation. In December, *Female Studies II* was published. It was an anthology of 66 course outlines and bibliographies collected by the Commission on the Status of Women of the Modern Language Association and edited by Florence Howe (1970). With Howe's leadership, the commission had begun to function as a "clearinghouse" for information in the new field (Chamberlain, 1988).

The rapid growth of women's studies reflected the widely shared perception that changing what and how women (and men) study about women could and would affect the way women live. It offered a new opportunity for students and scholars to redefine themselves and their experiences around the world. It also allowed for discussion about whether there was a definitive separation between the women's movement and academia. Victoria Schuck (1974) perceived three rounds in the history of the women's movement, of which only the third posed a challenge to academia. Contemporary feminism, through women's studies, "aimed at destroying the sexual stereotypes bequeathed by nineteenth-century male academics" (pp. 413–414).

To Florence Howe (2000), women's studies represented a third phase in American women's struggle for education. First, in the early and mid-nineteenth century, proponents of improving female education accepted cultural assumptions about women's nature and demanded a higher education appropriate to woman's role as a moral teacher. Next, in the late nineteenth century, they began to stress the identity of male and female intellectual capacities and to call for access to the standard courses. Only in the third phase did they challenge the male hegemony over the content of college courses and the substance of knowledge itself.

The double purpose of women's studies—to expose and redress the oppression of women—was reflected in the widespread attempts to restructure the classroom experience of students and faculty. Circular arrangement of chairs, periodic small group sessions, use of first names for instructors as well as students, assignments that required journal keeping, reflection papers, cooperative projects, and collective modes of teaching with student participation all sought to transfer to women's studies the contemporary feminist criticism of authority and the validation of every woman's experience. These techniques borrowed from the women's movement also were designed to combat the institutional hierarchy and professional exclusiveness that had been used to shut out women (Rossi & Calderwood, 1973). Indeed, collaboration in teaching and program governance has been a vital contribution of the women's movement to educational innovation.

The responsibility of women's studies to the larger feminist community also became a debated issue in the early years. Bitter conflict developed between factions who weighed differently the political and academic aims of the campus movement. White, middle-class, heterosexual feminists were attacked for attempting to separate women's studies from the radical women's movement (Forfreedom, 1974).

More fearful that women's studies would be destroyed by internal conflict if not by external opposition, Catharine Stimpson (1973) analyzed the sources of the inner turmoil. She identified the problems as women's acceptance of cultural stereotypes of femininity and their consequent distrust of women in power, as well as ideological conflict among five categories of women's studies practitioners: "pioneers" who had taught about women before women's studies, "ideologues" who had come to women's studies through feminism, "radicals" who had been politicized, "latecomers" who became interested after women's studies began, and "bandwagoners" who found women's studies useful for their careers. Stimpson saw hope for survival in the "buoyancy that comes from sensing that to work for women's studies is to belong to a historical tide" (p. 314).

Adrienne Rich (1976a) addressed the issue of women's studies' possible co-optation within the university system. She found that, despite its tenuous hold on the university, women's studies continued to be a place where students may claim an education, demand to be taken seriously, and are taught what they really need to know to live as women in the world. Rich envisioned a university transformed by feminist principles, with competition replaced by cooperation, fragmentation by wholeness, and even the line between campus and community shaded. It was a goal that depended on women learning to use their power constructively as an agent of change. Rich wanted students to claim their knowledge and use it in their everyday life, not just keep it in the classroom.

With the increasing integration of women's studies in to the educational establishment, a new constituency of students entered the classroom. Unlike the students of the early 1970s, they were less likely to identify themselves as feminist, or sometimes to even understand such basic concepts as sexism and feminism. Susan Snaider Lanser (1977) was startled to find her students not only apolitical but still suffering the burden of traditional sex-role expectations.

Consciousness raising, (hooks, 2000) borrowed from women's liberation to become a teaching device in early women's studies classroom, took place less often. Cheri Register (1979) identified four stages in both the classroom process and the development of women's studies and the women's movement. Moving from compensating, to criticizing, to collecting and constructing, and finally to conceptualizing anew, students and teacher would pass through despair to emerge with a new and positive basis for understanding and living with a feminist perspective.

New perceptions of women's studies were accompanied by new structures. To facilitate communication among practitioners and to enhance the development of scholarship and teaching, the National Women's Studies Association was founded in San Francisco in 1977. After careful preparation, it was designed to express both professional and feminist values. A complicated structure allowed for equitable representation of various constituencies—regional groups, students, staff, elementary and secondary teachers, lesbians, Third-World women, community women, etc. The intent was to counter the tendency toward exclusiveness and exclusion that characterizes many other professional organizations. Sliding registration fees for conventions provided funds to equalize transportation costs for residents of nearby and distant places. Widespread participation would be encouraged by eliminating keynote speakers (Greene, 1976).

In fulfillment of the commitment of women's studies to be inclusive of all women and all women's concerns, programs for the NWSA conferences in the late 1970s and early 1980s included hundreds of sessions. Even with all this diversity, women's studies faced challenges from within. The most extensive debates addressed the relationship of women's studies to the feminist movement and the integration of activist and academic goals, inside as well as outside the classroom. Although these debates served to stimulate and to enrich women's studies, they also provided a source of potential conflict among constituent groups and required that the NWSA perform a delicate balancing act (Davis & Frech, 1981). These sorts of debates continue at the NWSA conference even today.

Conviction remained strong that women's studies must be explicitly political, consciously an academic arm of women's liberation, and actively part of a larger social movement that envisions the transformation of society (Gordon, 1975). Unlike other academic pursuits, it must not separate theory from practice. Since feminism made women's studies possible, women's studies must in turn make feminism possible. Today's women's studies practitioners and programs enter into innumerable community activities in many ways: teachers are taking women's studies into prisons (Bergeron, Lempert, & Linker, 2005), studying the socialization of girls (Lipkin, 2009), and examining feminist mothering (O'Reilly, 2008).

Challenges from lesbians and women of color to make women's studies truly inclusive continued. Much of the writing from this period directed the movement toward becoming more mainstream (Code, 2003). Others believed that women's studies should be integrated into general education by redefinition and expansion of basic required courses rather than offered as an alternative general education curriculum (Lougee, 1980). Some feminist educators saw this approach as a threat to the survival of separate women's studies courses or questioned whether content could be abstracted from a feminist framework or taught by faculty at large without sacrificing essential goals. Others found classroom dynamics transformed by the presence of students seeking mainly to fulfill degree requirements (Ness & Brooks, 1980).

Christine Garside Allen (1975) argued that women's studies should combine introductory and advanced-level interdisciplinary courses with intermediate course work in the disciplines. Greta Hoffman Nemiroff (1978) analyzed the difficulties and value of interdisciplinary work. Because women's studies challenged the discipline-based categories in which the structure and economy of most universities are grounded, she felt it could not be easily assimilated within the academy. Practitioners have advanced women's studies development by systematic efforts to examine and expand its interactions with other disciplines.

Being an interdisciplinary program or department is important to women's studies in academia. Gloria Bowles said, "Perhaps one day the Renaissance man will be replaced by the interdisciplinary woman" (as cited in Bowles & Duelli-Klein, 1983, p. 40). Although Bowles has pioneered a course on theories of women's studies, she cautioned against the potential danger of what Mary Daly (1985) called "methodolatry" (p. 11). Instead of artificially creating a system of ideas, women's studies instructors should locate their questions in the women's movement and obtain techniques suitable to women's survival needs.

It is specifically this feminist endeavor to improve women's lives that Bowles and Duelli-Klein (1983) considered important to the improvement of women's studies' methodology. The way to avoid sexist methods such as context stripping is to ground theory in feminist action research. Researchers must abandon the pretext of value-free objectivity for conscious subjectivity more appropriate to studies explicitly intended to be for as well as about women.

Duelli-Klein's examination of feminist methodology draws on Marcia Westkott's (1979) analysis of how sexist content, method, and purposes influence representations of women. Westkott recommended other ways of thinking about reality that link subject and object, rather than separating them. Feminist thought typically uses methods of analyzing self and other, person and society, consciousness and activity, past and future, and knowledge and practice. It is open and compelling, instead of closed and controlling. It reinforces understanding with active dedication to improve the condition of women. Westkott finds that these feminist critiques of content, method, and purpose are the building blocks of women's studies theory (1979).

The feminist theory of the 1990s includes discussions that evolved from the women that gathered in Beijing for the fourth United Nations Conference on Women. These women attempted to articulate a common global agenda for change in women's lives. In September 1995, the group at Beijing released a declaration that included this passage:

> *We reaffirm our commitment to: The equal rights and inherent human dignity of women and men and other purposes and principles enshrined in the Charter of the United Nations, to the Universal Declaration of Human Rights and other international human rights instruments, in particular the Convention on the Elimination of All Forms of Discrimination against Women and the Convention on the Rights of the Child, as well as the Declaration on the Elimination of Violence against Women and the Declaration on the Right to Development. (United Nations, 1995, para. 8)*

There were 38 specific points made in the declaration, but the focus on the rights of every person is really inherent to feminism and the theories behind it. By specifically referencing discrimination, they emphasized that not everyone is equal worldwide and that should be a major part of ensuring everyone's human rights.

The 1990s to the present mark the era commonly associated with the third wave of the feminist movement. Third-wave feminism seeks to challenge or avoid what it deems as the weaknesses to the second wave's definitions of femininity, which often assumed a universal female identity and over-emphasized experiences of upper middle class white women. Third-wave theory usually incorporates many elements of feminism including queer theory, transgender politics, anti-racism, womanism, post-colonial theory, critical theory, postmodernism, and ecofeminism (Heywood & Drake, 1997).

Also considered part of the third wave is a celebration of sexuality as a positive aspect of life, with broader definitions of what sex means and what oppression and empowerment may mean in regards to sex. This includes reconsiderations of the second-wave oppositions to pornography and sex work. Many proponents of the third wave of feminism challenge existing beliefs that participants in pornography and sex work cannot be empowered (Johnson, 2002).

Advocates of third-wave feminism believe that it allows women to define feminism by incorporating their own identities into the belief system of what feminism is and what it can become. In their introduction to the idea of third-wave feminism in *Manifesta*, authors Jennifer Baumgardner and Amy Richards (2000) suggested that feminism can change with every generation and individual:

> *The fact that feminism is no longer limited to arenas where we expect to see it—NOW, Ms., women's studies, and redsuited Congresswomen—perhaps means that young women today have really reaped what feminism has sown. Raised after Title IX and "William Wants a Doll," young women emerged from college or high school or two years of marriage or their first job and began challenging some of the received wisdom of the past ten or twenty years of feminism. We're not doing feminism the same way that the seventies feminists did it; being liberated doesn't mean copying what came before but finding one's own way—a way that is genuine to one's own generation. (p. 47)*

Third-wave feminism began as a response to alleged failures of the second wave and also as a response to the backlash against initiatives and movements created by the second wave. Feminist leaders rooted in the second wave such as bell hooks, Audre Lorde, Maxine Hong Kingston, and many other feminists of color, sought to negotiate a space within feminist thought for consideration of subjects related to race (Gillis, Howie, & Munford, 2007).

Some third-wave feminists prefer not to call themselves feminists, as the word feminist can be misinterpreted as insensitive or elitist by critics. Others have kept but redefined the term. Third-wave feminism seeks to challenge any universal definition of femininity (Henry, 2003). Third-wave feminism deals with issues that seem to limit or oppress women, as well as other marginalized identities (Siegel, 1997). Consciousness raising activism and widespread education is often the first step that feminists take toward social change.

> *Consciousness among women is what caused this, and consciousness, one's ability to open their mind to the fact that male domination does affect the women of our generation, is what we need . . . The presence of feminism in our lives is taken for granted. For our generation, feminism is like fluoride. We scarcely notice we have it—it's simply in the water. (Baumgardner & Richards, 2000, p. 17)*

This body of work revolves around responses made to multiple challenges from within feminist culture as well as intellectual and global changes outside its borders. The internal critiques come from those who still feel excluded from feminism in academia, including women of color, poor and working-class women, women with disabilities, and older women. The external influences on feminism include lesbian, gay, bisexual, and transgender (GLBT) theories, reproductive technologies, postmodern works, and shifts in global power to name a few (Heywood & Drake, 1997). Feminist theorists have tried their best to delve into these changing landscapes with creativity and openness.

Breakout: The BSU WGS Program

History of the Ball State Women's and Gender Studies Program

The atmosphere was set for change in the 1970s at Ball State University. People were reading *The Feminine Mystique*, *Ms. Magazine*, and hearing about Roe v. Wade in the news. Things really got started for Women's Studies at Ball State University in the summer of 1971. The History Department sponsored a series of films and presentations, entitled, "Adam's Angry Rib: Women on the Move." Many of the speakers were prominent national feminists and large groups of people attended.

After one of these presentations, a group of people went out for conversation and drinks. The idea of creating a course in Women's Studies was discussed. Aware that there was a national trend toward programs and departments, this group felt that Ball State should be part of the movement. They made the decision to start the arduous paperwork process. The two people most influential women in this process were Sharon Seager and Betty Newcomb. They were aided in their efforts by Victor Lawhead, Dean of Undergraduate Programs, who offered his support during the process.

With this support and because of these individuals' hard work, the first Women's Studies class (ID 210) was taught in the Spring of 1972. ID was the title for the interdisciplinary aspects of the class, and it was team taught by Seager, Newcomb, and Marie Vogel. It was comprised of 60 students, a huge class compared to those is taught in Women's and Gender Studies today. No one had been trained in Women's Studies, not at Ball State, not anywhere. The instructors relied on helpful librarians for books, as well as guest lecturers from campus and the local community.

The movement continued with more speakers, such as Shirley Chisholm, and more classes. An informal Women's Studies Committee was formed in 1974. In 1975, Richard Burkhardt, the Dean of Faculties, gave the committee official status and asked them to create a program that would house a minor in Women's Studies.

Althea Stoeckel, a professor from the History Department, became the first chair of the Women's Studies Committee. The committee worked on getting more courses approved, and by 1977, there were 12 new courses being taught in several disciplines. Securing these approvals they shifted their focus to getting the minor approved, and that was accomplished in December 1980.

The decade of the 1980s led to several further changes, including the naming of a new chair of the Women's Studies Committee. In addition, a quarterly newsletter was published for started, published for a few years, and then discontinued. In lieu of a newsletter, *The Purple Sheet* began later in the 1980s. Publication was sporadic, having been stopped for a few years, but was later resumed so friends and alumni of the program could be updated to the news from the program. In 1986, Women's Studies received their first office space, in North Quad room 113/114. Moreover, in this decade, the committee was at long last given official program status, and underwent a title change, to become known as the Women's Studies Program. By the end of the decade (1988), Michael Stevenson was given the title of Director.

Not yet satisfied with the new program name, a larger discussion about what to title the program began in the 1980s. It was not until 1989 that this was resolved and the program was renamed Women and Gender Studies. Still, not everyone involved with the program was happy about the change and by 2001 the title reverted back to the Women's Studies program. A name change occurred again in 2009 when the program was renamed the Women's and Gender Studies program.

The 1990s was a time of continued growth for the program. Women's Studies originally gained more room in North Quad for the expanding program, but by 1999, the program moved to its current space, Burkhardt Building 108. Throughout this decade, the program continued its outreach and activism activities. Over time, the program has sponsored a Lunchtime Book Discussion Series, the Winterfest Information Fair, and Women's Week. The Women's Studies program is a member of the National Women's Studies Association, and has had a collaborative, work relationship with several community agencies. Some of these include the American Association of University Women, A Better Way, League of Women Voters, Ball Memorial Hospital, Planned Parenthood, Habitat for Humanity, and the National Organization for Women.

From 1994 until 2009, the Director of the program was Dr. Kim Jones-Owen. She was instrumental in moving the program forward with classes designated specifically as Women's Studies classes, as well as the new major in Women's Studies. In 2005, the very first major in Women's Studies graduated, and many more have followed. Julee Rosser was named the Acting Director of the program in 2009. The Dean of the College of Science and Humanities appointed a new Director, Dr. Lisa Pellerin, from Sociology. She has been the Director from the summer of 2009 to the present day (2015).

Feminist Activism

Feminist activism not only focuses on women's issues but has spread throughout many other areas of political and social action including (but not limited to): environmental topics, body politics, feminist art, identity issues, reproductive rights, gender issues, animal rights, GLBT rights, and minority civil liberties. These forms of activism can include letter writing, boycotting, protesting, the visual arts, bodily demonstrations, education, and leafleting. Currently, the focus of feminism has shifted to include a viewpoint and passion for equality—pinpointing unjust systems and powers around the world that have an impact on all types of lives. Feminist activism investigates the intersections of social, political, and cultural histories, their consequences, and commits time and energy to the freedom of all people from inequalities.

Merely learning or being a student of women's and gender studies can be seen as activism in it of itself, just look at what the Ball State WGS program has been through in its history. There are also those that consider women's studies to be an academic field, separate from the feminist movement. You can incorporate activism into education, but you can also choose to focus on research. Feminism and Women's & Gender Studies are both all about choice.

Myths

Myth #1: All feminists are hairy lesbians and bra-burning radicals who hate men.

Fact: Being feminist has nothing to do with sexual orientation or man-hating. In addition, body hair or lack thereof has absolutely nothing to do with it either. Feminists come from all different backgrounds and cultures to support equality.

Myth #2: Feminism has made women equal now, so we don't need the women's movement anymore.

Fact: Women are still behind in many different ways; they continue to be paid less on average than men, many jobs are not friendly to mothers, and women continue to be responsible for the majority of household work (men averaging 7 hours a week while women average 14 hours). The United States needs affordable child care options and paid family leave and the women's movement will continue to work on those issues, among many others.

Myth #3: Women can't be girly and be a feminist at the same time.

Fact: Feminism is fundamentally about giving women choices, not about finding new ways to limit their self-expression. People can choose to be girly (whatever that means to them), provided that they recognize that the choice to act in a traditionally feminine manner is just that—a choice. It is totally acceptable and even common within the feminist movement.

Myth #4: Feminism is really only for middle-class white women.

Fact: Feminism is historically a multicultural cause. Feminists today are a diverse group of women, men, and those with other identities who strive for an end to racism, sexism, ableism, classism, ageism, etc.

Myth #5: Feminism specifically liberates women at the expense of men.

Fact: Feminism doesn't just liberate women; it also liberates men by breaking down the standards that society has put in place for both women and men. Men are taught in this society to be macho, emotionless, and to never show weakness. These socially constructed patriarchal rules cause men to be socially confined. Feminism says that it's okay for men to show weakness, be followers, and to show their emotions. Women can show manly traits and be strong leaders. Feminism is all about equality for everyone.

Conclusion

So by now, you should have a small (or bigger) idea of what Women's & Gender Studies is. You should also be able to discuss the larger history of feminism, where the WGS field originated. The reading for this chapter is Adrienne Rich's "Claiming an Education." It encourages you as a student to take seriously your right to be taken seriously and invites you to understand the relationship between your personal biography and the wider forces in society that affect your life. Consider the history of the women's movement and the fight for women to receive higher education as you examine the reading.

Suggested Readings

Berger, M., Ed. (2006). *We don't need another wave: Dispatches from the next generation of feminists.* Emeryville, CA: Seal Press.

Freedman, E. (2002). *No turning back: The history of feminism and the future of women.* New York: Ballantine.

Henry, A. (2004). *Not my mother's sister: Generational conflict and third-wave feminism.* Bloomington: Indiana University Press.

Hernandez, D., & Rheman, B., Eds. (2002). *Colonize this! Young women of color on today's feminism.* New York: Avalon.

Siegel, D., & Baumgardner, J. (2007). *Sisterhood, interrupted: From radical women to girls gone Wild*. New York: Palgrave Macmillan.

Valenti, J. (2007). *Full frontal feminism: A young woman's guide to why feminism matters*. Emeryville, CA: Seal Press.

References

Allen, C. (1975). "Conceptual history as a methodology for women's studies." *McGill Journal of Education, 10*, 49–58.

Association of College & Research Libraries. (n.d.). *Core list of journals for Women's Studies*. Retrieved October 2, 2009 from http://libr.org/wss/projects/serial.html

Banaszak, L. (Ed.). (2005). *The U.S. women's movement in global perspective*. Lanham, MD: Rowman & Littlefield Publishers.

Baumgardner, J., & Richards, A. (2000). *Manifesta: Young women, feminism, and the future*. New York: Farrar, Straus and Giroux.

Beauvoir, S. (1949). *The second sex*. New York: Knopf.

Bergeron, S., Lempert, L., & Linker, M. (2005). "Negotiating the politics of space: Teaching women's studies in a women's prison." *NWSA Journal, 2*, 199–207.

Bergoffen, D. (1997). *The philosophy of Simone de Beauvoir: Gendered phenomenologies, erotic generosities*. Albany: State University of New York Press.

Bowles, G., & Duelli-Klein, R. (1983). *Theories of Women's Studies*. London: Routledge.

Boxer, M. (1982). *When women ask the questions: Creating women's studies in America*. Baltimore: Johns Hopkins University Press.

Chamberlain, M. K. (Ed.). (1988). *Women in academe: Progress and prospects*. New York: Russell Sage.

Code, L. (2003). *Encyclopedia of feminist theories*. New York: Routledge.

Conway, J. K., Bourque, S. C., & Scott, J. W. (1989). *Learning about women: Gender, politics and power*. Ann Arbor: University of Michigan Press.

Cott, N. (1987). *The grounding of modern feminism*. New Haven: Yale University Press.

Daly, M. (1985). *Beyond God the Father: Toward a philosophy of women's liberation*. Boston: Beacon Press.

Davis, B., & Frech, P. (1981) "Diversity, fragmentation, integration: The NWSA balancing act." *Women's Studies Quarterly, 9*, 33–35.

DiGeorgio-Lutz, J. (2002). *Women in higher education: Empowering change*. New York: Praeger Publishers.

Evans, S. (1980). *Personal politics: The roots of women's liberation in the civil rights*. New York: Random House, Inc.

Forfreedom, A. (1974). *Whither women's studies? Report on the West Coast Women's Studies Conference*. Sacramento, CA: Sacramento State University Press.

French, M. (1985). *Beyond power: On women, men, and morals*. New York: Summit Books.

Friedan, B. (1963). *The feminine mystique*. New York: Norton.

Gillis, S., Howie, G., & Munford, R. (2007). *Third wave feminism: A critical exploration*. London: Palgrave Macmillan.

Ginsberg, A. E. (2008). *The evolution of American women's studies: Reflections on triumphs, controversies, and change*. New York: Palgrave Macmillan.

Gordon, L. (1975). "A socialist view of Women's Studies: A reply to the editorial." *Signs: Journal of Women in Culture and Society, 1*, 559–566.

Greene, E. (1976). "The case for a national women's studies association." *Women's Studies Newsletter, 4,* 1–3.

Henry, A. (2003). *Not my mother's sister: Generational conflict and third-wave feminism.* Bloomington: Indiana University Press.

Heywood, L., & Drake, J. (1997). *Third wave agenda: Being feminist, doing feminism.* Minneapolis: University of Minnesota Press.

hooks, b. (2000). *Feminism is for everybody: Passionate politics.* Cambridge, MA: South End Press.

Howe, F. (1970). *Female studies II.* Pittsburgh, PA: Know.

Howe, F. (2000). *The politics of women's studies: Testimony from thirty founding mothers.* New York: Feminist Press.

Johnson, M. (Ed.) (2002). *Jane sexes it up: True confessions of feminist desire.* New York: Four Walls Eight Windows.

Kennedy, E. L. & Beins, A. (2005). *Women's studies for the future: Foundations, interrogations, politics.* Piscataway, NJ: Rutgers University Press.

Kent, S. K. (1993). *Making peace: The reconstruction of gender in interwar Britain.* Princeton, NJ: Princeton University Press.

Lipkin, E. (2009). *Girls' studies.* Berkeley, CA: Seal Studies.

Lougee, C. (1980). "Women, history, and the humanities: An argument in favor of the general studies curriculum." *Women's Studies Quarterly, 9,* 4–7.

Martinez-Alemán, A. M., & Renn, K. (2002). *Women in higher education: An encyclopedia.* Santa Barbara, CA: ABC-CLIO Press.

Moi, T. (1999). *What is a woman? and other essays.* New York: Oxford University Press.

National Women's Studies Association. (1977). "NWSA constitution preamble." *Women's Studies Newsletter, 5,* 6–8.

National Women's Studies Association. (n.d.) *NWSA/MS. Magazine guide to Women's & Gender Studies.* Retrieved August 28, 2009 from http://www.nwsa.org/research/theguide/index.php

Nemiroff, G. (1978). "Rationale for an interdisciplinary approach to women's studies." *Canadian Women's Studies, 1,* 60–68.

Ness, E., & Brooks, K. (1980). *Women's studies as a catalyst for faculty development.* Women's Studies Monograph Series. Washington, DC: National Institute of Education.

O'Reilly, A. (2008). *Feminist mothering.* Albany, NY: State University of New York Press.

Paz, O. (1988). *Sor Juana, or, the traps of faith.* Cambridge, MA: Belknap Press.

Reed, E. (1975). *Woman's evolution from matriarchal clan to patriarchal family.* New York: Pathfinder Press.

Register, C. (1979). "Brief amazing movements: Dealing with despair in the women's studies classroom." *Women's Studies Newsletter, 7*(4), 7–10.

Rich, A. (1976a). "Women's studies: Renaissance or revolution?" *Women's Studies, 3,* 121–126.

Rich, A. (1976b). *Of woman born: Motherhood as experience and institution.* New York: Norton.

Rossi, A., & Calderwood, A. (1973). *Academic women on the move.* New York: Russell Sage Foundation.

Schuck, V. (1974). "Sexism and scholarship: A brief overview of women, academia, and the disciplines." *Social Science Quarterly, 55,* 563–585.

Siegel, D. (1997). "The legacy of the personal: Generating theory in feminism's third wave." *Hypatia, 12*(3), 46–75.

Lanser, S. S. (1977). "Beyond the Bell Jar: Women Students of the 1970s." *The Radical Teacher, (6),* 41–44. Retrieved December 16, 2015 from http://www.jstor.org/stable/20709092

Stimpson, C. (1973). "What matter mind: A theory about the practice of women's studies." *Women's Studies, 1,* 293–314.

Stocking, G. (1995). *After Tylor: British social anthropology, 1888–1951*. Madison, WI: University of Wisconsin Press.

Sullivan, S. (2000). "The work of Simone de Beauvoir: Introduction." *Journal of Speculative Philosophy, 14*(2), v–vi.

Tobias, S. (Ed.). (1970). *Female Studies I*. Pittsburgh: Know.

Trecker, J. (1971). "Women's place is in the curriculum." *Saturday Review, 54*(October 16), 83–86.

United Nations. (1995). *The fourth world conference on women Beijing declaration*. Retrieved January 15, 2009 from http://www.un.org/womenwatch/daw/beijing/beijingdeclaration.html

Westkott, M. (1979). "Feminist criticism of the social sciences." *Harvard Educational Review, 49*, 422–430.

Wollstonecraft, M. (1792). *A vindication of the rights of woman*. London: Walter Scott.

Discussion Questions

1. What's your personal definition of feminism?

2. Who wrote A Vindication of the Rights of Women?

3. What does the concept of consciousness raising mean to you?

4. Would you rather read The Second Sex or The Feminine Mystique or both? Why?

5. Do you identify as a feminist? Why or why not?

Claiming an Education

by Adrienne Rich

Speech delivered at the convocation of Douglass College, 1977

For this convocation, I planned to separate my remarks into two parts: some thoughts about you, the women students here, and some thoughts about us who teach in a women's college. But ultimately those two parts are indivisible. If university education means anything beyond the processing of human beings into expected roles, through credit hours, tests, and grades (and I believe that in a women's college especially it might mean much more), it implies an ethical and intellectual contract between teacher and student. This contract must remain intuitive, dynamic, unwritten; but we must turn to it again and again if learning is to be reclaimed from the depersonalizing and cheapening pressures of the present-day academic scene.

The first thing I want to say to you who are students, is that you cannot afford to think of being here to receive an education: you will do much better to think of being here to claim one. One of the dictionary definitions of the verb "to claim" is: to take as the rightful owner; to assert in the face of possible contradiction. "To receive" is to come into possession of: to act as receptacle or container for; to accept as authoritative or true. The difference is that between acting and being acted-upon, and for women it can literally mean the difference between life and death.

One of the devastating weaknesses of university learning, of the store of knowledge and opinion that has been handed down through academic training, has been its almost total erasure of women's experience and thought from the curriculum, and its exclusion of women as members of the academic community. Today, with increasing numbers of women students in nearly every branch of higher learning, we still see very few women in the upper levels of faculty and administration in most institutions. Douglass College itself is a women's college in a university administered overwhelmingly men, who in turn are answerable to the state legislature, again composed predominantly of men. But the most, significant fact for you is that what you learn here, the very texts you read, the lectures you hear, the way your studies are divided into categories and fragmented one from the other—all this reflects, to a very large degree, neither objective reality, nor an accurate picture of the past, nor a group of rigorously tested observations about human behavior. What you can learn here (and I mean not only at Douglass but any college in any university) is how men have perceived and organized their experience, their history, their ideas of social relationships, good and evil, sickness and health, etc. When you read or hear about "great issues," "major texts," "the mainstream of Western thought," you are hearing about what men, above all white men, in their male subjectivity, have decided is important.

Black and other minority peoples have for some time recognized that their racial and ethnic experience was not accounted for in the studies broadly labeled human: and that even the sciences can be racist. For many reasons, it has been more difficult for women to comprehend our exclusion, and to realize that even the sciences can be sexist. For one thing, it is only within the last hundred years that higher education has grudgingly been opened up to women at all, even to white, middle-class women. And many of us have found ourselves poring eagerly over books with title like: The Descent of Man: Man and His Symbols: Irrational Man: The Phenomenon of Man: The Future of Man: Man and the Machine: From Man to Man: May Man Prevail?: Man, Science and Society: or One Dimensional Man —books pretending to describe a "human" reality that does not include over one-half the human species.

Less than a decade ago, with the rebirth of a feminist movement in this country, women students and teachers in a number of universities began to demand and set up women's studies courses—to claim a women-directed education. And, despite the inevitable accusations of "unscholarly," "group therapy," "faddism," etc., despite backlash and budget cuts, woman's studies are still growing, offering to more and more women a new intellectual grasp on their lives, new understanding of our history, a fresh vision of the human experience, and also a critical basis for evaluating what they hear and read in other courses, and in the society at large.

But my talk is not really about women's studies, much as I believe in their scholarly, scientific, and human necessity. While I think that any Douglass student has everything to gain by investigating and enrolling in women's studies courses, I want to suggest that there is a more essential experience that you owe yourselves, one which courses in women's studies can greatly enrich, but which finally depends on you in all your interactions with yourself and your world. This is the experience of taking responsibility toward yourselves. Our upbringing as women has so often told us that this should come second to our relationships and responsibilities to other people. We have been offered ethical models of the self-denying wife and mother; intellectual models of the brilliant but slapdash dilettante who never commits herself to anything the whole way, or the intelligent woman who denies her intelligence in order to seem more "feminine," or who sits in passive silence even when she disagrees inwardly with everything that is being said around her.

Responsibility to yourself means refusing to let others do your thinking, talking, and naming for you; it means learning to respect and use your own brains and instincts; hence, grappling with hard work. It means that you do not treat your body as a commodity with which to purchase superficial intimacy or economic security; for our bodies to be treated as objects, our minds are in mortal danger. It means insisting that those to whom you give your friendship and love are able to respect your mind. It means being able to say, with Charlotte Bronte's Jane Eyre: "I have an inward treasure born with me, which can keep me alive if all the extraneous delights should be withheld or offered only at a price I cannot afford to give."

Responsibility to yourself means that you don't fall for shallow and easy solutions— predigested books and ideas, weekend encounters guaranteed to change your life, taking "gut" courses instead of ones you know will challenge you, bluffing at school and life instead of doing solid work, marrying early as an escape from real decisions, getting pregnant as an evasion of already existing problems. It means that you refuse to sell your talents and aspirations short, simply to avoid conflict and confrontation. And this, in turn, means resisting the forces in society which say that women should be nice, play safe, have low professional expectations, drown in love and forget about work, live through others, and stay in the places assigned to us. It means that we insist on a life of meaningful work, insist that work be as meaningful as love and friendship in our lives. It means, therefore, the courage to be "different"; not to be continuously available to others when we need time for ourselves and our work; to be able to demand of others—parents, friends, roommates, teachers, lovers, husbands, children—that they respect our sense of purpose and our integrity as persons. Women everywhere are finding the courage to do this, more and more, and we are finding that courage both in our study of women in the past who possessed it, and in each other as we look to other women for comradeship, community, and challenge. The difference between a life lived actively, and a life of passive drifting and dispersal of energies, is an immense difference. Once we begin to feel committed to our lives, responsible to ourselves, we can never again be satisfied with the old, passive way.

Now comes the second part of the contract. I believe that in a women's college you have the right to expect your faculty to take you seriously. The education of women has been a matter of debate for centuries, and old, negative attitudes about women's role, women's ability to think and take leadership, are still rife both in and outside the university. Many male professors (and I don't mean only at Douglass) still feel that teaching in a women's college is a second-rate career. Many tend to eroticize their women students—to treat them as sexual objects—instead of demanding the best of their minds. (At Yale a legal suit [Alexander v. Yale] has been brought against the university by a group of women students demanding a stated policy against sexual advances toward female students by male professors.) Many teachers, both men and women, trained in the male-centered tradition, are still handing the ideas and texts of that tradition on to students without teaching them to criticize its antiwoman attitudes, it's omission of women as part of the species. Too often, all of us fail to teach the most important thing, which is that clear thinking, active discussion, and excellent writing are all necessary for intellectual freedom, and that these require hard work. Sometimes, perhaps in discouragement with a culture which is both antiintellectual and antiwoman, we may resign ourselves to low expectations for our students before we have given them half a chance to become more thoughtful, expressive human beings. We need to take to heart the words of Elizabeth Barrett Browning, a poet, a thinking woman, and a feminist, who wrote in 1845 of her impatience with studies which cultivate a "passive recipiency" in the mind, and asserted that "women want to be made to think actively: their apprehension is quicker than that of men, but their defect lies for the most part in the logical faculty and in the higher mental activities." Note that she implies a defect which can be remedied by intellectual training; not an inborn lack ability.

I have said that the contract on the student's part involves that you demand to be taken seriously so that you can also go on taking yourself seriously. This means seeking out criticism, recognizing that the most affirming thing anyone can do for you is demand that you push yourself further, show you the range of what you can do. It means rejecting attitudes of "take-it-easy," "why-be-so-serious," "why-worry-you'll-probably-get-married-anyway." It means assuming your share of responsibility for what happens in the classroom, because that affects the quality of your daily life here. It means that the student sees herself engaged with her teachers in active, ongoing struggle for a real education. But for her to do this, her teachers must be committed to belief that women's minds and experience are intrinsically valuable and indispensable to any civilization worthy the name: that there is no more exhilarating and intellectually fertile place in the academic world today than a women's college—if both students and teachers in large enough numbers are trying to fulfill this contract. The contract is really a pledge of mutual seriousness about women, about language, ideas, method, and values. It is our shared commitment toward a world in which the inborn potentialities of so many women's minds will not longer be wasted, raveled-away, paralyzed, or denied.

CHAPTER 2
Learning Gender & Privilege

Gender & Biology

Gender can be explained as the way society produces, forms, and rewards our understandings of femininity and masculinity, or the process by which certain manners and activities are attributed to "women" and "men." Society constructs and prescribes perceived differences among humans and then gives us "feminine" or "masculine" people. Quotation marks are used here on purpose to emphasize that these concepts are fluid and socially constructed. They are created by social practices that reflect the numerous mechanisms of power in society. Therefore, gender is culturally and historically changeable. There is nothing essential, intrinsic, or static about femininity or masculinity. They are merely social categories that mean different things in different societies and in different time periods throughout history.

Gender is entrenched in culture and the numerous types of knowledge accompanying any given community. What it means to be feminine in one culture is totally different than the culture next door. Same goes for masculinity. This implies that people growing up in different societies in different parts of the world have different gender expressions. Moreover, what gender means in US society now, isn't exactly what it meant for Americans living in the 1800s, 1920s, or even the 1990s.

In addition, contemporary life in the twenty-first century, which involves more and more global systems of consumerism and communication, means that the assumptions of gender that we have in the United States is spread world-wide more easily. They are progressively more linked to forms of global economic organization. Keeping that in mind, we should consider the social and economic forces of globalization (such as appropriation of indigenous peoples, communication across global markets, and militarism and political expansion) and how they have shaped gender arrangements and relations. Whatever our location, it is important to consider how we each interact with other cultures and also how the media shapes our ideas about femininity and masculinity.

People often get confused between the terms sex and gender. ***Sex*** refers to biological differences between males and females, for example, chromosomes (female XX and male XY), reproductive organs (ovaries and testes), and hormones (estrogen and testosterone). ***Gender*** refers to the cultural differences expected (by society/culture) of men and women according to their sex. A person's sex does not change from birth, but their gender can. In the past, people tend to have very clear ideas about what was appropriate to each sex and anyone behaving differently was regarded as deviant (World Health Organization, 2015).

Today, we accept a lot more diversity and see gender as a continuum rather than two categories. Therefore, men are free to show their "feminine side" and women are free to show their "masculine traits." The biological approach suggests that there is no distinction between sex & gender, thus biological sex creates gendered behavior. Gender is determined by two biological factors: hormones and, as mentioned above, chromosomes. Hormones are chemical substances secreted by glands throughout the body and carried in the bloodstream. The same sex hormones occur in both men and women, but differ in amounts and in the effect that they have upon different parts of the body (Geary, 2009).

Biology is connected to culture. An example of that is how children with ambiguous sex characteristics are handled at birth. ***Intersex*** children have reproductive or sexual anatomies that do not seem to fit the typical male or female definitions. When intersex children are born, families and physicians often make a sex determination that is then sometimes followed with hormone therapy and surgery. These steps are taken to try and force children to fit into our societal binary categories. Physicians and families use gendered norms to construct the bodies of these ambiguously sexed children.

A focus on gender assignment, identity, and expression includes three methods to comprehend the forces that shape gender. This focus can also help explain how we understand and express gender as individual people. ***Gender assignment*** is given to children at birth, determined by body type, either as male or as female. This is the first classification a person receives from a physician or a parent. From that point on, our behavior, dress, activities, and everything else we do in our daily lives correspond to whatever assignment we were given at birth. ***Gender expression*** is how we express our gender externally. ***Gender identity*** is how we feel about ourselves and our own gender internally. Based on these definitions, we can see that gender is a prominent theme in our lives and in the world. It shapes our social lives, attitudes, behaviors, and our own unique sense of selves. It is one of the foundational ways that societies are arranged (Carlson, et al., 2008).

In actuality, gender is a practice in which all people participate. It is something that we perform daily in our lives. Gender is something we "do" rather than something we "have." ***Gender acquisition*** is a process that has people practice the aspects of gender and learn the "right" behaviors for girls or boys. Many people all over the world still struggle with the idea that not everyone relates to the gender assignment from birth, particularly boys who like pink or want to dress up or play with "girly" items. Ironically, history shows us that color has not always been associated with gender. It wasn't until the 1940s that pink was associated with girls and blue with boys (Mealey, 2000).

Gender expression isn't always the same as gender identity for some people. It also might not match our assigned gender at birth. According to GLAAD (2015), ***transgender*** is the state of one's gender identity or gender expression not matching one's assigned sex. Transgender is independent of sexual orientation so transgender people may identify as heterosexual, homosexual, bisexual, asexual, etc. People who identify as transgender often feel that the gender assignment that they were given at birth, based on their genitals, is a false or incomplete description of themselves. In comparison to transgender, cisgender identity is one where gender identity and expression match the assignment given at birth. They practice conformity among their gender assignment, identity, and expression.

Often, the terms transgender and transsexual are used interchangeably. There are differences between the terms. Transsexual people could refer to themselves as trans men or trans women. Transsexual people want to create a permanent gender role in the gender with which they identify. Many transsexual people engage in medical interventions (surgeries or hormone therapy) as part of the progression of expressing their gender.

Additionally, transgender as a category overlaps with cross-dressing, but cross-dressing is different than transvestism. Cross-dressers wear clothes of the opposite sex, where transvestites wear clothes of the opposite sex for sexual pleasure. Transgender people who are cross-dressers are not automatically connected to the drag community, although some are. Drag queens are men who do female impersonations and drag kings are women who are male impersonators. There are those within the drag community that do pass as another gender and are also active in the trans community. Each person is different and can choose their own identity (Prince, 2005).

Transgender is also different from the concept of androgyny. ***Androgyny*** is defined as a lack of gender differentiation or a balance between masculine and feminine characteristics. Androgyny is an example of transgender behavior since it tries to break down feminine and masculine categories.

Transgender does not imply any specific form of sexual identity, but that statement is often confusing since transgender communities are linked to GLBTQ alliances and coalitions about sexual rights. Transgender theory is also influenced by queer theory and its assertion about fluid identities.

Genderqueer is another term that can sometimes cause confusion. It typically describes a person who is a nonconformist in challenging existing constructions and identities. It is also seen as a social movement that resists the traditional categories of gender (Prince, 2005).

Systems of Privilege & Inequality

Society recognizes the ways people are different and assigns group membership based on these differences, like with our discussion of gender above. At the same time, society also ranks the differences and institutionalizes them into the fabric of society. ***Institutionalized*** means formally placed into an organized classification or set of practices. This suggests that meanings related to difference exist beyond the intentions of individual people. For example, masculine is placed above feminine, thin above fat, and rich above poor. These rankings produce a hierarchy in which some ways of being, like being able-bodied or heterosexual, are valued more than others, like being disabled or homosexual. Some have advantages in utilizing resources while others are disadvantaged by unequal or lack of access to opportunities. There are some Americans that are unable to exercise the rights of citizenship while others in the United States have clearer pathways in the pursuit of happiness.

The tiered status of difference is fashioned from social practices that have patterns of difference become systems of privilege and inequality. Inequality for some and privilege for others is the result of these practices. ***Privilege*** can be defined as advantages people have by virtue of their status in society. This can be differentiated from earned privilege that results from earning a degree or fulfilling responsibilities. Those born with privilege may look down on those that have earned privilege.

It is easier to concede that others are disadvantaged than to divulge being privileged. Men might be sympathetic of women's rights but recoil at the suggestion that their own actions are in need of change. White people might be disturbed by the stories of racial injustice but still not comprehend that automatic white privilege is part of the problem. This is comparable to the debate where being supportive of women's rights does not inevitably translate into an understanding of how masculine privilege works.

Systems that facilitate privilege and inequality include: racism (African American, Asian American, Latino/Latina, Native American, etc.), religious discrimination such as anti- Semitism and hatred of Muslims; sexism; classism; ageism; sizeism (concerning body image); and ableism. Systems of oppression can be defined as systems that discriminate based on supposed or actual differences among people. So then sexism discriminates on the basis of gender, resulting in gender stratification, racism discriminates on the basis of racial and ethnic differences, and so forth for classism, ageism, sizeism, and ableism. Privilege can be identified and utilized in that same format.

Every woman is in multiple places within these systems. She might not have access to race and gender privilege because she is African American and a woman; she might have access to heterosexual privilege because she is heterosexual and class privilege because she lives in a family that is financially secure. This is the converging of various identities. Lives are not one-dimensional, but rather experienced as a daily struggle with the inequalities in our lives. Various identities concerning these systems of equality and privilege are usually thoroughly blended and potentially shifting depending on who we are, how we identify, and even where we live. This means that cultural forces of race, class, age, and ability are all factors of gender.

People experience race, class, gender, and sexual identity differently depending on the various factors mentioned above. This means that people of the same race or same age will experience race or age differently depending on their location in gender, class/level of employment, as well as sexual identity, and so on.

Systems of inequality such as racism, sexism, and classism intersect and work together to impose inequality and privilege, each supporting the other. The interconnections of racism and classism are often demonstrated by poverty statistics in the United States. Age discrimination is very much connected to sexism, as many women cringe when someone guesses they are older than they really are. This is part of the quest for youth and beauty that encourages women to satisfy gender stereotypes. Similarly, Homophobia can function as a tool of sexism. ***Homophobia*** is the fear and dislike of lesbians and gay men. Homophobia acts as a menace to keep women separate from one another in the patriarchy, consequently supporting sexism (Adams, Bell, & Griffin, 2007).

Power & Institutions

The feminist interpretation of power is fairly simple. Feminists believe that power in society is disproportionately, and unreasonably, balanced toward men. This leads to the discrimination against women, with men using their power to control women's lives. Examples of patriarchal power are often categorized into two "spheres," the public and the private spheres. Even many feminists would concede that in the public sphere, such as the workplace and politics, the balance of power is becoming more equal. For example, there are more and more female politicians being elected nationally. There are also prominent female coaches in the NBA & NFL.

However, an argument can be made that the greatest inequality lies in the private sphere. Women often work many hours both inside and outside of the home, including those women who are sole caregivers for their children. Carol Pateman (1988) terms this the "triple-shift" and said that this inequality directly stopped women from gaining power in the public sphere. Feminist theories have been very useful in contributing to our understanding of power, without feminists raising issues surrounding gender inequalities women might still be as emasculated today as they were 100 years ago (Harding, 2004; Lorde, 1983; MacKinnon, 1989).

The dominance of men is evident in virtually every aspect of modern life. It shapes the social status of men and women in our society. Male dominance in our culture can be described in many ways and from a range of viewpoints. An evolutionary standpoint might state that gender roles have changed over huge stretches of time in a way that naturally selected men and women into the roles they hold today.

From a religious standpoint, Christian practitioners are taught to believe that God created the world as is so everything is as it should be. Though there have been changes through time and a reflection on history suggests that women have "come a long way" in establishing their basic worth and value. From a feminist perspective, women haven't gone far enough and achieved total equality.

There are other viewpoints that suggest that the male domination in society is a function of patriarchy that not only prefers men but also represses women in our society. However explained, in our society, men are the dominant group and women are the subordinated group. Equality has not been achieved.

Patriarchy supporters would list the numerous perceived benefits society enjoys because of male dominance and gender roles. Feminist activists then share the great suffering women have faced over the years and the discrimination encountered every day. There will always be extremists on both sides and the facts suggest that these arguments will go on for the foreseeable future. In the long run, the purpose of the book (and most likely the class you are reading it for) is to educate people about the different facets of feminism along with women's and gender studies. We are not necessarily here to right every wrong and validate every good idea. The focus here is on the many structures of power, privilege, and influence in society. These structures make up the oppressive system of inequality that is frequently seen in patriarchal culture.

Institutions are societal groups that include recognized patterns of behavior planned around specific purposes. Functioning through social norms and established laws, major institutions include the family, marriage, politics, government, the military, religion, education, health and medicine, mass media, and sports. Major societal institutions have been historical factors in political, military, legal, and socioeconomic decisions made over centuries. Institutions are envisioned to meet the needs of society, but they meet some people's needs better than others.

These organizations are fundamental in creating systems of inequality and privilege because they structure differences among women in specific ways. Institutions are significant networks for the endurance of what Patricia Hill Collins (1989) calls "structures of domination and subordination." Institutions can fight back against systems of inequality and privilege. For example, positive portrayal of women and people of color in media or the activities of churches and many community organizations for civil rights.

Institutions encourage numerous systems of inequality into all aspects of women's lives. In terms of resources, institutions also support systems of inequality and privilege. Institutions assign a variety of roles to women and men. They are also places of employment where people do gendered work.

Educational institutions, for example, have historically employed a substantial number of women. The number of white males in these positions increases, along with higher salaries, depending on the level of education. Furthermore, it is often difficult for openly lesbian teachers to find K-12 teaching positions. Several cities and states are trying to pass laws preventing lesbians and gay men from teaching in publicly funded schools.

Institutions can allocate resources and distribute privilege differently also. Athletics is a good example of this, as the field has traditionally been male dominated. Men's sports are more highly valued than women's sports. Women's professional sports are clearly diminished. Despite Title IX of the 1972 Educational Amendments Act, which barred discrimination in education, many colleges still are not in compliance and spend considerably more money on men's sports than on women's. Female athletes on some campuses complain that men receive better practice times in shared gymnasiums and more up-to-date equipment. Some women's teams at the collegiate level even fight to have locker room space. With just these few statements, it is obvious that sports and athletics are an example of where resources are inequitably distributed within a large societal institution.

Prejudices are assimilated or integrated into our thoughts and behavior daily. We as humans need to use our free will to learn and resist stereotypes. We can negotiate these issues, accepting, or resisting them as we see fit. If we don't learn and grow from these issues, it can mean individuals are encouraged to believe that they are not worthy of social justice and equality are less likely to seek equality. We must fight against internalizing negative messages. Internalizing oppression means that we are not working toward equality, but sitting stagnant or blaming others. When people direct the resentment and anger they have about their situation onto those who are of equal or of lesser status, this process is called ***horizontal hostility***. As a strategy, it is similar to the idea of "divide and conquer" where groups are encouraged to fight each other in order to avoid alliances. Just imagine a season of *Survivor* or *Big Brother*. Women do this when they jealous someone's appearance or put other women down with verbal attacks.

Language is another key aspect of ideologies that support systems of inequality and privilege. Language is an amazingly challenging progression of symbols that we learn early in life and take for granted. Language gives us the space to name the bits and pieces of our experience but also to relate them to other things. It basically creates as well as reflects our reality. It creates thought and influences our daily lives. Unfortunately, the English language is organized in such a way that it preserves sexism and racism. The English language helps us to try and understand gender, but also limits women's options for self-definition and advocacy. Think about how language shapes our reality and structures women's lives. When you grow up learning 20 synonyms for the word slut, you learn something powerful about our society's views of female sexuality and the issues we have with gender.

Breakout: Disability

Tyler/Mckay/shutterstock.com

In her essay, "The Social Construction of Disability," Susan Wendell reasons that society forms disability by working under the supposition that everyone in that society fits in an able-bodied, white, middle-class, male paradigm, which subsequently precludes the physically impaired from completely participating in that society. Wendell critically studies the social and cultural issues that lead to the social construction of disability.

Instead of disability existing within the body, Wendell maintains that society is constructed to accommodate young, able-bodied men thereby forming disabling environments for those who are not the stereotype. Wendell's main focus is the way in which society forces disability on people with varied impairments. She also mentions other instances where society causes impairments. According to her model of social construction, some people are born with impairments and experience disability for their entire their lives. Others begin their lives as able-bodied and healthy, later becoming disabled for a variety of reasons that then affect them physically and socially.

Although Wendell makes a strong argument that disability is a socially constructed concept, disability affects a large portion of the world's population, particularly in just staying alive. Individuals with disabilities often struggle to keep up with societal expectations and what is necessary for their survival. In the United States, some individuals with disabilities receive money from the government for the income they are unable to work for. Many people with disabilities want to work and have the degrees and skills necessary to do so, but are unable to find meaningful work because of the stereotypes and prejudices that are prevalent in American culture. In order to make the world a place where people with disabilities will not feel shunned by a society that fails to accommodate them, infrastructural changes need to be made. We can implement a labor force of educated people with a variety of disabilities, improve the public health system, and create more universally designed homes, offices, and buildings.

When I think about a society without disabilities, I do not see a culture where all disabilities are cured. In its place, I see a fully accessible society, where there is widespread recognition that all structures and all activities must be created for the largest practical variety of abilities. In this world, no one would be considered disabled because every major kind of activity would be accessible. I know that it isn't realistic to expect every person to be able to do every activity there is, but that we should live in a world where major life activities are as accessible as they can be to as many people as possible.

I use the words accessibility and ability instead of the words independence or integration because independence and/or integration are not always suitable goals for people with disabilities. Some people cannot live independently because they will always need attendant care. Some people with disabilities, like those who identify as deaf, do not want to be integrated into non-disabled society; they choose their own separate culture and social lives. Ultimately, everyone should have access to opportunities to improve their abilities, to have gainful employment, and to take part in any public and/or private activities available.

Conclusion

In this chapter, the basics of gender and biology were examined first. Then, the focus was on the social construction of difference and how systems of inequality and privilege operate and exist. The ultimate emphasis of this chapter has been on systems of inequality and privilege and how they are maintained through the presence and power of institutions and the interconnected workings of ideologies and language.

In concluding this chapter, the need for social change to better the conditions of women's lives is underscored. The message in this chapter is the need to identify difference, to comprehend how the implications associated with difference and the conditions of everyday lives relate to privilege and inequality, and to celebrate difference through partnerships for social justice and other activism. Continue thinking about these themes as you examine the reading, *There Is No Hierarchy of Oppression* by Audre Lorde.

Suggested Readings

Cole, J., & Guy-Sheftall, B. (2003). *Gender talk: The struggle for women's equality in African American communities.* New York: Ballantine.

Collins, P. (2006). *From black power to hip-hop: Racism, nationalism, and feminism.* Philadelphia: Temple University Press.

Hooks, b. (2002). *Where we stand: Class matters.* New York: Routledge.

Lorde, A. (1984). *Sister outsider.* Freedom, CA: Crossing Press.

Mihesuah, D. (2003). *Indigenous American women: Decolonization, empowerment, activism.* Lincoln, NE: Bison Books.

Smith, B., & Hutchison, B. (2004). *Gendering disability.* New Brunswick, NJ: Rutgers University Press.

Stein, A. (2002). *The stranger next door: The story of a small community's battle over sex, faith, and civil rights.* Boston: Beacon Press.

References

Adams, M., Bell, L., & Griffin, P. (2007). *Teaching for diversity and social justice: A sourcebook.* New York, NY: Routledge.

Carlson, N., Miller, Jr., H., Heth, D., Donahoe, J., & Martin, G.N. (2008). *Psychology: The science of behavior* (7th Ed.). New York: Pearson.

Collins, P. H. (1989). "The social construction of black feminist thought," *Signs 14* (Summer): 745–773.

Geary, D. C. (2009). *Male, female: The evolution of human sex differences.* Washington, D.C.: American Psychological Association.

Harding, S. (2004). *The feminist standpoint theory reader: Intellectual and political controversies.* New York: Routledge.

Lorde, A. (1983). "The master's tools will never dismantle the master's house." pp. 94–101. In C. Moraga, & G. Anzaldua (Eds.). *This bridge called my back: Writings by radical women of color.* New York: Kitchen Table, Women of Color Press.

MacKinnon, C. (1989). *Toward a feminist theory of the state.* Cambridge, Mass.: Harvard University Press.

Mealey, L. (2000). *Sex differences.* NY: Academic Press.

Pateman, C. (1988). *The sexual contract.* Stanford: Stanford University Press.

Prince, V. (2005). "Sex vs. gender." *International Journal of Transgenderism. 8*(4).

World Health Organization. (2015). *Glossary of terms and tools.* Retrieved December 16, 2015 from http://www.who.int/gender-equity-rights/knowledge/glossary/en/

GLAAD. (2015). Transgender Issues. Retrieved December 16, 2015 from http://www.glaad.org/reference/transgender

Discussion Questions

1. How do you identify your own privileges and biases?

2. How do ideologies show up in the institutions that most affect your life?

3. How do institutions maintain gender inequality? Have you experienced gender inequality in particular institutions?

4. How do we create an equal power structure in our society?

5. Remember the definitions of sex and gender. How do we allow for more acceptance of varied behaviors and sexual identities?

There Is No Hierarchy of Oppression

by Audre Lorde

I was born Black, and a woman. I am trying to become the strongest person I can become to live the life I have been given and to help effect change toward a livable future for this earth and for my children. As a Black, lesbian, feminist, socialist, poet, mother of two, including one boy, and a member of an interracial couple, I usually find myself part of some group in which the majority defines me as deviant, difficult, inferior, or just plain "wrong."

From my membership in all of these groups I have learned that oppression and the intolerance of difference come in all shapes and sizes and colors and sexualities; and that among those of us who share the goals of liberation and a workable future for our children, there can be no hierarchies of oppression. I have learned that sexism (a belief in the inherent superiority of one sex over all others and thereby its right to dominance) and heterosexism (a belief in the inherent superiority of one pattern of loving over all others and there by its right to dominance) both arise from the same source as racism-a belief in the inherent superiority of one race over all others and thereby its right to dominance.

"Oh," says a voice from the Black community, "but being Black is NORMAL!" Well, I and many Black people of my age can remember grimly the days when it didn't used to be!

I simply do not believe that one aspect of myself can possibly profit from the oppression of any other part of my identity. I know that my people cannot possibly profit from the oppression of any other group which seeks the right to peaceful existence. Rather, we diminish ourselves by denying to others what we have shed blood to obtain for our children. And those children need to learn that they do not have to become like each other in order to work together for a future they will all share.

The increasing attacks upon lesbians and gay men are only an introduction to the increasing attacks upon all Black people, for wherever oppression manifests itself in this country, Black people are potential victims. And it is a standard of right-wing cynicism to encourage members of oppressed groups to act against each other, and so long as we are divided because of our particular identities we cannot join together in effective political action.

Within the lesbian community I am Black, and within the Black community I am a lesbian. Any attack against Black people is a lesbian and gay issue, because I and thousands of other Black women are part of the lesbian community. Any attack against lesbians and gays is a Black issue, because thousands of lesbians and gaymen are Black. There is no hierarchy of oppression.

It is not accidental that the Family Protection Act, which is virulently antiwoman and antiblack, is also antigay. As a Black person, I know who my enemies are, and when the Ku Klux Klan goes to court in Detroit to try and force the board of education to remove books the Klan believes" hint at homosexuality;' then I know I cannot afford the luxury of fighting one form of oppression only. I cannot afford to believe that freedom from intolerance is the right of only one particular group. And I cannot afford to choose between the fronts upon which I must battle these forces of discrimination, wherever they appear to destroy me. And when they appear to destroy me, it will not be long before they appear to destroy you.

Note:

1. A 1981 congressional bill repealing federal laws that promoted equal rights for women, including coeducational school-related activities and protection for battered wives, and providing tax incentives for married mothers to stay at home.

CHAPTER 3
Pop Culture & Media

Social Media & the Internet

As we read in Chapter 1, the third wave of feminism has had a bigger focus on online activism. More recently, its most powerful weapon has been the hashtag. The third wave has embraced online feminism and uses the Internet as a means to share information widely. Previously, feminism relied on paper flyers and word of mouth to spread information. Before Twitter and Facebook burst out as prominent news sources, participating in rallies was limited to those who lived in the area, or those who could afford to take time off work and travel. Letters, brochures, and flyers were created by feminist groups with major funding. Social media gave feminist activism to the masses, allowing for participation for anyone with a Twitter account, Instagram, and/or Facebook page and a desire to fight the patriarchy. By eliminating the obstacles of distance and location, social media sites have made activism much more available. Social media is enabling public discussions and crafting a platform for mindfulness and revolution.

In 2013, women in Texas wanted to protest an abortion bill. Many local women gathered together at the Texas State Capitol for a rally, but many more who couldn't be there in person protested online using the hashtag #StandWithWendy. All of these people, either in person or online, were supporting State Representative Wendy Davis through her 13-hour filibuster. When a protest was started about sexist t-shirts for children, people flooded the company's Facebook page until they removed the product.

More recently, The Representation Project (http://therepresentationproject.org/) has protested the numerous shallow red carpet questions female actors are asked by using the hashtag #askhermore. Reese Witherspoon mentioned the hashtag on air during the Academy Awards and listed potential substantive questions to ask on Instagram (Pulver, 2015). Additionally, the hashtag #NotBuyingIt was used during the Super Bowl to call out sexism in commercials in real time during the game.

During the Ray Rice domestic violence scandal, many new sources questioned why Janay Rice had stayed with her husband, so other women took to twitter sharing their stories of domestic violence with the hashtag #WhyIStayed. #BringBackOurGirls trended internationally to raise awareness of the more than 200 Nigerian girls who had been kidnapped by Boko Haram.

But feminist social media activism doesn't just raise awareness, it also produces tangible results. Companies and groups have changed policies and advertising as a result of social media backlash created by everyday people and their tweets. In 2012, the #StandWithPP hashtag was created after the Susan G. Komen Foundation announced it would be withdrawing its funding of Planned Parenthood because the organization provides abortions (among the many other health care services it provides). Supporters of Planned Parenthood used #StandWithPP on Twitter and Facebook to voice their support and pressure Komen to reverse their decision. Komen responded to the backlash and reversed their decision. Planned Parenthood is still under attack from conservative groups and so feminists continue to use the #StandWithPP hashtag to show support.

"Hashtag activism" is a term that has been badmouthed, but it has been effective at forcing politicians and organizations to change. Now, many groups carefully watch social media conversations about themselves. They pay attention to the negative social media chatter about them and have their PR staff go into battle mode.

Several potential 2016 presidential candidates are learning this in their campaigns. Jeb Bush fired a staffer for his tweets that called women "sluts" and Scott Walker fired a campaign staffer over tweets that disparaged the significant primary state of Iowa. Other candidates are trying to use social media to their benefit and news sources are analyzing that potential benefit during the course of the campaigns.

Cynics have claimed that social media doesn't provide any real outlets for activism. They also say that hashtags are meaningless. There may be some truth to that. There are plenty of social media campaigns that have been effective at raising awareness around the issues they're tackling, but not many of them have created tangible results.

For all the awareness that #BringBackOurGirls created, Boko Haram still has yet to release the 200 schoolgirls who were kidnapped. The girls are still missing and Boko Haram continues to kidnap other young women. The Nigerian government is trying to help, but progress is slow going (Kaze, 2015).

Social media activism alone won't solve the world's problems, but it has been a powerful force to fight against sexism. Social media activism will never completely replace traditional protests, demonstrations and rallies. Social media can provide a space for those who might feel voiceless. It lifts the voice of one person with a Twitter account, a Facebook page, a Tumblr, or an Instagram to a national story, no matter who that person is.

Television

Television is one of the most dominant types of media because it's everywhere. Most households in America own at least one. Many children grow up with a TV in their bedrooms. Television influences family life because it inspires impassive contact, usually replacing conversations or other interactive activities. Television is a graphic medium that shows numerous pictures on a frequent basis. Before, families would gather around and watch TV. Some still do that, but many other people record shows rather than watch them when they air, watch video on YouTube, and view television shows through mobile devices. Even though TV viewing habits are becoming increasingly diverse, these images are still seen as representing the reality. TV and other video influence people's understanding of the world they live in. This is especially true for children in America, who watch TV from an early age. Much of it is educational, but it still influences their ideas about the world significantly.

The multitude of channels available has not meant access to a wider range of positive images of gender. Reality shows strengthen prevailing ideas of gender and beauty standards. Some shows, like Teen Mom, show inconsistent messages about the challenges of unplanned pregnancies. Advertising companies control the content of commercials and when they are shown. Turn on an MLB game, see commercials are for beer, cars, and other products targeted at a male audience. Watch a soap opera and see commercials focused on beauty and household products. The influence commercial sponsors have over the content of programming is blatantly obvious. Commercial sponsors shape television content with the checks they write to the networks for space.

Traditional gender roles are everywhere on TV. Think of your favorite television show. You may think: "Look at all the diverse characters! That one is gay and that woman plays the main character. Look at that character with an obvious disability." Those statements are all true and good, but what about the plot lines? Is the woman longing for a heterosexual relationship? Does the gay man fit all the usual stereotypes? And is the disability mentioned over and over again? Just so you don't forget it's there?

The format of shows is also gendered. Soap operas focus on relationships and family and switch between multiple story lines. Crime shows such as Castle and NCIS are shown later in the evening, when children are supposed to be asleep. Other shows, like Mad Men & Downton Abbey, reminisce about the past, which was by and large dominated by men. Similarly, Game of Thrones shows sex, violence, and misogyny, with some really excellent female characters worked in. All of these shows focus on male-dominated relationships and reinforce gendered societal positions. The women are present and often main characters, but ultimately their plot lines revolve around men in the shows.

A related investigation can be made of shows that help normalize gay life in American society, even while they depend on outdated stereotypes. Some TV shows specifically feature empowered LGBTQ characters such as Pam De Beaufort and Tara Thornton in True Blood. Modern Family, Grey's Anatomy, and The Good Wife include LGBTQ characters with major plot lines.

Glee, until it ended recently, was a popular show with gay-friendly writing and some empowering parts and lessons about gender roles. At the same time, the show also included many women who are physically attractive and highly sexualized. There are numerous other examples in crime dramas. Shows like Law & Order SVU and Rizzoli and Isles provide strong, smart women as main characters, but these characters are all beauty stereotypes at the same time. They use their brains to solve mysteries and wear fashionable clothes and makeup at the same time. Regrettably, a majority of the victims on these shows are women also. It would be excellent to see a show that focuses on intelligence instead of beauty standards.

We can't forget about the news. Where local news may try to be as unbiased as possible, there are plenty of one-sided alternatives. Fox News is known for its support of conservative political opinion. Fox News supports the conservative Republican agenda, including hosting debates for potential Republican presidential nominees. Media critics list MSNBC as the more liberal counterpart to Fox News, but MSNBC doesn't boast the same viewership as Fox News. Satire news shows such as The Daily Show and Last Week Tonight with John Oliver provide alternative, more liberal takes on domestic and international news.

Mary Richards, from *The Mary Tyler Moore Show*, is often recognized as a major feminist icon from television. She was a great role model for working women in the 1970s, but she never actually said she was a feminist. If we stick with the 1970s, Bea Arthur from *Maude* was an outspoken feminist, who had an abortion on the show. She continued that trend playing the outspoken Dorothy on *The Golden Girls* in the 1980s.

Best friends Tina Fey and Amy Poehler have also had a feminist impact on television. Liz Lemon was a fictionalized version of *30 Rock* creator Tina Fey. She was constantly in a struggle to balance her personal and professional lives, and in her late 30s, felt the pressure to either adopt or have a child of her own, which can sometimes be mistaken for baby fever. In one episode, she bought a wedding dress, despite the fact that she didn't have a boyfriend, saying she'd get the dress then have a baby and do things her way.

Amy Poehler had her own success on her show *Parks and Recreation* as Leslie Knope. Leslie was a loyal, passionate, and determined woman. We could laugh at Leslie's weird obsessions like waffles, but never at her as a feminist. She asked, "What kind of lunatic would want to be Cleopatra over Eleanor Roosevelt?" and she was sincere. She even invents Galentine's Day, a holiday celebrated on February 13 with her lady friends. Leslie was not the token feminist of that show. Several other characters, both male and female, presented feminist ideals as normal, important beliefs. The characters didn't continually talk about feminism, but their ideals impacted their decisions, just like in real life.

Another popular show with feminist characters was *The Gilmore Girls*. Born to an unwed, teen mother, Rory, played by Alexis Bledel, was a super smart, well-behaved teen, who was valedictorian of her prep school and went to Yale. She was often seen reading feminist novels, and wanted to be like Christiane Amanpour when she graduated. At Yale, her dorm room was decked out with Planned Parenthood posters and Gloria Steinem stickers.

Let us not forget feminism in cartoons. Lisa Simpson is a vegetarian, environmentalist, and feminist. She adores ponies, struggles with body image issues, and has a love/hate relationship with her Malibu Stacy dolls. She will sometimes chastise Marge, her stay-at-home mother, for her seemingly traditional gender role, but ends up learning a lesson about how things aren't always what they seem. Marge has her own feminist traits in the show too.

Daria was the ultimate 90s girl with her outfit of combat boots, an army jacket, and an anti-everything attitude. She was the girl that made it okay for us to un-follow the status quo and face the patriarchy with sarcasm. She never actually claimed to be a feminist, like Lisa Simpson did, but her ideals often match the movement.

Movies

Feminist film theorist Laura Mulvey (1975) identifies ***the male gaze*** a major topic for learning about gender in filmmaking. Mulvey contends that movies are basically made through and for the male gaze and satisfy a voyeuristic need for men to look at women as objects. Viewers should "see" the movie through the eyes of the male lead character. The focus is on the production of meaning in a film. This includes how it imagines viewers, the movie production aspects that shape the representation of women, and also the reinforcement of systems of inequality and privilege. Mulvey points out that typical female subjects in films are not meaning making. Meaning making in Hollywood emphasizes gender ranking through such genres as gangster films, action films, and westerns that celebrate heteronormative topics and characters. In other words, these films portray heterosexuality as the norm.

Some feminist scholars have proposed the idea of ***subversive gazing*** by moviegoers who refuse to gaze the way filmmakers expect (Ellsworth, 1990; Greenhill, 2015; Humm, 1997; Smelik, 1998). An important part of this criticism is identifying how identities are constructed and performed. From a black feminist perspective, bell hooks (1992) wrote about ***the oppositional gaze***, encouraging women of color to reject and critique stereotypical characters in movies. Furthermore, film theorists are progressively taking global perspectives, critiquing white, European, straight and economically privileged viewpoints.

Feminist film theorists such as Claire Johnston (1975) emphasized that alternative films can function as ***counter cinema*** by incorporating nontraditional cinematic images and by allowing for women to be directors and producers. Last but not least, the incorporation of LGBT topics and themes in film attempts to disrupt traditional Hollywood plots. The Queer Film Society (http://www.queerfilmsociety .org/) is an association of LGBT film critics, historians, artists, and scholars. Their work is focused on the creation and celebration of queer films, characters, and storylines in international cinema. One of their mottos is "We're here, we're queer, we're watching movies."

The Bechdel Test (http://bechdeltest.com/) is a simple test that asks is a movie features at least two women who talk to each other about something other than a man. Bonus points are given to the film if the women are also named in the movie. Only about half of all films meet these requirements. The test is used as an indicator for the active presence of women in films and to call attention to gender inequality that is rampant in traditional Hollywood movies. The Bechdel Test is named for the cartoonist Alison Bechdel, in whose comic strip *Dykes to Watch Out For* it first appeared in 1985. Bechdel credits the idea to a friend, Liz Wallace, and to the writings of Virginia Woolf. If you have the time, click on the link above and see what recent movies pass the test. The website also tells you which films do not pass the test. Does any film on the list surprise you? Or are those that you thought would pass the test that didn't?

Romantic comedies have become the films created for female audiences. Their heteronormative formula reinforces myths about romantic love and marriage as the most important keys to women's happiness. This popular genre sometimes contains glimpses challenging the patriarchy, but not often. These films are packed with not-so-subtle gender stereotypes. For example, think of all the romantic films that Julia Roberts has been in. Yes, in many of them she is a strong, independent woman. But for most, the storyline revolves around her latching on and falling in love with a man. I think the same could be said for Sandra Bullock, Cameron Diaz, or Drew Barrymore. They are smart and funny, but often rely on their looks in the end. In the Shrek series of movies, the princess choosing to become an ogre, exhibiting her own sense of self and agency. She abandons traditional beauty standards, but she still embraces the roles of wife and mother in the standard patriarchal way.

Pornography is another example of the male gaze. It also highlights the normalization of violence against women. Porn extends the sexualization and objectification of women's bodies for entertainment not on in film, or print, but also online. In traditional porn, women are typically reduced to body parts. The porn actresses are also usually shown deriving pleasure from being dominated.

Racism interconnects with sexism in pornography when women of color are portrayed as "exotic" and are fetishized in particularly disparaging ways. Many feminists, myself included, oppose pornography for a variety of reasons. There are others, particularly those termed as "sex radicals," feel that porn can be a form of sexual self-expression. They argue that women who take part in the production of pornography are taking control of their own sexuality and are profiting from control of their own bodies. There is also a genre known as feminist porn which gives the actors and actresses a voice in their roles and storylines.

Some of the more persistent and long-lasting gender images in U.S. culture derive from Disney films. Disney Corporation is one of the biggest media conglomerate in the world in terms of revenue. It's not just movie sales, but toys, music, clothes, sheets, curtains, lunchboxes, etc. For the most part, Disney characters reflect white, middle-class, hetero-patriarchal norms. More recent Disney movies have tried to be more inclusive, but still rely largely on these traditional norms. Newer Disney female characters are empowered to make choices for themselves, but still tend to be represented with very stereotypical beauty ideals.

A very popular young adult novel turned movie is Suzanne Collins's book *The Hunger Games*. The film shows the main character, Katniss, wily and skilled, with qualities usually associated with boy characters, who jeopardizes herself to save her sister and another girl. Her portrayal is the opposite of Bella from the Twilight series in that she is not boy-obsessed, and contrasting Hermione of the Harry Potter books and films, she is the main character and not just a friend of the lead. With all that being said, Katniss is not without her flaws. She doesn't make very many of her own decisions, often protected by other male characters, and succeeds with lots of luck and assistance. An argument can be made that just because it is written by a woman and the main character is a woman, then it doesn't necessarily automatically mean it's a feminist work. If you have read or watched *The Hunger Games*, what do you think?

Music

Women have been involved in music for many, many years. There have been works from female composers and musicians (such as by Fanny Mendelssolm Hensel and Clara Schumann) that have been ignored or not noticed until after their deaths. Early on, it was mostly white, wealthy women who were able to devote themselves to music. In 1893, Margaret Ruthven Lang was the first American female composer to have one of her compositions performed by a symphony orchestra in the United States (George & Mauro, 2012). Nadia Boulanger was the first woman to conduct a symphony orchestra in the early twentieth century and was known as one of the best music teachers of her time (Patmore, 2015).

Historically, women were limited in music by the gendered nature of certain musical instruments. Some were deemed "inappropriate" for women. Throughout the nineteenth century, instruments such as the keyboard and harp were considered the only appropriate things for women to play. Even now, women are still encouraged to play certain instruments. Beyoncé often travels with an all-female backing band to create space for female musicians. Women continue to struggle to create a place for themselves.

The genre known as ***Women's Music*** is music by women, for women, and about women. The genre emerged as a musical expression of the second-wave feminist movement as well as the labor, civil rights, and peace movements. The movement in the US was started by lesbians such as Cris Williamson, Meg Christian, Margie Adam and peace activist Holly Near. Other prominent members in the movement included African-American musicians Linda Tillery, Mary Watkins, and Gwen Avery along with the super group Sweet Honey in the Rock. Women's music as a whole also includes anyone else working in the music industry in any role who also happen to identify as women (Garofalo, 1992).

Olivia Records, the first women's music record label, was created in 1973 by a group of women led by Meg Christian. Successfully, exclusively selling by mail order and at women's music festivals, Olivia was able to release Meg Christian's *I Know You Know* and Cris Williamson's *The Changer and the Changed*. Williamson's album was "one of the all-time best selling albums on any independent label" at that time, and was also the first LP (long play record) to be entirely produced by women (Garofalo, 1992).

Just as rock music mobilized rebellion in the 1960s, hip-hop music been influential in recent history as a critique of racial cultural politics. Originating in the 1970s, rap was influenced by rhythm and blues and rock and quickly spread into TV, film, and, in particular, music videos. At the same time that rap and hip-hop have been able to raise the issues of racism, poverty, and social violence, it has also perpetuated misogyny and violence. There are women performers in hip-hop and female rappers are receiving much more attention, but their status in the industry is far below that of men in the industry. Women's success in hip-hop is illustrated by the success of such artists as Queen Latifah, Lil' Kim, and Missy Elliot. Elliott in particular is known not only as a writer and performer but also as a producer of other artists' music. The success and fame of Nicki Minaj is also a step in the right direction, as she often raps about women's issues, notwithstanding the controversies that follow her frequently.

Music videos became popular in the 1980s with the beginning of MTV, a music video station that now ironically plays very few music videos. Music videos are basically advertisements for record companies and are usually for popular music that gets played on the radio. Other genres, like country, will sometimes make videos in other formats. Most music videos are predictable in the ways they exploit and sexualize women, sometimes in violent ways. Women are generally present in videos to be looked at, even when they are the artist performing the song. Also, music videos featuring male musicians are aired in greater numbers than those featuring female musicians, if these videos are ever aired on TV at all. Many musicians try other avenues to share their music, like YouTube or SoundCloud.

The argument can also be made that music videos have allowed women to literally find their voice and to create music videos from their perspective. This opportunity gave women popularity and industry backing. Music videos also provided the potential to disrupt traditional gendered perspectives. In the mid-1980s, MTV helped such women as Tina Turner, Cyndi Lauper, and Madonna gain success. Madonna is often cast as both perpetuating gender stereotypes about sexualization and an important role model for women to express themselves freely. Lady Gaga is similarly mentioned as an icon who supports and resists female sexuality. Madonna and Lady Gaga have been regarded as returning the male gaze by staring back at the patriarchy. Beyoncé, has also been known for feminism and female empowerment, with songs like "Single Ladies (Put a Ring on it)," "***Flawless," and Destiny's Child's "Independent Women." Other artists like Rihanna, Christina Aguilera, and Pink are also celebrated in much the same way.

There are also "indie" artists and bands whose music is produced within networks of independent record labels and underground music venues. Indie is also seen as a distinct genre of rock music with a specific artistic aesthetic that includes many artists. Singer-songwriters such as Ani DiFranco, the Indigo Girls, Tracy Chapman, and Tori Amos were important in providing feminist music as also were the "riot grrl" fem punk artists and bands of the 1980s. Many of these artists continue to serve as role models for young women seeking to gain a more independent place in contemporary music.

Breakout: Feminist Music (Kathleen Hanna)

© Jackie Roman/The Hell Gate/Corbis

Kathleen Hanna is a feminist musician and activist. In the 1990s, she was the lead singer of the band Bikini Kill and then started the group Le Tigre with Johanna Fateman and JD Samson. Hanna is currently working with a musical group called The Julie Ruin. Each of these groups have supported feminism through their work.

Kathleen Hanna is well known for being an outspoken feminist and many people often credit her for helping start third-wave feminism with the riot grrrl movement. At concerts, Hanna encourages women to move to the front of the stage to avoid harassment. The "girls to the front" concept helped women feel comfortable at concerts and more welcome to participate without feeling threatened.

Inadvertently, Hanna came up with the name for Nirvana's single, "Smells Like Teen Spirit". She wrote "Kurt Smells Like Teen Spirit" on Kurt Cobain's wall. Kurt was unaware of the deodorant by that name, geared toward young women. He just really liked the phrase (Azerrad, 1994).

Kathleen Hanna has also openly discussed her decision to have an abortion when she was younger. She believes that talking about her abortion will encourage other women to openly discuss the topic as well, helping to decrease the social stigma of abortion and further the pro-choice movement (Barcella, 2004). In her activism, Hanna has also been critical of politicians who do not support pro-choice laws or women's health in general.

Magazines

Women's magazines are a great (?) way to study how gender works in U.S. society. I include the question mark because while magazines may have lots of information about gender in our society, not all of it is great. In fact, most of it is awful. Women's magazines are one of the main parts of the multi-billion-dollar industries that produce cosmetics, fashion, and help shape the social construction of "beauty." Alongside these advertising campaigns are bodily standards against which women are encouraged to measure themselves. Because almost no one measures up to these artificially created and often computer-generated standards, the message is to buy these products and your life will improve.

Women's magazines come in several varieties. First are the fashion magazines that focus on beauty, self-improvement, and satisfying men. Examples of these include Glamour, Vogue, Cosmopolitan, Marie Claire, and Ebony. Seventeen would also be in this area, even though it is geared toward teens. Another variety of women's magazines are those that are geared toward cooking and home decoration. Examples of this are Better Homes and Gardens, Redbook, Good Housekeeping, HGTV magazine, and the Food Network magazine. Not only can readers get recipes and decorating tips, but these magazines promise relationships tips also. There are also women's magazines that appeal to specific women such as Parents magazine or Sports Illustrated for Women. There are also feminist magazines like Ms., Bitch, and Bust magazines.

Again, just as in music, technology has provided a way for women to express their voices through publishing. "Zines" are quick, cheap, cut-and-paste publications that have been around since the riot grrl movement. These publications, which range in quality, often provide a forum for alternative views on a wide variety of subjects, especially pop culture. Zines provide an opportunity for feminists to resist ideas in main stream publications that sustain women's subordination. Zines usually focus on a specific topic even while they critique racist, and patriarchal social structures. Members of the student group Feminists for Action at Ball State University have been creating zines annually for several years. It is a great creative outlet for the students and also an excellent advertisement for the group as a whole.

Literature & Books

In "'Thinking About Shakespeare's Sister," Virginia Woolf responds to the question "Why has there been no female Shakespeare?" Woolf wrote her essay in the late 1920s, but still today many critics and professors of literature raise the same questions about women's abilities to create great literature. British literature classes rarely acknowledge women authors. Lit majors often only read women such as Woolf, Jane Austen, or Emily Dickinson. The usual justification is that women simply have not written the great literature that men have that is important enough to be in the canon.

Women have always been writing, even in the time of Shakespeare, but their works were often neglected by the arbiters of the literary canon because they fell outside the narrowly constructed definitions of great literature. Even today, authors like J.K. Rowling submit work using male names or initials so as to have their work read or published.

Traditionally, women's novels have dealt with the subjects of women's lives: family, home, children, and love. As the canon was defined according to white male norms, women's writing and much of the writing of people of color were omitted. Jane Austen is still a popular novelist despite having written her books two centuries ago. Her current popularity is based in part on the dramatization of her work in a series of movies as well as the fact that Austen was both a romantic and a feminist. The continually relevant plots in her work offer a basis for her solid assessment of sexism and classism.

More women began to publish novels and poetry, and these have eventually been included in the canon. Toni Morrison (who received the Nobel Prize for literature), Alice Walker, and Maya Angelou have written about the dilemmas and triumphs faced by black women in a white, male-dominated culture. Feminist playwrights like Eve Ensler and feminist comedians such as Wanda Sykes, Margaret Cho, Tina Fey, Amy Poehler, and Amy Schumer have also been very influential in providing new scripts for women's lives.

So the feminist book canon grows larger and more diverse every day, which is important. Classics like Betty Friedan's *The Feminine Mystique*; Simone de Beauvoir's *The Second Sex*; Arlie Hochschild's *The Second Shift: Working and the Revolution at Home*; Naomi Wolf's *The Beauty Myth*, and bell hooks' entire oeuvre (a good start is *Feminism Is for Everybody*), stand the test of time and should be included in any comprehensive feminist reading list.

So maybe you would like to read some more updated titles, along with the oldies but goodies listed above. Here are my recommendations for you:

1. *Bad Feminist*, by Roxane Gay. "I embrace the label of bad feminist because I am human," she writes. Gay is true to herself and examines the cultural atmosphere of feminism today. We can't all be perfect feminists and what does that even mean, anyways?
2. *We Should All Be Feminists*, by Chimamanda Ngozi Adichie. Sure, quotes of this essay are included in a Beyonce song. That's enough reason to read it, right? But, seriously, this originated as a TEDx talk and Adichie does a great job explaining why we should all claim the title of feminist.
3. *Full Frontal Feminism: A Young Woman's Guide to Why Feminism Matters*, by Jessica Valenti. First out in 2007, this book has been a must-read for young feminists ever since. The second edition addresses cultural changes since then along with updates about topics ranging from pop culture to reproductive rights.
4. *Men Explain Things to Me*, by Rebecca Solnit. Check this out for Solnit's experiences with "mansplaining" and the silencing of women's voices. She also writes about marriage equality, sexual harassment, and Virginia Woolf.
5. *How to Be a Woman*, by Caitlin Moran. My British feminist hero. Like I mentioned with hooks above, read anything you can get your hands on by Moran. She's fantastic.

Art

Just as female writers have been ignored, misrepresented, and trivialized, so too female artists have faced similar struggles. Women's art has often been labeled "crafts" rather than art. This is because women, who were often barred from entering the artistic establishment, have tended to create works of art that were useful and were excluded from the category of fine art. Often, female artists, like other women who were writing novels, used a male pen name and disguised their identity in order to have their work shown. With the influence of the women's movement, women's art is being reclaimed and introduced into the art history curriculum, although it is often taught in the context of "women's art" or "feminist art history." This emphasizes the ways the academy remains androcentric, with the contributions of "others" in separate courses.

Female artists such as Frida Kahlo, Georgia O'Keeffe, and Judy Chicago have revitalized the art world by creating women-centered art and feminist critiques of masculine art forms. Similarly, graphic artists such as Barbara Kruger and mixed-media artists such as Jennifer Linton have incorporated feminist critiques of consumerism and desire. Photographers such as Cindy Sherman and

Lorna Simpson have also raised important question s about the representation of women and other marginalized people in media and society. Joyce Wieland has famously created quilted art pieces using a traditionally feminine form. More recently, Carol Rossetti is a designer, illustrator, and artist who has created images focusing on a variety of women's issues. They have been widely shared on social media. Last but not least, the "Guerrilla Girls," an anonymous feminist group wearing gorilla masks, use the names of dead female artists to highlight the ways women and people of color are disproportionately excluded from the art world through posters, postcards, and public appearances (http://www.guerrillagirls.com/).

Conclusion

This chapter could go on and on about the topics covered. So many women are creating activism on social media and so many more women artists, authors, musicians, etc., have been left out of history. Their works need to be taught, promoted, discussed, and shared, if only for us to achieve feminist equality in these areas. Let's continue the discussion with the questions below and the reading about Beyoncé.

Suggested Readings

Bay Area Video Coalition. (2015). *Does pop culture affect your views on feminism?* Retrieved December 14, 2015 from http://blogs.kqed.org/education/2015/04/07/how-are-women-of-color-changing-pop-culture/

Buszek, M. (2006). *Pin-up grrrls: Feminism, sexuality, popular culture.* Durham: Duke University Press.

Carson, M., Lewis, T., & Shaw, S. (2004). *Girls rock! Fifty years of women making music.* Lexington: University Press of Kentucky.

Jervis, L., & Zeisler, A. (2006). *BITCHfest: Ten years of cultural criticism from the pages of Bitch Magazine.* New York: Farrar, Straus and Giroux.

Jones, A. (Ed.). (2010). *The feminism and visual culture reader.* New York: Routledge.

Karlyn, K. (2011). *Unruly girls, unrepentant mothers: Redefining feminism on screen.* Austin: University of Texas Press.

New, S. (2005). *Feminism and popular culture.* Retrieved December 14, 2015 from http://www.thefword.org.uk/2005/11/feminism_and_popular_culture/

Whelehan, I., & Gwynne, J. (2014). *Ageing, popular culture and contemporary feminism: harleys and hormones.* New York: Palgrave Macmillan.

Zeisler, A. (2008). *Feminism and pop culture.* Berkley: Seal Press.

References

Azerrad, M. (1994). *Come as you are: The story of Nirvana.* New York: Doubleday.

Barcella, L. (2004). "The A-word". Salon. Retrieved December 14, 2015 from http://www.salon.com/2004/09/20/t_shirts/

Ellsworth, E. (1990). Feminist spectators and personal best. In P. Erens (Ed.), *Issues in feminist film criticism* (pp. 183-196). Bloomington: Indiana University Press.

Garofalo, R. (1992). *Rockin' the boat: Mass music & mass movements.* Cambridge, MA: South End Press.

George, D., & Mauro, L. (2012). An American woman forgotten. Retrieved December 14, 2015 from http://hampsongfoundation.org/margaret-ruthven-lang-on-the-40th-anniversary-of-her-death/

Greenhill, P. (2015). "The Snow Queen": Queer Coding in Male Directors' films. *Marvels & Tales, 29*(1), 110–134. Detroit: Wayne State University Press.

hooks, b. (1992). *Black looks: Race and representation.* Boston: South End Press.

Humm, M. (1997). *Feminism and film.* Edinburgh: Edinburgh University Press.

Johnston, C. (1975). Feminist politics and film history. *Screen, 16*(3), 115–125.

Kaze, R. (2015). Retrieved December 16, 2015 from http://news.yahoo.com/suspected-islamists-kill-six-abduct-50-cameroon-soldier-130151831.html

Mulvey, L. (1975). Visual pleasure and narrative cinema. *Screen, 16*(3), 6–18.

Patmore, D. (2015). Nadia Boulanger. Retrieved December 16, 2015 from http://www.naxos.com/person/Nadia_Boulanger/27093.htm

Pulver, A. (2015). *Reese Witherspoon talks up #AskHerMore on the Oscars red carpet.* Retrieved December 14, 2015 from http://www.theguardian.com/film/2015/feb/23/reese-witherspoon-talks-up-askhermore-on-the-oscars-red-carpet

Smelik, A. (1998). *And the mirror cracked. Feminist cinema and film theory.* London: Macmillan.

The Queer Film Society. (2015). Retrieved December 14, 2015 from http://www.queerfilmsociety.org/

The Representation Project. (2015). Retrieved December 14, 2015 from http://therepresentationproject.org/

Discussion Questions

1. How do you discover new music or books to read? Do you think about who creates these works as you choose them?

2. What can be done to support new women authors, artists, musicians, etc.? How do we make room for them in the history books?

3. What other feminists should be included in this chapter? Who would you write about?

4. Are you involved in activism on social media? If not, how would you like to be involved?

5. More and more celebrities are claiming to be feminists in public. How would you like to see feminism in mainstream media?

Beyonce's Fierce Feminism

by Janell Hobson
March 7, 2015

The singer/actor/popular-culture icon known simply by her first name—Beyoncé—does not hesitate to embrace the feminist label. She has especially shined a light on women's power: The power to perform in a male-dominated music industry; the power to acquire fame and fortune; the power to delight in one's beauty and sexuality; the power to cross over into mainstream media while championing a "girl power" anthem. Yet when women like Beyoncé proudly proclaim feminism, they tend to invite more debates than affirmation.

There was no denying the sheer audacity of Beyoncé's performance at this year's Super Bowl in early February, as she strode confidently on a stage that highlighted her silhouetted figure. The spectacle invoked goddess power, represented by Oshun—an African orisha (spirit or deity) known for her self-love, generosity and wealth—and Durga, the Hindu warrior goddess whose multiple hands emerged via digital screen as an extension of Beyoncé's essence. Beyoncé also summoned the collective power of women—representing diverse racial and ethnic backgrounds—by having an all-woman 10-piece backing band (The Sugar Mamas), women back-up singers and 120 women dancers. There was even a moment when the fans in the mosh pit seemed to be all women.

And while Beyoncé and troops captivated hundreds of millions of Super Bowl spectators and TV viewers with their overtly sexual moves, lead guitarist and music director Bibi McGill was given a spot-light moment to appr priate rock-star masculinity with her pyrotechnic guitar playing. In 13 minutes, Beyoncé exploded all the symbols associated with the Super Bowl: football, male virility and violence. Even the omnipresent objectification of women in Super Bowl ads momentarily lost its power.

"Lights out!!! Any questions??" tweeted Beyoncé's marital and music partner, Shawn "Jay Z" Carter, when the New Orleans Superdome had a power failure after his wife's halftime show.

If this is what Beyoncé had in mind when she prophetically sang, "Run the World (Girls)," I say: Bring it on!

But despite this performance of feminism for a mass audience, Beyoncé's critics still question her brand of female empowerment. There were those who wanted her to wear more clothes on stage, or not be so sexy in her dance moves.

And others who came to her defense.

In an article for The Telegraph in the U.K., Emma Gannon wrote, "If we accept that Lena Dunham [of the much-debated HBO series *Girls*] likes to take her clothes off and celebrate her body (with the majority of the media giving her a firm thumbs up), then how come Beyoncé is branded 'not a feminist' for doing the same?"

Blogger David R. Henson similarly interrogated our discomfort on Patheos by arguing that Beyoncé's provocative dress and dancing suggest "power, not sex." "It takes a warrior to be able to do something like that," wrote Henson. "No surprise then...that the Hindu warrior goddess Durga shows up, incarnated by Beyoncé. Against the pop-up screen, hands emerge and encircle Beyoncé from behind. These are not male hands. These are not Justin Timberlake's hands threatening to disrobe her in a 'wardrobe malfunction' [as happened with Janet Jackson during the 2004 Super Bowl halftime show]. These are her hands and they reach out and around her, not to possess her but to expand her power."

Aishah Shahidah Simmons, documentary filmmaker of NO! The Rape Documentary and a writer for the Ms. Blog and the Feminist Wire, agrees.

"Her Super Bowl performance clearly turned patriarchy on its head," says Simmons. "Her inclusion of an all-woman band, owning her sexual power, her presentation of such a diverse group of women (African Americans, Latinas, Asians)—she was definitely in a place of power. There was so much estrogen on stage and [there were] open spaces for queer desire and performance."

So does this performance cement her status as a feminist?

"I think I am a feminist in a way," Beyoncé once revealed in an interview with Jane Gordon of the U.K.'s *Daily Mail*. "It's not something I consciously decided I was going to be; perhaps it's because I grew up in a singing group [Destiny's Child] with other women...I never want to betray that friendship because I love being a woman and I love being a friend to other women." Beyoncé also identified as a "modern-day feminist" who believes in gender equality, in a recent interview with Jo Ellison for *British Vogue*.

However, not everyone acknowledges Beyoncé's version of feminism. Danielle Belton of the blogs Black Snob and Clutch Magazine sees Beyoncé as "mere entertainment." "Other pop icons like Madonna and Lady Gaga certainly seem more informed and more passionate about their gender politics," Belton muses. "Whereas Beyoncé seems not as passionate. It seems more like marketing."

Brittney Cooper, who blogs as Crunktastic in the Crunk Feminist Collective, thinks Beyoncé is much more complicated than that, but admits that, for some, the pop star is perceived to be an "untrustworthy feminist." On the one hand, she and her fellow Destiny's Child members Kelly Rowland and Michelle Williams sing about being an "Independent Woman" or a "Survivor"; on the other hand, they sing about pleasing men and conforming to their desires in a song like "Cater 2 U."

Belton similarly argues that "Beyoncé is reflective of a generation of women growing up with conflicted feelings about the double standards for women, and she's doing it on a massive scale. She's [a] super-empowered [woman] who has her husband and child in tow. She sings about being an 'Independent Woman' but also craves traditional marriage and motherhood."

But do such conflicted feelings negate Beyoncé's feminism? After all, feminists do marry and become mothers. They might then bring their feminist politics into traditional spheres, attempting to disrupt these identities and complicate the politics of respectability.

"I don't think Beyoncé has aspirations toward respectability," says Cooper. "She's interested in exploding those categories, in which one can be a wife and mother and still be very sexual. But if Beyoncé is hypersexual—and therefore 'inappropriate'—do we have a model for how women can be 'appropriately sexual' in the public sphere? When can a woman own her sexual power from a self-defined sexual standpoint?"

Not only that, but shouldn't a woman who sings about independence and female power also be multifaceted in her expressions, whether about romantic desire, heartache or dominating the music scene? Is a feminist not allowed to contradict herself? Other pop icons, such as Madonna and Lady Gaga, routinely appropriate conventional portrayals of femininity and sexuality even as they invite us to contest their meanings.

Tamika Carey, a feminist rhetorician at the University at Albany, would certainly like to see feminists give Beyoncé that space. "I refuse to let a constricted definition of feminism blind us to her innovative engagements with female performance and artistic expression," she says.

Filmmaker/blogger Simmons, however, believes that those who hesitate to view Beyoncé in feminist terms may be unduly influenced by racial politics. "If Beyoncé were white, she would definitely be called a feminist. But mainstream culture often doesn't recognize women of color in that way," she says. "As black women, we aren't even viewed as acting, as performing. Everything we do is supposed to be based in reality. So, if there are any contradictions, you don't get to be the face of feminism. Even though Bey is definitely in control of her image."

Cooper-aka-Crunktastic acknowledges this racial element as well, noting that, "White women may have trouble seeing Beyoncé as a feminist because she is racialized as a woman of color. And for women of color, the politics of respectability limits who we're willing to hold up as our role models in the public sphere, since it's so easy to tear us down."

In this year of the snake, 2013, Beyoncé is certainly feeling its tightening coil as criticisms have piled up against her—first with the report that she lip-synched the national anthem during President Barack Obama's inauguration, and later with the online outrage over what many perceived to be a betrayal of her "girl power" motto with a leaked track containing the hook "Bow down, bitches." It's a return to Southern-style hip-hop, in which the Houston-born singer borrows from the rap "diss track" tradition of bravado and dirty-dozen vernacular put-downs, but these "anti-feminist" lyrics and gender-bending masculine style (including a deepening of her vocals) seemed to undermine her feminist credentials. It also didn't help that she decided to entitle her tour "The Mrs. Carter Show World Tour."

Yet the "Mrs. Carter" title is hardly reflective of Beyoncé's reality, as she legally hyphenated her name to Knowles-Carter, and there are even rumors that her husband, too, goes by the legal surname Knowles-Carter. If this is how they privately identify, doesn't that suggest that "Mrs. Carter" is simply a public rhetorical performance—just as she performed as a "single lady" (or as her alter ego Sasha Fierce) at a time when she had recently changed her single status by marrying Jay-Z? As she reminds us in her "Bow Down/I Been On" track: "But don't think I'm just his little wife." We have to take clues about Beyoncé's feminist beliefs from these lyrics, since she typically projects a public persona while barely revealing her private life, even in the recent documentary *Life Is But a Dream*, for which she was a codirector and executive producer.

The talented and successful entertainer has been performing in show business since the age of 15, but we need not dismiss Beyoncé's brand of feminism as mere marketing. Feminism is political consciousness, not a product, and as Cooper notes, "Beyoncé has certainly evolved in her thinking about feminism—where before it was about her women friends, now she's critiquing patriarchy."

Here Cooper refers to Beyoncé's interview earlier this year with Amy Wallace in *GQ*, in which the pop star declared: "I truly believe that women should be financially independent from their men. And let's face it, money gives men the power to run the show. It gives men the power to define value. They define what's sexy. And men define what's feminine. It's ridiculous."

Beyoncé has been advocating for women's financial independence since her early Destiny's Child years, singing about unreliable lovers careless with their money in "Bills Bills Bills," or later, during her solo career, admonishing her ex to "not touch her stuff" as he exits "to the left/ to the left" in "Irreplaceable." Especially telling is her financial bravado in a song like "Suga Mama" ("Puttin' you on my taxes already...I promise I won't let no bills get behind..."). In a culture that focuses too much on consumerism, we may rightly feel uncomfortable with this emphasis on materialism, but Beyoncé's recognition of the economic inequalities between men and women certainly fuels her rhetoric and performance of what our society defines as "power."

Without a doubt, Beyoncé holds both financial and cultural power, and it will be intriguing to watch how they unfold. Blogger Danielle Belton would like to see the pop star more informed about women's realities: "There needs to be more substance behind the girl-power mantle she's been carrying." For Aishah Shahidah Simmons, Beyoncé is already practicing feminism—even if it's confined to the music industry.

"I hope Beyoncé inspires young women artists to have a women's band," she offers. "I know for the women in her band, Beyoncé has changed their lives and given them so many opportunities [to get] other gigs. That's the kind of model she gives us within the context of music and entertainment, so maybe she can inspire us to do similar work in other arenas. As far as I'm concerned we need all hands on deck [in ushering feminist social movements]."

Despite Beyoncé's contradictions—finding it "ridiculous" that men still define what's sexy while she maintains her body and image through conventional portrayals of sexiness and white beauty standards, or preaching "girl power" while calling us "bitches" in the next breath—her albums and soundtracks provide more than enough catchy beats and hooks to empower and encourage solidarity. If a battered woman can feel empowered to leave her abuser while booming "I'm a survivor/I'm not gon' give up" in her getaway car, or if a woman running for public office can make "Run the World (Girls)" her campaign slogan, need we expect more from our pop stars?

"Beyoncé just needs to wear a T-shirt that says, 'This is what a feminist looks like,'" Simmons suggests slyly. "Maybe she'll wear it on her Mrs. Carter world tour."

I can see it now. *Lights on! Any questions?*

CHAPTER 4
Body Image

Our bodies show lots of obvious gender expressions. The inscription of gender on the body is partly how we as a society recognize masculine and feminine. Bodies that are not easily recognizable as fitting with in this binary often cause anxiety when we cannot place them neatly into masculine or feminine boxes this binary aspect of bodies as either this way or that way is so taken for granted that we rarely question these by binaries.

Actions performed by our bodies provide a sense of agency and are shaped by social forces that give the meaning that gender performances are not only what we do they are also who we are or become. This implies that we are what we do and what we do is shaped by culture, social practices, and institutions that give those everyday actions meaning.

Race, age, and ability are factors in this category as well with various stereotypes of these categories that are persistent in society. These ideas have been used to control different communities just as with the expectations that certain people are naturally good at sports, science, math, etc. Those expectations have function to reinscribe racial discourses on human bodies. There are also discourses about the aging body that regulate behaviors just as there are for ability or disability.

The very notion of disability or differently abled as a bodily impairment implies a lack rather than a different set of attributes. The definition of being impaired only comes with something compared to being normal. In this way, bodies are contextualized in cultural meanings informed by our ideas about gender and other identities. Many of these cultural ideas for example come from the media (covered in a later chapter).

The focus of this chapter is on the social construction of the body and beauty ideals. Beauty is one of the most powerful discourses, associated with gendered bodies. Beauty norms regulate our lives, affecting what we do and how we think. I'm sure that you have a specific idea of what the word beautiful is, maybe even a person that pops into your head. Ultimately though, this notion of beauty is constantly in flux and varies across time and culture. This chapter provides some methods for negotiating beauty and also includes a discussion of eating disorders.

Historical Constructs

Body image ideals, such as race and gender, are social constructs that have grown out of a combination of history, politics, class, and moral values. One need look back only a few generations, or across cultures, to see that attitudes about thinness and fatness are fluid and ever changing.

During the late 1800s, actress Lillian Russell, who was said to weigh 200 pounds, was a famous performer and ads about her could be found all over the country (Schwartz & Bowbeer, 1997). During this era, in fact, there were more programs to help people gain rather than lose weight. Up until most recent history, stoutness was associated with good health, affluence, and social status. Skinny people were viewed as poor or lower class, because they most likely didn't have enough money to feed themselves regularly. From the beginning of history, art objects such as Venus figurines and sculptures of fertility goddesses showcased larger sizes as signs of health and wellness. "Rubenesque" depictions of women as plump and curvaceous were in favor for centuries throughout Europe (Belkin, 1998).

According to Peter Stearns, obesity became associated with gluttony and sin more during the late nineteenth century. Protestant values became more prominent and there was an increase in food and consumerism. During World War I, food shortages led media outlets to claim that gaining weight was unpatriotic. Anti-fat attitudes took over, and medical interventions (surgery, drugs, counseling, etc.) were encouraged to rid Americans of their fat (Stearns, 2002).

Later on, Twiggy, Kate Moss, and Victoria's Secret models replaced more curvaceous figures like Marilyn Monroe as the new ideal of beauty. In the same way, the popular media has also encouraged males to become more trim and hard-bodied.

Social Construction

From a social construction standpoint, the way to understand the body is to recognize attributes as arising out of cultures in which the body is given meaning. For example, as mentioned earlier, in some parts of history, being heavier was considered more beautiful than being thin and other times being very thin was seen as beautiful. There has never been an actual fixed definition of beauty in American culture or internationally, for that matter.

On the flip side of this is the concept of ***biological determinism*** where a person's biology or genetic makeup rather than culture or society determines her or his or their destiny. This approach sees people in terms of the reproductive and biological bodies. This allows people to transcend cultural norms and not feel stuck in traditional masculine and feminine roles.

It may seem obvious, but societies don't often follow the idea of biological determinism. For example, menstruation has often been seen a smelly taboo and distasteful. Menstruation has often been regarded negatively and describe with euphemisms like the curse or on the rag. Girls are still taught to conceal menstrual products from others, especially men. Gloria Steinem (1978) suggests that if men could menstruate, ads and products would be everywhere in mainstream media, including the commercial breaks of professional sports.

Bodies can be seen as cultural artifacts. Culture becomes embodied and is represented through the body. These ideas can be seen through more women, especially white women, that want to shrink their bodies. This can be compared to men who are more likely to want bigger bodies physically. The fact that many more women than men would willingly want to be characterized as small is an example of gender norms associated with the body.

Another important aspect of the social construction of bodies is ***objectification***, that is seeing the body as an object in separate from its context. This is most often supported by the media, entertainment, and fashion industries. All bodies can be a objectified, although the context for female identified bodies is different. There is much more cultural and societal support for female objectification. Men can be objectified, but the contexts and consequences are vastly different for those that identify as female.

As objectification becomes more prominent in our society, many people focus more on the body as something to control and use to express identity. As a result, the body becomes something to be fashion and in control of. The ability to express ourselves through clothing (or tattoos or piercings) has become synonymous with personal freedom. The argument could be made that this isn't really freedom because we have to purchase and fashion ourselves around what is available from different stores and sizes. The other argument against this would be that focusing on fashion and clothing would take away from other political and economic concerns that should be more important.

In the Classroom

Size bias is something children learn early in America. Students who do not fit narrow ideals of health and beauty are scorned and ostracized by their peers, and many adults either fail to see it or unconsciously believe that fat children are to blame for their own inadequacies. Understanding the social and political factors that shape attitudes toward body size can help educators to look beyond their own cultural lenses when it comes to the lives of their students. From such a vantage point, they can be more compassionate role models and help students to understand that while variations in body shape and size are natural, expressions of bias never are.

Breakout: Fashion (Bing)

Courtesy of Ashleigh Bingham

Ashleigh "Bing" Bingham is an Indiana-based doctoral student and blogger. Her website "I Dream of Dapper" is a project she single-handedly created few years ago to explore her love of menswear while also critiquing outdated American gender norms. Besides her own blog, Bing also writes for Qwear and Autostraddle.

Indiana is known for being a very conservative state. Growing up there, Bing struggled to fit in with her peers. Like many other people, she didn't really come into her own identity until college. She found friends who shared similar ideas about identity and supported her work. Since then, she has tried to inspire, challenge, and encourage individuals everywhere to feel comfortable in their own skin (and clothes).

Bing has almost 15,000 followers on her blog. She also has a tutorial on YouTube to teach the brave how to recreate her famous hairstyle, The Queer Pomp (www.youtube.com/watch?v=gx9_EVpS91c). That video has almost 1,500 views on YouTube.

Bing is an amazing young feminist challenging gender norms through fashion and education. She has accomplished much in her life so far and will only continue to become more successful. For even more thoughts from Bing, check out the reading at the end of this chapter.

Beauty Ideals

With the rise of mass media throughout the twentieth century, the popular image of women in America has undergone a substantial change. From Tyra Banks to Kendall Jenner, the body shapes of the most admired models have remained consistently slimmer than that of the average American woman, representing a nearly impossible ideal.

This has resulted in a severe rise in weight anxieties and negative body image among women and girls. Dissatisfaction with weight is nearly universal among women, while dieting is pervasive. Girls as young as 6 are commonly unhappy with their weight. This trend has likewise been reflected around the world wherever this media culture has become dominant. The result has been the massive spread of previously rare eating disorders and lifelong unhappiness toward one's own body.

It's not just a women's issue, men are affected also. Baldness, penis size, and weight gain are just a few of the issues that men are told to be concerned with. Ultimately, though, because women's worth is more tied to bodily appearance than the men's worth, portrayals of female beauty are more significant in women's lives. This is called the ***double standard*** associated with beauty ideals. What this means is that despite the increasing focus on male bodies in society and popular culture, women are particularly vulnerable to having their worth measured by their bodies.

Historically, beauty standards have varied. Let's see how we got to the ideals that are prevalent today.

1900s–1910s: The Gibson Girl

The Gibson Girl, a creation of illustrator Charles Dana Gibson, was an iconic image of the popular beauty ideals at the turn of the century. Rarely are beauty standards so clearly defined, but Gibson did his research and based his illustrations on thousands of American girls. This feminine ideal was depicted as skinny and tall, along with a substantial bust and hips. The exaggerated look was achieved by way of corseting. Gibson Girls were portrayed as both fashionable and stylish (Library of Congress, 2015). Visit the link in the References to see the Gibson Girl illustrations.

1920s: The Flapper

Women known as flappers came along as American culture took a liberal turn. These women were far more casual than before. The flapper was a young woman who had little regard for uptight older generations and behavioral norms. Flappers wore loose dresses and skirts that flashed ankles, knees, and legs. The women wore this type of clothing in order to be able to dance to jazz, the popular music at the time. They also cut their hair short. Women were known to tan and wear dark makeup during this time (U.S. History, 2015).

1930s–1940s: Fashion in Wartime

The Great Depression brought back a traditional style to women's fashion and body image. Women continued to have short hair, but the skirts became longer. When World War II began, requisitioning of fashion materials such as silk, nylon, and clothing dye became necessary. Women became practical, with simple shirts and jackets. Women even tailored the unused suits of men at war, remaking them into everyday women's wear. Women at this time aspired to become more curvy and feminine. In particular, advertisements told women how they could avoid a too-skinny look (Olds, 2001).

1950s: Post-War

In the 1950s, the ideal body image for women remained fuller-figured. Marilyn Monroe and Grace Kelly are great examples of this ideal. Hollywood films propelled glamorous models such as Monroe to celebrity status. Rationing ended, so fashion choices extended for women. Once again, makeup and hair products gained popularity. Women wanted to use a variety of ways to meet beauty ideals during this time (The People History, 2015).

1960s: Hippies

The 1960s brought a new standard of beauty, similar to that of the flappers of the 1920s. Straying away from the curvy images of the 1950s, the sexual revolution of the 1960s celebrated thinness and androgyny. Twiggy, a popular supermodel at the time, embodied this idealized body type. Twiggy is small, with short hair, and a boyish look (Lawson, 2015). This new beauty ideal abandoned all curves and focused on young looks. Also at this time, the "hippie" look including long, straight hair became popular later in the 1960s (Wild, 2015).

1970s: Thin Is In

The 1970s saw the continued prominence of a thin ideal, which often encouraged women to go to dangerous lengths to achieve this beauty standard. Anorexia gained popularity at this time, with deadly consequences for many women, including Karen Carpenter (Latson, 2015). More information on eating disorders is found later in the chapter. Actress Farrah Fawcett was also known as a sex symbol of the time. She was well known for her layered hair and one-piece swimsuits. Women of the time copied her look with long hair and natural makeup.

1980s: Let's Get Physical

The beauty ideal of the 1980s focused on fitness. Toned bodies were now encouraged and aerobic videos became a widespread trend. Diet and exercise became the main focus of many women's lives. Media depictions of women in the 1980s glamorized tall, skinny women. The fashion of the time included headbands, tights, leggings, leg warmers, and anything made of spandex. Business attire for women was bold colored suits and shoulder pads. This decade also saw the rise of supermodels such as Naomi Campbell, Cindy Crawford, and Claudia Schiffer (Sherrow, 2001).

1990s: Baywatch

Throughout the 1990s, the skinny ideal became even more exaggerated. Women were expected to be thin, but also have large breasts. Pamela Anderson popularized this look on the TV show "Baywatch." Also popular during this time were beauty ideals called the "waif look" and "heroin chic." Kate Moss is the supermodel who made bony thin her signature look.

2000–now: Rise of Plus-Size

We are coming full circle, to where women are beginning to have curvier bodies. Mainstream media and fashion designers are beginning to take notice as well. Recently, Tess Holliday became the first woman of her size (26) to land a modeling contract. She's also the founder of the #effyourbeautystandards movement, also making the cover of People magazine and several other news shows. She and other body positivity supporters are reminding us all that every body is beautiful.

Overall Trends

American body ideals for women have changed somewhat throughout the twentieth century. In recent decades, these two conflicting images appear to have merged into what is considered beautiful: an almost unhealthily thin and bony frame, combined with a substantial bust. A movement for plus-size standards is growing, but is still not the ideal of beauty.

A number of factors contribute to women's negative self-image and body dissatisfaction. The media and its portrayal of beauty have been found to be associated with eating disorders and the urge to be thin. As family and friends absorb these media messages, this adds to an increased pressure for women to aspire to this ideal. This pressure can work its way into all aspects of our lives.

As women pursue this unattainable ideal, they can become more dissatisfied with their appearance. Most will struggle with trying to attain this ideal and will be unhappy with their looks. Anxiety over body image and frequent dieting have become common enough to be considered a normal, unhealthy lifestyle for women.

Beauty norms can take over a significant amount of time in women's lives. It is interesting to think about these everyday behaviors that maintain the body. The seemingly trivial rules and practices some scholars call **_disciplinary body practices_**. They are practices because they involve taken for granted behaviors such as shaving legs, applying makeup, and curling or coloring hair. They are disciplinary because they involve social control in the ways that we spend time, money, and effort. These practices that regulate our lives are directly connected to the production and consumption of various beauty products. It's a vicious circle.

Think of how many disciplinary beauty practices in which you or your friends take part in daily or weekly. For some people, it's not just products, but also facelifts, eye tucks, rhinoplasties, collagen injections, Botox, liposuction, tummy tucks, stomach stapling, breast implants, and breast reductions. Women are also undergoing vaginal cosmetic surgery, which like the other procedures mentioned, comes with its own set of risks. It is important to understand that the aesthetics of the pelvic area are related to norms about gender, the body, and sexuality and especially norms created by media and contemporary pornography.

Where many women strive to attain the beauty ideals on an ongoing basis, there are just as many women who are choosing not to participate in the rituals. They are not supporting the industries that produce the beauty products. These women are also actively creating other definitions of beauty. Some are actively appropriating the standards by highlighting and or exaggerating the very norms and standards themselves. They are using fashion and cosmetics for their own empowerment, fighting against existing cultural standards.

A critical response to resisting beauty ideals comes in the form of a question: What's wrong with being beautiful? The feminist answer is that it is not beauty that's the issue but rather the way beauty has been constructed by popular culture. We shouldn't just focus on one type of beauty and conform to that. Instead, we need societies that recognize a variety of beauty ideals.

Another common question: Can you wear makeup and feminine accessories and still identify as a feminist? The answer, of course, is yes. Many third-wave feminists joined the movement for this cause alone. The third wave of the feminist movement encourages people to dress as they feel comfortable. They champion the freedom of self-expression. Therefore, there are plenty of feminists who wear makeup, dresses, and high heels, just as there are feminists who refrain from makeup and other stereotypical feminine fashions.

Eating Disorders

Eating disorders are compulsive issues that include a variety of different behaviors. There are several different types: anorexia nervosa (self-starvation), bulimia nervosa (binge eating with self-induced vomiting and/or laxative use), compulsive eating (uncontrolled/binge eating), and muscle dysmorphia (fear of being inadequately muscled). Outside of these disorders are other general eating behaviors that may be problematic including: occasional binge eating and fasting, overly compulsive food habits, fear of public eating, and general problems associated with compulsive dieting and/or over-exercising. The latter list of generalized disordered eating/exercising is becoming more widespread among North American women.

These disorders are directly associated with the politics of gender and sexuality. It appears that the number of eating-disordered women in any given community is proportional to the number of individuals who are dieting to control weight. Dieting seems to trigger the onset of an eating disorder in vulnerable individuals.

Eating disorders, excluding muscle dysmorphia, affect women primarily. These issues are even more prevalent in college-aged and young women. According to the National Association of Anorexia Nervosa and Associated Disorder, 91% of women surveyed on a college campus had attempted to control their weight through dieting. 22% dieted "often" or "always." By age 20, 86% report onset of eating disorder, and 43% report onset between ages of 16 and 20 (ANAD, 2015).

Anorexia is the third most common chronic illness among adolescents. 95% of those who have eating disorders are between the ages of 12 and 25 (ANAD, 2015). 25% of college-aged women engage in bingeing and purging as a weight-management technique (Wade, Keski-Rahkoneb, & Hudson, 2011).

The mortality rate associated with anorexia nervosa is 12 times higher than the death rate associated with all causes of death for females 15–24 years old. Over one-half of teenage girls and nearly one-third of teenage boys use unhealthy weight control behaviors such as skipping meals, fasting, smoking cigarettes, vomiting, and taking laxatives. In a survey of 185 female students on a college campus, 58% felt pressure to be a certain weight, and of the 83% that dieted for weight loss, 44% were of normal weight (ANAD, 2015).

The media continues to play a role in how people, and women, specifically, define themselves and their bodies. The body type portrayed in advertising as the ideal is possessed naturally by only 5% of American females (Wade, Keski-Rahkoneb, & Hudson, 2011). Although eating disorders have the highest mortality rate of any mental disorder, the mortality rates reported on those who suffer from eating disorders can vary considerably between studies and sources. Those who suffer from an eating disorder may ultimately die of heart failure, organ failure, malnutrition, or suicide. Those medical complications are reported as the cause of death instead of the eating disorder. According to a study done by the *American Journal of Psychiatry*, eating disorder mortality rates were 4% for anorexia nervosa, 3.9% for bulimia nervosa, and 5.2% for eating disorder not otherwise specified (Crow, et al., 2009).

Should the huge number of women who are always on a diet overly concerned with weight issues, compulsive about what they do or do not eat be included in the statistics on eating disorders? If so, then the number of women with these problems increases exponentially. Because food and bodies are central preoccupations in so many women's lives, we might ask, why women and why food?

Historically, women have long been associated with food preparation and that has been a large part of female cultural norms. Women have been relegated to the private sphere of the home more than the public world, where food consumption is again part of the norm. In American culture, food has been associated with comfort and celebration, especially for holidays. For better or for worse, lots of people use food as a way of dealing with the anxiety and unhappiness in life. Combine all these ideas together and food becomes the object of compulsion. Add in the beauty ideal stereotypes, which brings up a whole new set of anxieties, and eating disorders can appear.

Eating disorders can show how many women want self-control in their lives. Within context of limited power and autonomy reflected in American society, these women look for ways to have any control. Women try to control their bodies and achieve an impossible perfection because they don't have power in other parts of their lives. The pressure in our society for women to measure up to cultural standards of beauty is central to understanding eating disorders. This is often called the "culture of thinness." These standards infringe on all women's lives whether we choose to live with them or actively resist them. Messages are everywhere in the media telling women that they're not good enough. Mass media is encouraging them to constantly change any part of their lives with various products and practices.

Although the focus is on girls, young women and women of all ages really, boys, and men are also a part of this issue. Girls and boys learn early on that they must aspire to some unattainable standards of physical perfection. Again, media messages like this distract people from other issues and focus them on disciplining their bodies to unattainable standards. The focus and energy they put on their bodies in turn affect their self-esteem. This can lead to internal struggles and long-term psychological harm. In these ways, eating disorders can be seen as cultural statements about gender.

Conclusion

Female beauty standards in America have remained unrealistic and extreme for many years. Mass media and popular images of thinness show an ideal that is more and more unattainable for the average woman. Celebrity culture along with TV and films are prime examples of these stereotypes. This trend has been reflected numerous times in many first-world nations. Although the focus of this chapter is American culture, it should be mentioned that women in developing nations typically lack this anxiety over their weight.

The problematic media images promote thinness, peer pressure, and personal levels of anxiety or depression. Women develop those conditions that are then exacerbated by the continual unsuccessful pursuit of an impossible goal. This continued problem has shown a rise in weight concern in even very young girls. Dieting and anorexia are also being tried by young women with more frequency. While the severity of this problem is receiving increasing attention in the public sphere, these anxieties remain so common as to be normal among women. A cultural shift is desperately needed in America. We need to build up the self-esteem of children from a young age and encourage people to see beauty in all sizes. The focus should be on health, not a scale or pants size. Only then will our society become better as a whole.

For more information about learning to accept yourself and others, no matter what clothing they wear, check out Bing's reading at the end of this chapter.

Suggested Readings

Steinem, G. (1978). *If men could menstruate.* Ms. Magazine.

Brumberg, J. (1998). *The body project: An intimate history of American girls.* New York: Random House.

Grossman, M. (2010). "Beating anorexia and gaining feminism," in Martin, C., & Sullivan, J.C. *Click!: When we knew were feminists.* Berkley: Seal Press.

Martin, C. (2007). *Perfect girls, starving daughters: The frightening new normalcy of hating your body.* New York: Free Press.

Newsome, J. (2011). *Miss representation.* Retrieved December 14, 2015 from http://therepresentationproject. org/film/miss-representation/

Weitz, R. (2004). *Rapunzel's daughters: What women's hair tells us about women's lives.* New York: Farrar, Straus and Giroux.

Wolf, N. (2002). *The beauty myth: How images of beauty are used against women.* New York: Harper Collins.

Wykes, M., & Gunter, B. (2005). *The media and body image: If looks could kill.* London: Sage Publications.

References

ANAD. (2015). "Eating Disorder Statistics." Retrieved December 14, 2015 from http://www.anad.org/get-information/about-eating-disorders/eating-disorders-statistics/

Belkin, K. (1998). *Rubens.* London: Phaidon Press.

Crow, S.J., Peterson, C.B., Swanson, S.A., Raymond, N.C., Specker, S., Eckert, E.D., & Mitchell, J.E. (2009). "Increased mortality in bulimia nervosa and other eating disorders." *American Journal of Psychiatry,* 166, 1342–1346.

Latson, J. (2015). *How Karen Carpenter's death changed the way we talk about anorexia.* Retrieved December 14, 2015 from http://time.com/3685894/karen-carpenter-anorexia

Lawson, T. (2015). *Fashion.* Retrieved December 14, 2015 from http://www.twiggylawson.co.uk/fashion

Library of Congress. (2015). Retrieved December 14, 2015 from http://www.loc.gov/exhibits/gibson-girls-america/the-gibson-girl-as-the-new-woman.html

Olds, L. (2001). "World War II and Fashion: The Birth of the New Look," *Constructing the Past.* 2(1). Retrieved December 14, 2015 from http://digitalcommons.iwu.edu/constructing/vol2/iss1/6

Schwartz, D., & Bowbeer, A. (1997). *Lillian Russell: A bio-bibliography.* Westport, Conn.: Greenwood Publishing.

Sherrow, V. (2001). *For Appearance' sake: The historical encyclopedia of good looks, beauty, and grooming.* Westport, Conn.: Greenwood Publishing.

Stearns, P. (2002). *Fat history: Bodies and beauty in the modern West.* NYU Press.

Steinem, G. (1978). *If men could menstruate.* Ms. Magazine.

The People History. (2015). *1950s fashion.* Retrieved December 14, 2015 from http://www.thepeoplehistory.com/50sclothes.html

U.S. History. (2015). *Flappers.* Retrieved December 14, 2015 from http://www.ushistory.org/us/46d.asp

Wade, T. D., Keski-Rahkonen A., & Hudson J. (2011). "Epidemiology of eating disorders." In M. Tsuang and M. Tohen (Eds.), *Textbook in Psychiatric Epidemiology* (3rd ed.) (pp. 343-360). New York: Wiley.

Wild, C. (2015). *Hippie high school.* Retrieved December 14, 2015 from http://mashable.com/2015/01/16/hippies-high-school/

Discussion Questions

1. What do you think about gender norms in our society? Should they be changed?

2. Will body ideals and fashion continue to change over time? Do you think history repeats itself when it comes to these ideas?

3. Eating disorders are a serious issue. What are some ways we can use mass media to combat this issue?

4. Popular culture often dictates American beauty ideals. How can we change the message to include all shapes and sizes?

5. How do body image issues affect men and women differently. Do they?

Stop Selling It Short(s)

by Ashleigh Bingham

There is a deafening internal groan that occurs when the discussion turns to "body image". That is not to say that body image is not an important topic but rather that we have been having the same conversation for decades and so very little has changed. I remember in junior high when they split up the girls and the boys and we, a group of braced-faced teens, talked about body image while the boys were elsewhere being taught how to change the oil in a car or something to that stretch of the imagination. I remember the various lessons on eating disorders, exercise, and the importance of a well-balanced diet (which has actually changed more than the entire discussion of body image). These lessons didn't stop my friends and I from skipping meals to feel better about our pre-pubescent pudginess nor did it encourage us to look at body image as a symptom of a bigger issue. I will admit that teenagers' understanding of beauty is about as deep as the pools that they are able to swim in unsupervised but it was those concepts that we used as reflection ponds to judge ourselves. I could list off each body part of a celebrity and how we one day dreamed to have bodies like theirs but the underlying motivation was to be desirable. We were young, we were learning, and we so desperately needed to know that who we were was acceptable and even wanted.

Now this is where my school bus of thought is going to take a big left turn away from the "you-don't-need-other-people's-approval" direction that this could very easily take. Instead I'm going to issue you the challenge of reexamining the conversations you have had with a different focus. How many times have you talked about body image as being anything other than weight? Other than beauty? What about gender identity expression? What about how you see yourself as a girl/boy/human in the body you were born into? What about that form of body image?

It wasn't until I was about 20-something that I was able to look into a mirror and see myself in it. No there was nothing wrong with my eyes but for the longest time, there was something off about the person looking back at me. You see, I had spent years learning and perfecting the image of my body, its femininity. I had mastered the liquid eyeliner, could curl an entire head of hair in a flash, and boy could I leap tall buildings in a single bound in my skin-tight jeans but for me, it was skin-deep, a false image that allowed me to move throughout my world comfortably and yet not at all. I would later learn that Judith Butler calls gender a performance and I would be forever changed. I had, in fact, learned to play a character. I framed my body, my being in femininity but with each compliment my uneasiness grew. I was uncomfortable in this body that I had crafted and it began to show in the ways in which I would push it to be better, thinner, more feminine whatever it was, I was searching for a sense of authenticity. I was searching for a version of myself that would feel like home, a version that fit like a glove or even more rare like the perfect pair of shorts for a hot summer day.

I once own a pair of shorts that I swear could breathe rainbows into the cloudiest of days. These were not your typical cargo shorts but rather they had the unthinkable ability to fold up into their own back pocket. Now this may not seem like magic today but at the time, they were life changing. Now the shorts were perfect, nothing is, their one flaw was the department that sold them, the men's department. Growing up in the Midwest with a conventionally conservative mother, shopping in the men's section was a no-go but my dreams were bigger. Naturally, I begged and pleaded, worked out a payment plan with my allowance, and then walked around the store like a pitiful puppy to really get my point across like the mature human being I would one day grow up to be. Believe it or not, it actually worked.

From that day forward those shorts and I were inseparable, in my mind there is a slow-motion flashback where we are climbing trees, riding scooters, laughing and blowing bubbles to the tune of some sappy song about friendship. I would go as far as to call them my first love, which only turns this sickly sweet summer into a mystery plot when one day they went missing. After some topnotch sleuthing I found them tucked in the trashcan at the end of our curb...much to my mother's displeasure I will soon find out. By the look on my mother's face, I had just spoiled her mastermind plan to rid her house of the shorts once and for all. From them on I dubbed myself the short's full time bodyguard. Whenever they were washed, I was there. When they were dried, I was there. When they were folded haphazardly and throw in front of my bedroom door, I was there. I was always there...well except for the inevitable day that I was not. There are rumors of a used-clothes donation; others say they found their way out with the trash after all, but all I know is that that was my first taste of betrayal.

Betrayal may seem a bit strong from the outside but this was just one of many lessons I would learn about what was acceptable and what was not. I learned to stop asking for certain things. "Boy" things. Of course I still wanted them more than anything but I knew my chances were slim and it would inevitably end badly. Thus my alter-ego was born. When I look back at photos, I of course have to laugh at the hideous chunky highlights and excessive eye makeup. It's absolutely laughable because I tried so hard to be someone likable only to dislike myself. It wasn't until I was well into my third year of college that I decided that I was going to stop running from who I was. I went to a thrift store, bought a few button-ups and a tie and never looked back. It was truly liberating. I was shattering the distorted image of myself and replacing it with a person I could recognize, love, and celebrate.

As time went on I bought my first chest binder, those of you with breasts can relate to the unfortunate gap that occurs between buttons when one is frontally well-endowed. I had a certain picture of myself in my head that was ruined by the push-up bras of my past. Flattening my chest was the second greatest change I was able to make and I was instantly astounded by how much happier I was. I felt secure, I felt in control of my body, and most of all I felt like myself. Now as you can imagine, not everyone understood what I was doing. Not everyone could see that I was finally becoming who I wanted to be, or at least how I wanted to look. They couldn't see how my chest binder was no more taboo than their spandex body suits or that my ties were comparable to their necklaces. We were all using our resources to create an image but mine was different, it was "masculine" and because gender expression was never discussed in and around body image, I became an outcast. How could a girl who identifies with her body want to look anything but feminine?

Awful things can come out of feeling alone, unaccepted. Lives are cut short, relationships are lost, and years are spent in misery when they could instead feel magical. I refused to believe that I was the only person who felt like their body image was entirely acceptable no matter how "gender non-conforming" it was. I couldn't believe that what I had felt my entire life was somehow wrong so I took to social media and started to document my journey. I posted photos, questions, quotes that meant something to me and my journey towards a positive body image. I soon found that I was one of many who had been deterred from this manner of self-expression. We created a community, a family of people who were finally living their lives by their rules. We refused to be called less because we wanted more out of our lives. We had been told lies by the world around us and we were finally seeing them for what they were. We could be women in ties, we could be women in suits, we could look however we wanted and embrace it no matter what society said.

Maybe you think this is a fluke, maybe you think this is a small incident and this doesn't effect that many people. If you are under this impression, you are sadly mistaken. Little girls and boys are growing up each day with the message with how they want to look, how they know their true selves to look is unacceptable. I know this because they write to me, they submit photos of their own journeys, and I get to share and celebrate the work they are doing to find themselves in a world of unhealthy messaging. I run a blog called I Dream of Dapper, which is currently being followed by 14,000+ individuals and is growing rapidly. I challenge you to visit it. I challenge you open up your mind to the messages that have been taught to you through the absence of acknowledgement. Body image is far deeper than skin, much more than fat and bones; it's how you see yourself, how you perceive what you have to work with and how that functions in your life.

The truth of the matter is that we are who we are and there's no use in changing that. You can waste your entire life trying to look like someone else or you can take charge of your life and your body and celebrate the person that you are. Society teaches many lessons about what is acceptable and what is disgusting but you have the agency to decide what will be apart of your journey. Only you know your true self and only you can let that person shine. I may not currently own a pair of blue cargo shorts that can fold up into their own back pocket but I do get up each morning and smile to myself as I button up my shirt over my minimized chest. I walk with pride and purpose because when I pass those reflective surfaces, I know exactly who's looking back at me and I couldn't be happier.

CHAPTER 5

Sexuality

Let's face it, **sexuality** is a topic that interests most people. It can cause both happiness and frustration. Since our own societies and communities shape sexual desires and behaviors, it becomes clear that our ideals about sexuality are heavily regulated. Governing bodies and popular culture control the who, what, when, where , and why of sexuality. Laws that condone certain relationships and sexual identities are created and regulated. Those that have the power shape the norms and behaviors associated with sexuality.

A central focus of our discourse on sexuality is the assumption that everyone should experience sexual desire at some point in their lives. **Asexual individuals**, those people who do not experience sexual desire, challenge the normative patriarchal culture. Additionally, some feminist research uses asexuality to challenge feminist pro-sex theory (Cerankowski & Milks, 2010).

Counter to all the regulations on sexuality is the idea that sex, when consensual, can be liberating. Controlling and enjoying your own sexuality can be empowering. It can also be powerful and fulfilling to seek out and be in a sexual relationship.

Feminists frequently value the idea of **empowered female sexuality**. They also often disagree about the definition of that term. What does that empowerment look like? Might it be different for every woman? Couldn't it also change over time, depending on the age of the female?

Empowered female sexuality is a particularly important issue for teens and young adults. The United States needs better media literacy education and proficient, comprehensive sexuality education. Both types of education listed above are either completely nonexistent or scarcely provided in this country. Teaching these subjects and having a basic understanding of them are central to enhancing teen girls' sexual empowerment.

Sexual empowerment is a key theme in this chapter. The social construction of sexuality is discussed and key terms are provided. The politics of sexuality, including information about feminist ideas of pornography, are also shared.

Social Construction

Sexuality involves various interests, attractions, identities, and practices. It is constructed through societal **sexual scripts**. This means that humans perform sexuality the same way gender and other identities are performed. Sexual scripts are basic guidelines for how we are supposed to feel and act as sexual beings.

As mentioned earlier, sexuality has been an important concern for the feminist movement. The idea that sexuality is socially constructed is important to the feminist view of this topic. Many radical feminists maintain a separation between sex and gender. They use the term sex to refer to the biological differences between male and female bodies. They then use the word gender for identifying masculine and/or feminine behaviors, attitudes, etc. Sometimes these distinctions can be problematic. Defining the sex of one's body is also a form of interpretation because in doing so, a person is using social constructs to ascribe or impose gendered ideals on their bodies. Certain features of the body are deemed more important than others and then associated with a particular sex.

In *Gender Trouble,* Judith Butler (1990) argued that gender (including sex) is a performative utterance. She describes it as a discursive act which brings into being that which it names. Butler argues that sex as a category is inseparable from the power relations in which it is constructed.

Among the first feminist works to contest the idea of a "natural" sexuality existing prior to culture is In *Sex, Gender and Society,* Ann Oakley (1996) disagrees with the idea that natural sexuality existed before culture. Using anthropological evidence, she compared the sexual behaviors of several indigenous groups and her research showed a wide variety. Societal stereotypes of a significant difference between male and female sexuality are found to be culturally specific rather than universal. Indigenous groups were also found to vary widely in the meaning and importance given to sexual activity. Oakley and her research provided empirical support to patriarchal ideas of human sexuality.

Radical feminists have been important in creating theories about the political significance for women and sexuality. Adrienne Rich (1996), writing in the second wave of the feminist movement in the United States, defines **compulsory heterosexuality** and lesbian erasure. She wrote that the assumption that women have an innate orientation toward men coupled with the definition of lesbianism as less natural, deviant, a product of bitterness toward men, or an alternate lifestyle choice to the heterosexual norm is an important form of male power. She details male power, "ranging from physical brutality to control of consciousness (pg. 132)" which convinces women to identify with heterosexuality and away from lesbianism, and then furthers patriarchal stereotypes of female sexuality.

As mentioned above, sexuality is shaped by societies we live in and so are socially constructed. The focus on these sexual scripts emphasizes how we understand what is "normal." People are not naturally anything; individuals' sexual desires and identities change over the course of their lives. "Normal" is a historically constructed concept from our own societies. In other words, these scripts provide guidelines for sexual behaviors in particular cultures at different times. Foundational in this is the opposition between heterosexuality and homosexuality. This opposition shapes sexual feelings and expression. It helps define what is "normal."

Sexual scripts are sometimes misunderstood. The focus on virginity as an indicator of female moral worth, or being known as a "good girl," is troublesome. This notion is especially problematic since young women are increasingly sexualized and then also face abstinence movements that shame any sexual activity. Research shows that many teens who sign "virginity pledges" become sexually active regardless and then aren't educated or prepared to protect themselves against pregnancy and STDs (Kempner, 2014).

Sexual scripts influence how people develop their own sexual identities. We learn these subjects by accepting, rejecting, and/or negotiating the sexual scripts we see around us. These subjects are called **sexual self-schemas**. They are defined as ideas about sexual aspects of individuals that are established from lived experiences and guide sexual feelings and actions. The sexual self-schemas that you find acceptable may not be unacceptable to your friends and family. Everyone is different.

Sexual identity, one aspect of sexual self-schemas, is defined as a person's attraction to people of a certain gender. It is an individual's romantic/sexual identity with other people. Sexual identity does not require sexual experience, just how an individual sees themselves.

Heterosexuality is a sexual identity where romantic and/or sexual feelings are between people of the "opposite sex," commonly known as straight people. *Homosexuality* is a sexual identity where romantic and/or sexual feelings are between people of the "same sex," commonly known as gay. Gay and homosexual are labels that can be inclusive of women, although they are often used to describe men.

The term lesbian means the romantic and/or sexual feelings between women. You might also hear the terms dyke, butch, and femme. Dyke is synonymous with lesbian, although it usually is used to describe a masculine lesbian. Like queer, dyke is a word that is sometimes used in a derogatory manner. It has been appropriated or reclaimed by lesbians with pride.

Butch and femme are roles associated with gender that have been historically adopted by some lesbians. Butch means acting more masculine and femme means acting feminine. Lesbians now sometimes avoid these labels because there is no need to identify with traditional heterosexual relationships. There are still those who enjoy these identities and use them to suit themselves.

Bisexuality implies a sexual identification with both women and men. There are several negative biases associated with bisexuality. The stereotypes say that not only do these people have sex all the time, but they are doing it with both women and with men at the same time. Bisexuality just means that the choice of lover can be either a woman or a man. Unfortunately, there are still many stigmas associated with bisexuality.

The term *polysexual is* defined as being attracted to multiple genders. *Polysexual* people are attracted to individuals from the full range of sexual identities. This identity takes the gendering of "people" broader than woman and man. *Polysexuals* are attracted to diverse sexual identities from an array of gender identities. This term critiques the heterosexual/homosexual binary, highlighted in the term bisexuality. Those who identify as polysexual may be attracted to transgender people, two spirit people, or those who identify as genderqueer. They may also be attracted to cisgendered people. *Polysexuality* is different from *polyamory*, which is defined as the desire to be intimately involved with more than one person at once. Polyamory does not imply diverse sexual identities, only that a person seeks multiple, simultaneous romantic encounters and/or relationships.

The word *queer* was historically an insult when referring to one's sexuality. Recently, the term has taken on new meaning. It has been reclaimed for self-empowerment by some who reject the terms straight, gay, lesbian , and bisexual. It has also been reclaimed by individuals who try to live alternative sexual identities that are more fluid. So queer is not a synonym for GSRM (gender, sexual, romantic minorities) identity. Currently, queer is typically used as another alternative to lesbian and gay, creating a new sexual identity for individuals to utilize.

We just covered a lot of terms and some of them can be confusing when learning about them for the first time. A basic idea to try to remember is that gender is about the feminine and masculine, and sexual identity is about sexual feelings and behaviors. It is possible to have several combinations of individuals with various identities and sexual scripts.

Finally, the phrase *coming out* refers to someone identifying as gay, lesbian, bisexual, queer, or otherwise in a public manner. Coming out is a process where people recognize and identify this to themselves and then share it publicly. There are those individuals that never come out to families or others because they fear rejection or retaliation. For those that do take the chance, corning out means becoming part of an identifiable community. It also means that they learn to function as an outsider in a straight world. The world is becoming more open and welcoming place, but ultimately, most of the world is still heterosexual and patriarchal.

Instead of participating in the coming out process, some people choose to remain the *in the closet*. That means not being out at all. In the closet can indicate that a person considers themselves to be homosexual but is not out to others. Or it means a person is in denial and is not comfortable claiming a specific identity. Or all of those things combined.

Since homophobia and the bullying are still major problems in the United States, it is easy to understand why some people don't share their identities with everyone. ***Homophobia*** means a fear or hatred of gays, lesbians. bisexuals, and/or queer people. It can be especially hurtful to young people as gay youth are especially at risk for suicide.

By examining risk factors—the conditions or experiences that increase the likelihood of suicide—we can begin to try and understand suicidal behavior. Risk factors are greater and more severe for GSRM youth, especially in situations where there is bullying (Institute of Medicine, 2011). Substance abuse, lack of support, and higher rates of depression increase their risk of suicide. Homophobia, bullying, and institutionalized heterosexism lead to GSRM teen suicide.

Issues of power and why certain groups get to define "correct" sexual activity and how it is regulated should be included in this discussion. ***Compulsory heterosexuality***, the expectation that everyone should be heterosexual, is central to regulating sexual activity. The idea of heteronormativity or the assumption of heterosexuality as the norm regulates social policy.

Previously in U.S. history, anti-miscegenation laws tried to stop individuals from different races from being in relationships. "Don't Ask, Don't Tell" was a law that prohibited gays from openly serving in the military. Current marriage laws in many states also provide examples of compulsory heterosexuality in social policy. The current battle with certain county clerks over gay marriage is a case in point.

These ***sexual scripts*** can be varied, depending on differences like gender, race, class, age, ability, etc. Gender is significant, but it intersects with many other identities. For example, women with disabilities, particularly apparent ones, are often faced with stereotypes where it is assumed that they can't have sex or don't want to.

There are also stereotypes for women of color, including double standards that allow men to act certain ways that women can't; similarly white women are socially permitted to act certain ways opposed to women of color. The stereotypes of black women as promiscuous whores or sluts in rap videos highlight how sexual scripts are influenced by popular culture and mass media.

The increasing sexualization of young girls in media normalizes men's demands for younger sexual partners. The scripts teach girls that they must be sexual at younger and younger ages. Part of the feminist movement is to help children regain more of their childhood and erase these gendered norms of sexuality.

Politics & Violence

There are politics in sexual relationships since they happen in societies that assign power based on systems of inequality and privilege. The dominance associated with a gender conforming system that presumes heterosexuality is the norm, also known as ***heteronormativity***.

When people get involved in romantic relationships, the politics of those relationships means that people bring the baggage of their gendered lives with them. Although much of this is familiar, because we all have baggage right? Sharing your baggage with a person you are in a relationship with is seen as completely natural, but keep in mind that the experiences of different gendered lives imply power. The intersecting of identities also implies power in many ways.

Heterosexuality is organized within patriarchy so that the power men have in society gets carried into relationships. This presumed power can encourage women's subordination within the relationship.

This might mean that a woman sees herself through the eyes of the man she is with and tries to follow his image of who she should be. It might also mean that a woman feels that she should tend to a man's daily needs and take care of the household, all while still working outside the home.

There are plenty of women who choose this life, but many feminists would argue that this is still an example of male domination in our patriarchal society where men ultimately benefit. They have their emotional and domestic needs filled by women and are left free to do whatever they want. Women often freely choose arrangements like this because they want men to take care of them financially.

These intimate relationships are a source of support for many women, so it isn't heterosexuality that is the problem but the patriarchal society in which the relationship takes place. When a relationship is in unequal power, it becomes challenging for women and men to have healthy relationships. These same kinds of sexual politics come into play in GSRM relationships.

There are also issues that come into play that could be seen as unique to women. Some women come with the baggage of femininity to figure out. They may also have internalized homophobia to deal with as well. In the United States, our patriarchal society still encourages a lot of homophobia, and not just with women, but women, specifically, will try to deal with being platonic girlfriends or if the two are romantically interested in each other. These tricky situations are exacerbated in the context of heteronormativity and compulsory heterosexuality.

Heterosexual couples and dating are encouraged by American society. Historically, school dances and proms have had strict rules regarding couples, attendance, and dress codes, all influenced by compulsory heterosexuality. Additionally, popular mass media generally assumes heterosexual dating. Valentine's Day is a huge holiday that celebrates heterosexuality. Yes, gays and lesbians celebrate Valentine's Day and are also visible in the entertainment industry, but for the most part, heterosexual intimacy is still more prevalent on the Internet, in print media, as well as on TV and in the movies. Heterosexuality is still the norm in our society. That could be OK, as long as our society didn't degrade other forms of sexuality, as it does now.

Finally, there is marriage, an institution that historically has recognized two committed people, but only if one is a woman and the other a man. That changed recently, at least legally, because same-sex marriage has been legalized through federal legislation. There are societal stereotypes that still need to change. Non-heterosexual couples often encounter obstacles when adopting children. They might also face challenges with gaining custody of and/or raising their biological children.

Some Americans still believe ugly stereotypes about these sexual identities as an immoral and abnormal "choice" that could have negative consequences for children. It has generally been assumed by some that children of homosexual parents will grow up to be homosexual, which they view as immoral and wrong. All evidence about this issue shows that this is not the case, but not all people do research on topics before deciding on their viewpoints.

Another example of this is myth about lesbian parenting. Despite research that suggests that lesbians make great mothers, there are strong social imperatives against lesbian parenting. A similar prejudice is the idea that GSRM people abuse or convert children. These negative, uninformed, and hurtful stereotypes reinforce homophobia and heterosexism.

Again, it all comes down to dominant stereotypes in our culture. While GSRM people are seen as problems in our society, research actually shows overwhelmingly that heterosexual males are the major predators of children. In any event, because of these societal stigmas, GSRM parents encounter problems concerning parenting, and may not be welcome in occupations involving children in some places in the United States. In this way, sexual self-schemas develop in a social context and are framed by the various workings of power in society.

Breakout: Sexual Assault on College Campuses

miker/Shutterstock.com

Higher education institutions across the United States have been challenged recently on how best to deal with reports of rape and sexual assault on campus. Schools are working to revise their policies and procedures to prevent further incidents. According to a survey commissioned by the Association of American Universities (2015), more than 27% of female college seniors reported having experienced some form of unwanted sexual contact since while at college. Additionally, high-profile lawsuits have kept the topic of college sexual assault in the spotlight. In 2015, a former Florida State University student filed a lawsuit against the school for its handling of her sexual assault report. Another lawsuit was filed against former Florida State football star Jameis Winston, whom the student accused of raping her in 2012 (Larimer, 2015).

New research and information is being gathered on this issue. President Obama appointed the White House Task Force to Protect Students from Sexual Assaults ("Memorandum," 2014). The Rape, Abuse and Incest National Network (RAINN) provided the White House with an extensive list of recommendations. RAINN included research that suggests 90% of rapes at colleges are perpetrated by 3% of college men, which indicates a significant issue of repeat offenders (Lisak & Miller, 2002).

The CDC (2014) reports that only "125 college and university campuses across the U.S. have affiliations with CDC's Rape Prevention and Education program to facilitate the implementation of sexual violence prevention strategies and activities (pg. 13)." There are thousands of colleges and universities, so should they be working with this CDC project? Or are there other programs that schools are using to assist with this issue? It's fairly obvious that much more research is needed in order to determine best practices in preventing rape and sexual assault on campuses. The CDC does suggest that first steps should be for universities to work to build trust between administrators and the student body. They also recommend implementing routine anonymous surveys for students to safely express their experiences with sexual issues on campus.

In 2014, the White House released "Not Alone: The First Report of the White House Task Force to Protect Students From Sexual Assault." See https://www.notalone.gov/assets/report.pdf for the full report. The report's goal is to dramatically reduce the number of students who are sexually assaulted on campus. It makes a series of recommendations that begin with gauging the scope of the crisis through anonymous campus-wide surveys. The report also encourages universities to engage their male students and encourage them to step in when someone is in trouble and become part of the solution. The White House also created a website, NotAlone.gov, which provides more information and pathways for reporting problems.

Ultimately, schools should use the information provided by the federal government and other reputable sources to have visible, helpful reporting avenues for students. Additionally, many schools are known for their programming on campus, so they should channel those skills into sexual assault and/or consent awareness programs. The more education students receive about this issue, the better.

Pornography

Many mainstream feminists agree that the pornography industry is problematic in many ways. There are some feminists that are totally against porn. There are some that are very critical of the industry, but not against the actual existence of porn. There are then other feminists whose opinions lie in between. This section of the chapter is only meant to provide basic information about current mainstream pornography. You can make up your own mind about how you feel about this often controversial topic.

Let's begin with the ***anti-porn*** side. The porn industry is one that turns sex into a commodity that is more about power and profit than pleasure. The porn industry contributes to the commodification and objectification of bodies, particularly those belonging to women. Providing sexual pleasure for consumers is not intrinsically wrong; some form of this has existed for much of history, but there are problems with the ways porn is created, advertised, and sold.

The effects of porn go way beyond whatever actors do or say. Porn also has an extensive impact on more than just simple arousal. This holds true especially when parents and schools are not properly educating children and young adults about sex. When young people don't receive comprehensive sex education either at school or at home, they turn to other means of educating themselves. That can lead youth to porn for answers.

This trend is symptomatic of a bigger problem regarding sex education in America, but let's focus on the topic at hand. Porn is (in)advertently teaching its viewers about unsafe and nonconsensual sex. There are hundreds of revenge porn sites (sex tapes made with former partners posted without those partners' permission). Often no condoms are required during the filming of porn. It isn't porn's responsibility to teach its viewers about sex, but unfortunately, porn contributes to misconceptions about sex.

Porn also contributes to dangerous ideas about the role of women in sexual activities. While BDSM and other kinkery can be practiced safely and consensually in private, displaying these forms of sex as the sexual norm online and in video form can be extremely harmful. Scenes that depict performers choosing a safe word and discussing what they are comfortable with are often missing in porn.

Additionally, porn depicting rough sex shows viewers that potentially degrading acts can be done at any point during sex without proper communication and consent. Even porn without kinkery often depicts sex as violence toward women. Women are slapped, choked and used for male pleasure with little or no effort made for the pleasure of the women involved. Even lesbian porn is generally made with male viewers in mind.

Porn also sexualizes young women, using terms like "barely legal" and having them wear schoolgirl or cheerleader outfits. While acting out a fantasy can be fun and fulfilling, these tropes often lead to the exploitation of underage girls. Many sites also separate videos by race or identity which contributes to the fetishization of racial and other minorities. "Tranny" or "hermaphrodite" porn perpetuates stereotypes and uses harmful and derogatory language.

Pornography is marketed toward male viewers, which makes it a direct link to the patriarchy. The women who participate in pornography deserve dignity and respect, even if they are engaging in acts that perpetuate ideas about male domination over women. Performing in pornography turns women into sex objects and is a huge example of how deeply ingrained patriarchal oppression is today. As feminist Catharine MacKinnon (2007) said, "Pornography is a harm of male supremacy made difficult to see because of its pervasiveness, potency and, principally, because of its success in making the world a pornographic place (pg. 378)."

Let's now turn to the ***pro-porn*** side of the debate. Most feminists agree that it is true that porn is currently in a form that can encourage harmful ideas about sex and objectify the bodies of women and minorities. There are still many that do not believe that porn is inherently wrong. There is a genre of feminist porn that depicts sex as consensual and mutually enjoyable experience rather than only a male pleasure-focused activity. There are also instructional pornography videos that show viewers how to safely participate in fun and consensual sex. A Google search can lead to safe and helpful websites for porn purchasers. There are also many books about feminist porn available for readers.

As mentioned earlier, anti-porn feminists believe that porn is a central aspect of patriarchy that reduces women to sex objects. They also claim that porn is a main part of the oppression and degradation of women. From a pro-porn viewpoint, these claims rob the performers of control over their bodies. The performers are also shamed for participating in an industry that provides them with a way to make a living and the opportunity to explore their sexuality.

Many people assume that the women participating in porn are not enjoying it. Claims like that denigrate women and question their right to autonomy with their bodies. By hating porn and considering it to be a shameful profession, performers are then seen as lesser humans. Efforts to empower or legally protect those in the profession are also hindered by these stereotypes.

The problems within pornography definitely stem from larger patriarchal frameworks, so while the industry needs drastic improvement, pornography cannot be blamed for sexism and violence. This is particularly true when there are institutionalized policies that repeatedly shame and debase the female body, regardless of their profession. Instead of blaming pornography or censoring it, we should think critically about the way it is sold specifically for men rather than as a universally enjoyable way of exploring sexuality. If we are going to reform the pornography industry, we first have to work to destigmatize it. We might start with accepting it as a legitimate method of employment and also a fine way for women to find sexual enjoyment.

Conclusion

There are multiple forces and interests are involved in shaping sexuality. Sometimes, these forces act to try to force people into boxes and labels of sexuality. As mentioned earlier, culture helps define and normalize different definitions of sexuality. There are also other factors at play, many of them political, which both produce and constrain sexuality. Patriarchy is the key focus of feminist activism, but patriarchy is not the only problem, and there are other issues that must be challenged along with patriarchy. As Judith Butler (1996) made clear, women's oppression is multifaceted and there "is no one site from which to struggle effectively. There have to be many, and they don't [necessarily] need to be reconciled with one another." (pg. 123) So let's continue to discuss sexuality, specifically comprehensive sex education, with the reading at the end of the chapter.

Suggested Readings

Bordo, S. (1997). "The body and the reproduction of femininity" in Conboy, K., Median, N., and Stansbury, S., (Eds.). *Writing on the body: Female embodiment and Feminist theory.* 309–326. New York: Columbia University Press.

Carroll, R. (2012). *Rereading heterosexuality: Feminism, queer theory and contemporary fiction.* Great Britain: Edinburgh University Press.

Freedman, E. (2006). *Feminism, sexuality, and politics.* Chapel Hill: The University of North Carolina Press.

Jackson, S. and Scott, S. (1996). *Feminism and sexuality: A reader.* New York: Columbia University Press.

Shildrick, M. (2009). *Dangerous discourses of disability, subjectivity and sexuality.* New York: Palgrave Macmillan.

Smith, A. (2010). "Dismantling hierarchy, queering society." *Tikkun, 25*(4), p. 60.

Springer, K. (2008). "Queering black female heterosexuality." In Friedman, J. and Valenti, J. (Eds.). *Yes means yes: Visions of female sexual power & a world without rape.* New York, Perseus Publishing.

Valenti, J. (2010). *The purity myth.* Berkley: Seal Press.

References

American Association of Universities. (2015). *Report on the AAU campus climate survey on sexual assault and sexual misconduct.* Retrieved December 14, 2015 from http://www.aau.edu/uploadedFiles/ AAU_Publications/AAU_Reports/Sexual_Assault_Campus_Survey/Report%20on%20the%20 AAU%20Campus%20Climate%20Survey%20on%20Sexual%20Assault%20and%20Sexual%20 Misconduct.pdf

Butler, J. (1990). *Gender trouble.* London: Routledge.

Butler, J. (1996). "Gender as performance." In Osborne, P. *A critical sense: Interviews with intellectuals.* New York: Routledge.

Center for Disease Control. (2014). *Preventing sexual violence on college campuses: Lessons from research and practice.* Retreived December 14, 2015 from https://www.notalone.gov/assets/evidence-based-strategies-for-the-prevention-of-sv-perpetration.pdf

Cerankowski, K., & Milks, M. (2010). "New orientations: Asexuality and its implications for theory and practice." *Feminist Studies, 36*(3), pp. 650–664.

De Beauvoir, S. (1997) *The second sex.* UK: Vintage.

Institute of Medicine. (2011). *The health of lesbian, gay, bisexual, and transgender people: Building a foundation for better understanding.* Washington, DC: National Academies Press.

Kempner, M. (2014). *Just sign no: More evidence virginity pledges don't work.* Retrieved December 14, 2015 from http://rhrealitycheck.org/article/2014/08/21/just-sign-evidence-virginity-pledges-dont-work/

Larimer, S. (2015). *Jameis Winston's accuser, Erica Kinsman, files civil lawsuit over rape allegations.* Retrieved December 14, 2015 from https://www.washingtonpost.com/news/early-lead/wp/2015/04/17/ erica-kinsman-jameis-winstons-accuser-files-civil-lawsuit-over-rape-allegations/

Lisak, D. & Miller, P.M., 2002. "Repeat rape and multiple offending among undetected rapists." *Violence and Victims 17*(1), 73–84.

MacKinnon, C. (2007). "Pornography, civil rights, and speech." In O'Toole, L. L., Schiffman, J. R., & Edwards, M. L. K. *Gender violence: Interdisciplinary perspectives* (2nd ed.). New York: New York University Press.

Memorandum—*Establishing a White House Task Force to protect students from sexual assault.* (2014, January 22). Retrieved December 14, 2015 from https://www.whitehouse.gov/the-press-office/2014/01/22/ memorandum-establishing-white-house-task-force-protect-students-sexual-a

Moore, S. (2012). *Naomi Wolf's book Vagina: Self-help marketed as feminism.* Retrieved December 14, 2015 from http://www.guardian.co.uk/commentisfree/2012/sep/05/naomi-wolf-book-vagina-feminism

Oakley, A. (1996). "Sexuality" in Jacson, S. and Scott, S. (Eds.). *Feminism and sexuality: A reader.* Great Britain: Edinburgh University Press, pp. 35–39.

Rich, A. (1996). "Compulsory heterosexuality and lesbian existence" in Jacson, S. and Scott, S. (Eds.). *Feminism and sexuality: A reader.* Great Britain: Edinburgh University Press, pp. 130–143.

Discussion Questions

1. How is romance and love related to popular culture? Provide some examples.

2. Are you pro-porn or anti-porn? What's your argument for picking your side?

3. How do gender roles affect relationships?

4. Has radical feminism helped women's sexuality? Why or why not?

5. How does an emphasis on virginity and abstinence harm young people? Do you think that it does?

Do We Have to Consent to Social Norms?

By Tif Cannon Cooper, M.A. & Angie Vanderluit, M. A.

Right now, we would like to invite you to sit and think about *consent*. To explore that topic, we will discuss several different aspects of sex in culture and how vital consent is. In order for those involved in any sexual exploration to have a genuinely good time, true consent must occur. This means agreeing to participate in something about which you have been informed of, all in a context free of pressure or coercion (Friedman & Valenti, 2008, p. 8). Consent is what makes us feel safe, free, and respected in society as well as in sexual situations. Think about how sexual pressure is related to cultural pressure. For instance, is it necessary for us to participate in gender/sex roles simply because people may tend to think of these roles as "normal"? How do we separate healthy sexual choices, our true sexual expression, from what has been perpetuated by our society? What social privileges do people enjoy due to their being perceived as "normal" in the culture we live in? Throughout this discussion, we will visit various topics, from the role of biology in cultural construction to taboos and morality, while exploring the psychological effects of shame on marginalized groups such as LGBTQIA, kink, disabled, and a vast spectrum of "others."

When was the last time you said, "That is weird", in reference to another person? It could be that they dressed or acted differently, perhaps their vocabulary seemed odd in comparison to what you would do/say/wear. You know, in some way, that they are not the same as you and that makes them "weird". Cultural relativism teaches us that the standards of our society are not universal, and that we cannot judge other groups' behaviors by our own cultural standards (Burn, 2005, p. 358). Simply put, what we may think of as 'default settings' in our society, such as gender roles and heterosexual, monogamous relationships, are culturally constructed. To use a relatable example, the social construction of your sexuality, your sexual orientation, and even your gender identification was a process that began before you even entered this world. First thing was first, your biological sex needed to be established; people likely asked your parent/s, "Boy or girl?" because without that need-to-know info, most would not have had any idea what to gift at the baby shower. Without knowing the baby's gender, perhaps the wrong color or type of clothing would be given and that would not do. Everyone knows that if you put a baby girl into a pair of blue pajamas that she will indeed vanish into a puff of smoke, same as when you put a pink shirt on your baby boy. Puff of smoke and gone goes the baby! Now, obviously we are being sarcastic, however, the pink versus blue, 'boy' toys versus 'girl' toys, and on and on, is a very real thing in our society (Lorber & Moore, 2007, p. 68). All leaning back to the societal construction of our sexuality and how we will end up expressing this, intrinsic parts of the human condition not typically questioned by hetero, cisgender, and able-bodied peoples.

Before you even arrived from the womb, your biological gender was setting up a series of assumptions about the person you would likely become, all based on what the sonogram tech said, or even your XX or XY chromosomal configuration (if that was known)(Lorber & Moore, 2007, pp. 2, 15). Clothing was purchased to 'match' your biological gender, as well as toys and blankets and books and perhaps even the paint on the walls of your nursery was dictated by the "gender color scheme": blue and red for boys, pink and or purple for girls, with the occasional "gender neutral" choices of green and yellow.

When you were a newborn you looked exactly like every other baby all swaddled up and scrunch-faced. Thankfully, due to your either pink or blue cap or blanket, people would know whether or not to say you were "handsome" or "pretty". Making the mistake of telling new parents that their infant daughter looks "strong" is about as well received as saying that another couple's newborn son looks "delicate". Beyond gendered adjectives to describe you, some people might have even gone as far as to make further assumptions related to your inevitable sexual orientation. We have all heard many a time, "She's so pretty! You are going to hate it when she starts dating boys!" or, "He is so handsome! You just know the girls are going to be all over him when he grows up!" as though it is a given that all babies grow into adult heterosexual individuals, without exception. The idea seems ludicrous, but it is rarely given much thought when speaking to an expectant parent or visiting a newborn baby.

Consider this framework that is being constructed, even before you get here, but certainly upon your arrival; the choices based on gender identification, the reinforcement of gender through things as simple as color of clothing, the assumptions that spring from the gender identification, and is it not hard to see that the social construction of your sexuality was in progress well before you even joined in. Because you were raised in a culture that told you girls were made of "sugar and spice" while boys were made to "man up", the gender you were born into was further reinforced by societal norms and expectations that followed you all your life. Up until the age of about 8 or 9, boys show the same amount of emotion and affection as girls in the same range. However, this dramatically stops once boys hit about age 10 to 12 and they get the message from society that showing emotion is something that only females do (Shaffer & Gordon, 2005).

Couple this with the additional built-in perception that anything deemed female/feminine is wrong, bad, weak, the opposite of "manning up" and it is easy to see how the harm is dealt on both ends (Way, 2011). Women are weak and men are not to show emotion. Nobody wins. Aggression is linked to masculinity, while nurturing and putting others before you are traits culturally linked to femininity (Lorber & Moore, 2007, p. 115; Lee & Shaw, 2015, p. 125). You do not have to be a genius to figure out how this all plays into our individual sexuality and it's expression.

We really, really, REALLY did not want to talk about this next topic. We want this article to be uplifting and definitely not depressing. Still, the reality is that part of getting closer to a world where no one gets raped means talking about it, when it happens, how it happens, and how to purge our culture of it. Unfortunately, rape is a part of our culture and our history. Rape is taking advantage of another sexually without getting their informed (meaning they know what's going on and are not being pressured) consent. We cannot really be bias-free on this topic, either. We do not believe the rape myths that people continue to espouse: "some women make it up", "they reported it for attention", if a person was dressed or acted in a certain way then "that person deserved to get raped" (Lee & Shaw, 2015, p. 553). Just... no.

We know that rape statistics are problematic because of underreporting due largely to victim-blaming. However, we thought the following were important. According to Lee and Shaw (2015), "nearly 3 in 10 women and 1 in 10 men in the United States have experienced rape, physical violence, and/or stalking by a partner and report a related impact on their functioning," (p. 538), and "Rape victims are about 4 times more likely to contemplate suicide and 13 times more likely to make a suicide attempt" than people who have not experienced violation of their consent (p. 540). When women get raped, their sense of control and self-worth is disrupted and if they talk about it, their truth is questioned. When men get raped, the same happens and their masculinity is questioned. These damaging myths are so ingrained into our societal thinking that they make people who did nothing wrong feel horrible to the point they self-destruct. Our society blames the victim and it is alarmingly commonplace for anyone person's assault to be ignored. Why does it have to be this way? What needs to change?

Switching topics, consider your own experience with the onset of puberty. For most of the human species, puberty is awkward regardless of gender. For individuals whose gender identity does not match their biological gender, puberty can be and is often traumatic (Chen, 2015). Gender dysphoria among youth contributes directly to suicide attempts, drug addiction, and self-hatred (Maron & Grace, 2015). But for cis gender girls (whose gender identity matches their biological sex), with puberty comes shame and embarrassment of a completely different variety. Girls and women are culturally shamed or pressured into purchasing all sorts of things, all with the message that their bodies *need* fixing, in one way or another. The already self-conscious girl growing up in our culture, she is inundated with the direct message that her natural body is not good enough, clean enough, pretty-skinny-blonde-white-able-bodied enough, and *needs* to be "improved".

Going further with this theme of body shame, menstruation has been stigmatized by Western religions and social circles for centuries (Phipps, 1980). Instead of viewing the presence of blood as an awesome reminder of the strength and power of being a woman, we purchase products to keep us as far away from the blood as possible. Purchasing products that "absorb" the shame, ahem, blood before clogging up plumbing or ending up in the garbage where it becomes someone else's job to deal with. The tampon industry is supported through the medicalization of women's natural body processes and the notion that the only way to deal with menstruation is through disposable, "sanitary" products (Lorber & Moore, 2007, p. 87). There are healthy, reusable options such as menstrual cups and cloth pads that, when properly washed, accomplish the same goal as disposable products. The one catch is that the user may have brief contact with her menses. Many women, ourselves included, see this as a problem because it represents how disconnected they are from their bodies.

The story you were indoctrinated with is a tale that serves a purpose: to teach you what your gender's role is. This was presented to you through stories in books and movies, rearranged and repeated, recycled over and over, but always with the same plot: boy meets girl, boy woes girl, they fall in love, and they live happily ever after. The sunset fades away and that is the end, we never see whether or not that "ever after" part is a reality.

Disney has mastered this formula and built a multi-billion dollar empire entirely based on the heteronormative idea that this formula of love and relationships applies to every viewer. When you pause to think about any storyline of most any Disney movie, did you ever question why girl plus boy equals love eternal? If you never gave it a second thought that is understandable because you were never meant to question. That is the ugly truth behind the social construction of sexuality: it is a socially engineered process that the participants are, for the most part, completely unaware of. It is in the fabric of our culture. We simultaneously believe it to be natural and struggle with it, trying to save face by cramming our presentation of who we are into a box; thinking that no one else has to put in the same amount of effort that we do. We enforce our own constraints.

Should an individual feel that their sexuality is not represented in our media and given equal rights in our society, great efforts are put forth at making the heterosexual, monogamous lifestyle the standard by which all other lifestyles are then judged against. This is an effort to make any person question their own minds, invoking a sense of self-doubt when they do not feel that they fit into society's pre-ordained mold. Seemingly, the only societally acceptable way of life is the one that we all learned about in those stories and movies, repeated over and over. People on the margins of society outside of the traditional picture of what has been deemed "acceptable sexual behavior" see life through a different lens. Through that outsider lens, these individuals and groups are able to see how much is socially constructed. Even nursery rhymes were built on a projected ideology of a heterosexual society:

"John and Jaclyn sitting in a tree,

K-I-S-S-I-N-G,

First comes love,

Then comes marriage,
Then comes Jaclyn with the baby carriage."

This simple, little rhyme begins leading children to what society believes to be the 'right' path; that entails growing up, developing a heterosexual relationship, and fitting nicely into the prescribed gender roles. The rhyme even ends with the female being the one pushing the baby around, of course after the marriage line, which carries with it a further stringent morality message. This is not the only children's rhyme that plays out this societal expectation just as there is not a sole movie or story that presents heteronomativity as the only/right/correct way of life; the majority of these materials do and the one hope is that, moving on, more inclusive stories and movies will be created and shared.

Religious influence also seeps into sex education throughout our lifetimes. It does this through telling stories that teach us what behaviors are right and wrong, and what relationships are legitimate. It can also be used to administer judgment. Growing up in "the hometown" of a worldwide conservative evangelical church organization, in the wake of the Riot Grrrl movement, feeling like outsiders in this screwy culture and not fitting in makes some people transform the self-hating shame messages into cultural critique and efforts to radically change our life-worlds (cough cough). Feeling like you are going to hell just for feelings you cannot control is not a good basis for psychological health. Timeless Emma Goldman summed it up pretty well more than a hundred years ago when she spoke about puritanical influence on society: "It repudiates, as something vile and sinful, our deepest feelings; but being absolutely ignorant as to the real functions of human emotions, Puritanism is itself the creator of the most unspeakable vices" (Goldman, 1917, p. 170). Instead of preparing students with medically accurate information, mandated sex education in Indiana stresses abstinence only, leaving students unprepared for other events. Included in the long list of important topics that are missing in our government-supported sex education is consent communication, sexual diversity, and medically accurate information about sex in addition to protection from sexually transmitted infections and undesired pregnancy (Guttmacher Institute, 2015).

Masturbation, while stigmatized for people of all genders, is especially so for girls and women. Women are not encouraged to explore sexual pleasure through masturbation, which leads to not knowing what makes them feel good, leading to feelings of shame and inadequacy when heteronormative sex comes into the picture and sex is not all it has been cracked up to be. This manifests itself in gender inequality: women thinking they never can, never have, never will have an orgasm when sex is supposed to feel good and be pleasurable for all involved. It is also directly related to sexual scripts wherein sex is over at the conclusion of the man's orgasm whereas the woman's climax is incidental if it happens at all.

This sexual pleasure hierarchy where the male's pleasure is more important than the female's has a cascade of negative consequences, including the repression of female sexuality. In general, society already puts males over females. When women do not know how to give themselves pleasure and real sex education is not supported in schools, people get misinformation from peers and the media/pornography. We worry so much about what is normal that we ignore the possibilities (and preparations) for healthy sexuality.

While we do not buy into the classic "porn is bad for women" arguments, we do see problems with the traditional sex scripts' emphasis on male ejaculation and unrealistic sex in general (aka "porn sex"). We can see how this gender inequality is problematically disseminated and reflected through the media, extremely so in male-centered pornography. Women are culturally assigned the role of moral controllers of sexuality, as feminists for decades have pointed out with the virgin/whore dichotomy (Valenti, 2010, p. 21; Kraus, 1967).

Sex-positive radical feminists historically and to this day believe that "as feminists, we should reclaim control over female sexuality by demanding the right to practice whatever gives us pleasure and satisfaction" (Tong, 2009, p. 66). People with disabilities and people of color are erased and misrepresented respectively in media depictions of "normal" sexuality. Since we view sexuality as such an essential part of human life, asexualizing someone serves to dehumanize that person. There are also a lot of different ways that people can have sexual pleasure other than penis-in-vagina intercourse, as the body can develop many erogenous zones. There are also people who are asexual, and do not want to have sex and it does not distress them. Fringe sexuality groups such as the various facets of kink, LGBTQIA, non-monogamy, and gender nonconformity are all typically misrepresented or absent in the media, which has bad consequences for people with those identities. Misrepresentation communicates that these fringe groups are not good, valid, or healthy.

When we can question the messages about what sexuality and gender really mean instead of taking them for granted, we have the power to weaken the social pressure we have been discussing. As a society, we need to cultivate a culture of enthusiastic consent and respect for all forms of gender, sexuality, and their expressions. We have the power to de-construct sexuality and remove those constraints.

The first step is questioning it all.

References

Burn, S. M. (2005). *Women across cultures: A global perspective.* (2nd ed.). New York, NY: McGraw-Hill.

Chen, A. (2015, July 22). Health effects of transitioning in teen years remain unknown. *NPR News.* Retrieved from http://www.npr.org/sections/health-shots/2015/07/22/424996915/health-effects-of-transitioning-in-teen-years-remain-unknown

Friedman, J., & Valenti, J. (Eds.). (2008). *Yes means yes! Visions of female sexual power & a world without rape.* Berkeley, CA: Seal Press.

Goldman, E. (1917/1969). *Anarchism and other essays.* New York, NY: Varick Press.

Grace, L. J., & Maron, M. (2015, June 6). Episode 617: Laura Jane Grace. *WTF Podcast.* Retrieved from http://www.wtfpod.com/podcast/episodes/episode_617_-_laura_jane_grace

Guttmacher Institute. (2015). State policies in brief: Sex and HIV education as of February 1, 2015.

Kraus, H. (1967). Eve and Mary: Conflicting images of medieval woman. In J. Broude & M. D. Garrard (Eds.), *Feminism and art history: Questioning the litany* (pp.79-99).

Lorber, J., & Moore, L. J. (2007). *Gendered bodies: Feminist perspectives.* Los Angeles, CA: Roxbury Publishing Company.

Phipps, W. E. (1980). The menstrual taboo in the judeo-christian tradition. *Journal of Religion and Health, 19*(4), 298-303.

Shaffer, S., & Gordon, L. (2005). *Why boys don't talk—and why it matter: A parent's survival guide to connecting with your teen.* New York, NY: McGraw-Hill.

Shaw, S. M., & Lee, J. (2015). *Women's voices, feminist visions: Classic and contemporary readings.* (6th ed.). New York, NY: McGraw-Hill.

Tong, R. (2009). *Feminist thought: A more comprehensive introduction.* (3rd ed.). Boulder, CO: Westview Press.

Valenti, J. (2010). *The purity myth: How america's obsession with virginity is hurting young women.* Berkeley, CA: Seal Press.

Way, N. (2011). *Deep secrets boys, friends, and the crisis of connection.* Cambridge, MA: Harvard University Press.

CHAPTER 6
Reproductive Justice

Reproductive Justice (RJ) is the complete well-being of women, based on the achievement and protection of women's human rights by law. Within reproductive justice, it is important to fight equally for the right to have a child; the right not to have a child; and the right to parent the children we have. Women should also be able to control birthing options, including midwifery.

Reproductive Justice analyzes the ability of any woman to determine her own reproductive destiny and how it is linked directly to the conditions in her community, and not just individual choice and access. Reproductive Justice addresses the social reality of the inequality of opportunities to control our own reproductive destinies. This also includes obligations from the federal government for protecting women's human rights. Options for making choices have to be safe, affordable, and accessible.

Reproductive Justice also addresses the isolation of abortion from other social justice issues. Because reproductive oppression affects women's lives in multiple ways, a multi-pronged approach is needed to fight this exploitation and advance the well-being of women. The approach needs to include service delivery, addressing legal issues, and building the overall movement. These areas can work together to provide a crucial, comprehensive solution.

Reproductive Justice offers a framework for empowering women relevant to every family. Reproductive Justice analysis focuses on better lives for women, healthier families, and sustainable communities. This is a clear and consistent message applicable for all social justice movements. Using this analysis, multiple issues can be integrated and bring together people that are multi-racial, multi-generational, and multi-class in order to build a more powerful movement.

Reproductive Justice focuses on organizing women and their communities to challenge significant power inequalities in a process that links the personal with the political. Reproductive Justice can be used as a theory for thinking about how to connect the dots in our lives. It is also a practice, or a way of analyzing our lives through storytelling and sharing.

Criminal Justice System

Reproductive Justice (RJ) places reproductive health and rights within a social justice and human rights framework. As mentioned earlier, RJ supports the right of individuals to have the children they want, raise the children they have, and plan their families through safe, legal access to abortion and contraception. RJ will only be a reality when everyone has the economic, social, and political power to make healthy decisions about their bodies, sexuality, and reproduction.

Creating a more progressive criminal justice system is important to furthering the cause of reproductive justice. A criminal justice system that makes communities safer, protects personal liberty, and limits abuses of power by governmental authorities will also further the cause of reproductive justice. A progressive criminal justice system will help further the Reproductive Justice movement with rejecting mass incarceration; ensuring procedural safeguards and protecting the constitutional rights of the accused; as well as advocating for appropriate and humane sentences for convictions.

Reproductive Justice issues are criminal justice issues. For example, women nationwide have been prosecuted for their actions during pregnancy. These prosecutions penalize women for being pregnant. "Pregnancy crimes" tend to be drug-dependency; failing to follow a physician's orders or actions deemed "harmful" during pregnancy; and self-harm.

Pregnant women have been jailed or confined to try and keep them from abusing drugs or alcohol. In 2014, Tennessee made it a punishable offense to use drugs while pregnant. This law was passed even though it was opposed by the American Medical Association and other major medical groups. Under the law, women may be charged with assault or homicide for using narcotics during pregnancy (Beausman, 2014).

Some judges and prosecutors assert that these convictions discourage drug use by putting pregnant women into programs that are supposed to improve outcomes for the mother and the baby. Ultimately, though, these convictions and programs do very little to improve the health of those involved or address the actual addiction. RJ as a bigger movement is fighting against the convictions of women who use drugs during pregnancy. Drug use during pregnancy is a serious problem, but it doesn't need to lead to convictions. RJ can work with physicians and other health-care professionals that have pregnant patients to provide them with options to detox safely. This would also include realistic steps to be drug-free.

Other pregnant women have been targeted by criminal prosecution. Utah's laws allow a woman to be prosecuted for "causing" her miscarriage. Courts have stated that women could be held accountable for stillbirths if they do *absolutely anything* that could harm a pregnancy. This includes, but is not limited to, the use of both legal and illegal drugs, missed physician's appointments, and not seeking out "adequate" healthcare. There are some women in Utah that have been jailed for refusing to have a cesarean section and having a home birth (Larris, 2010).

Charges have also been brought up against a woman who attempted suicide while she was pregnant. In Indiana, Bei Shuai tried to commit suicide and afterwards was charged with murder and feticide. When her partner left her, she ate rat poison, but her friends were able to get Shuai to a hospital for treatment. Shuai's daughter was born several days later through a cesarean surgery. She survived the birth, but only lived a few days. Shuai was charged with murder and feticide after the birth. She eventually pled guilty to criminal recklessness and was then sentenced to time served (Penner, 2013). This example represents a gross misuse of state power and a violation of the very basic liberties of bodily autonomy and integrity. Shuai didn't need punishment; she needed mental health assistance.

Unfortunately, there is another more recent case with similar implications. In 2015, Purvi Patel became the very first woman in the state of Indiana to be convicted of feticide that was a result of her own miscarriage. Court documents allege that Patel bought pills online from China with the intention to abort. She apparently was trying to rid herself of pregnancy that resulted from an affair with a married man that she was concealing from her ultra-conservative family. According to law experts, Patel's 20-year sentence for feticide and neglect of a dependent is one of the most stern punishments a woman has faced in the United States for aborting her own pregnancy (Disis, 2015).

Many of Indiana's laws are outdated, including the one related to Patel's case, which is from 1979. With the exception of legal abortions, the law made it illegal to "knowingly or intentionally" end a pregnancy with a goal other than to produce a live birth or to remove a dead fetus (Disis, 2015).

According to legal experts, the law originated to fight unregulated, illegal abortion clinics, not to punish individual women. It brings up many questions on the rights of people as individuals. Could a woman who smokes or drinks during pregnancy be convicted? The law is so vague that practically anything is a possibility.

Sometimes, women are given more stringent sentences just because they are pregnant. Lacey Weld was convicted of conspiracy to manufacture methamphetamine in 2014. Weld was given a harsher sentence, more than 12 years in prison, because she was pregnant at the time the crime was committed. The prosecution argued that she put her fetus in harm's way during the crime (Department of Justice, 2014). Ultimately, her harsher penalty violates the main constitutional idea that requires equal treatment under the law.

Classism and economic status play a major role in this issue. Women who have health insurance and access to private health care providers are much less likely to be drug tested and/or be reported to the police. Women and families on public assistance must use hospitals that serve the poor. Those women are more likely to test for drug use and then report that drug use to police. Hospitals like that have a lot to lose if they don't maintain their compliance with state and federal regulations.

It is commonly assumed that all actions, positive or negative, pregnant women take will affect the fetus they are carrying. Many people also think that these actions are the only things that determine the health of the fetus. Throughout history, activities like alcohol use or eating fish have been declared to be either beneficial or harmful to pregnancy. These issues change frequently. Women have been prosecuted for small things like refusing to undergo surgery that could be seen as dangerous to the fetus.

Convictions of pregnant women are sometimes unfounded. It can be difficult to define causes of a miscarriage or stillbirth. There are many things, both positive and negative, that affect pregnancy outcomes. Women who abuse drugs are often impoverished, with little to no education. They typically also smoke and use alcohol. All of these can harm pregnancies. Court cases will often claim that drug use, or any other behavior, caused negative outcomes for pregnancies. When the courts only take one issue into consideration, they are ignoring other factors that can seriously affect pregnancy.

The threat of pregnancy crimes discourages women from seeking prenatal care and makes them afraid to share crucial information with their physicians. Medical staff may give private patient information to authorities, which can lead to questioning and arrests. For example, Anita Gail Watkins told her physician about her cocaine use before the birth of her son. The staff reported her to the Department of Human Services (DHS) and Watkins was charged with reckless endangerment (Paltrow & Flavin, 2013). Additionally, Sally Hughes DeJesus was turned in by her midwife when she used cocaine after 11 months of abstinence. Physicians performed a drug test on the healthy newborn and called the police when they had evidence that the baby had been exposed to cocaine. DeJesus was charged with felonious child abuse (Beiser, 2000). Cases like these discourage drug-dependent women from sharing their drug use or seeking help. Women fear that they will be convicted.

Prosecutions of pregnancy crimes can be based on outdated laws and discriminatory practices. They inexcusably view pregnant women differently under the law. The prosecutions of pregnancy crimes are not grounded in hard evidence and they discourage women from seeking needed prenatal or other care. These unconstitutional cases need to be dismissed.

How can you as an individual support reproductive justice? Advocate for concrete solutions that actually improve the health of pregnant women who are drug abusers. These women need substance abuse treatment and better access to prenatal care. Contact your politicians and those that run court cases. Tell them to refrain from bringing criminal charges when there are better options available.

Advocate for police and lawyer education, including information that says that the state should not interfere with women's bodily autonomy and integrity. We should also reject harsh sentences, probation, or parole that negatively influences the reproductive decision-making of individuals. See these sentences and convictions as human rights violations.

Important Court Cases

Historically, there have been several Supreme Court cases that were directly related to reproductive justice. The American Civil Liberties Union (ACLU) has assisted with many of these cases. Founded in 1920, the ACLU recognizes that reproductive rights are among our most important constitutional liberties. It has been a legal advocate for contraception choices, abortion rights, and the right to bear children. It is often involved in these issues through cases like the ones mentioned here. Check out the cases below to see the course of history reproductive justice has taken.

In ***Griswold v. Connecticut (1965)***, the Supreme Court struck down a state prohibition against the prescription, sale, or use of contraceptives, even for married couples. The Court held that the Constitution guarantees a "right to privacy" when individuals make decisions about intimate and personal matters such as childbearing.

United States v. Vuitch (1971) was the first case about abortion to reach the Supreme Court. In this case, a physician challenged the constitutionality of a law permitting abortion only to preserve a woman's life or health. The Court rejected the claim that the statute was too vague. It said that the word "health" should include both psychological and physical well-being.

Everyone has at least heard of ***Roe v. Wade (1973)***. This case challenged a Texas law prohibiting all but lifesaving abortions. The Supreme Court invalidated the law on the grounds that the constitutional right to privacy encompasses a woman's decision whether or not to terminate her pregnancy. The Court held that the state could not interfere with the abortion decision unless absolutely necessary. They said a woman had to have access to an abortion if it were necessary to preserve her life or health.

In ***Harris v. McRae (1980)***, the Supreme Court rejected a challenge to the Hyde Amendment. The Hyde Amendment banned the use of federal Medicaid funds for abortion except when the life of the woman would be endangered. Although this case wasn't successful, it did open the door to overturning many state bans.

In the ***City of Akron v. Akron Center for Reproductive Health (1983)***, the Court ruled that the city could not require minors under 15 to obtain parental or judicial consent for an abortion. They also said that the city couldn't require physicians to give women information designed to dissuade them from having abortions or impose a 24-hour waiting period after the signing of the consent form. Finally, the Court said that the city couldn't require that all second-trimester abortions be performed in a hospital.

Bolger v. Young's Drug Products Corporation (1983) challenged a federal law that made it criminal to send unsolicited ads for contraceptives in the mail. The Court said the law was unconstitutional because it impeded the transmission of information relevant to family planning and sexually transmitted disease prevention. In a similar way, ***Bowen v. Kendrick (1988)*** challenged the Adolescent Family Life Act, which authorized federal funding to teach the value of "chastity" in the context of social and educational services for young people. The Court rejected the claim, but after this, a lower court was asked to determine whether grants made from the Act were used to promote religious views without permission.

Webster v. Reproductive Health Services (1989) challenged a Missouri law that forbade the use of public facilities for all abortions except those necessary to save a woman's life and required other restrictions on abortion. The Supreme Court upheld the anti-choice law, which allowed for more state regulation of abortion. The Court did not allow for this case to be a catalyst to overrule Roe v. Wade.

Hodgson v. Minnesota (1990) is the case that provided teens with the option to go to court to obtain authorization for an abortion. This was a good option for them when they could not or would not comply with a law that asked for parental notification. *Rust v. Sullivan (1991)* is a case that challenged a rule barring abortion counseling or anything that isn't just prenatal care. It also barred referrals by family planning programs funded under Title X. The Court upheld the rule, but President Clinton rescinded the rule by executive order.

In *Planned Parenthood of Southeastern Pennsylvania v. Casey (1992)*, the Court maintained constitutional protection for the right to choose, but, at the same time, it adopted a new test for evaluating abortion laws. With the "undue burden test," state regulations can survive constitutional review so long as there isn't a "substantial obstacle in the path of a woman seeking an abortion of a nonviable fetus (Tribe, 1992, pg. 290)."

With *Schenck v. Pro-Choice Network of Western New York (1997)*, the Supreme Court endorsed a fixed 15-foot buffer zone around clinic doorways, driveways, and parking lot entrances. It did not support a floating 15-foot buffer around people or cars entering/leaving a clinic. *Stenberg v. Carhart (2000)* is a case also known as Carhart I. It struck down Nebraska's harsh abortion ban, which created a substantial obstacle for women and imposed an undue burden.

In *Ferguson v. City of Charleston (2001)*, the Court decided that the Fourth Amendment does not allow states to drug test pregnant women who seek care in a public hospital. The Court also insisted on the importance of confidentiality. In *Ayotte v. Planned Parenthood of Northern New England (2006)*, the Court re-emphasized its long-standing belief that abortion policies must contain safeguards for women's health. The case contested a New Hampshire law that mandated that physicians delay a teenager's abortion until 48 hours after parental notification, but lacked a medical emergency exception for protecting the teenager's health. The Supreme Court said the law must be blocked in those cases where teens face medical emergencies.

Gonzales v. Carhart and *Gonzales v. Planned Parenthood Federation of America, Inc. (2007)* are cases that the ACLU worked on to strike down the first-ever federal ban on abortion methods. The ban *specifically* fails to include an exception to protect women's health. The Court upheld the federal ban in a close vote, which undermines the core of Roe v. Wade, which is that women's health must continue to be vital in this issue. With this decision, the Court basically reversed its decision in Carhart I. Justice Kennedy evoked antiquated notions of women's place in society and called in to question their decision-making ability. Writing for the majority, he held that in "medical uncertainty," lawmakers could overrule a physician's judgment. He also wrote that the "State's interest in promoting respect for human life at all stages in the pregnancy" could be more important overall than a woman's health.

Breakout: Wilma Mankiller

© Peter Turnley/Corbis

"I've run into more discrimination as a woman than as an Indian."—Wilma Mankiller (Capriccioso, 2010)

Wilma Mankiller was the first female principal chief of the Cherokee Nation. She sought to improve the nation's health care, education system, and government. After leaving office, Mankiller remained an activist for Native American and women's rights until her death, on April 6, 2010, in Oklahoma (Verhovek, 2010).

(Continued)

Mankiller attended Skyline College and San Francisco State University in California before receiving her bachelor's degree in social sciences at Flaming Rainbow University in Oklahoma. In 1963, Wilma Mankiller married Hector Hugo Olaya de Bardi. The couple would later have two daughters: Felicia Olaya and Gina Olaya. Later on, Mankiller was greatly inspired by the attempts by Native Americans to reclaim the island of Alcatraz to become more active in Native American issues. Continuing her passion with helping her people, she returned to Oklahoma. After her move, she began working for the government of the Cherokee Indian Nation.

As the Cherokee Nation's principal chief, she made history as the first woman to serve in that role. She remained on the job for two terms, winning elections in 1987 and 1991. A popular leader, Mankiller focused on improving the nation's government, and health-care and education systems. Due to ill health, she decided not to seek re-election in 1995.

Mankiller shared her experiences in her autobiography, *Mankiller: A Chief and Her People. She also wrote Every Day Is a Good Day: Reflections by Contemporary Indigenous Women* (2004), featuring a foreword by Gloria Steinem. For her leadership and activism, Mankiller received many honors, including the Presidential Medal of Freedom in 1998 (Verhovek, 2010).

After learning of Mankiller's passing in 2010, President Barack Obama issued a statement about legendary Cherokee chief: "As the Cherokee Nation's first female chief, she transformed the nation-to-nation relationship between the Cherokee Nation and the federal government, and served as an inspiration to women in Indian Country and across America," he stated. "Her legacy will continue to encourage and motivate all who carry on her work (Obama, 2011, pg. 466)."

Planned Parenthood

Planned Parenthood (PP) is a not-for-profit organization that offers reproductive and maternal health services in America and worldwide. PP has its roots in Brooklyn, New York, where Margaret Sanger opened the first birth-control clinic in the United States. She founded the American Birth Control League in 1921, which changed its name to Planned Parenthood in 1942 (Cullen-DuPont, 1998). PP has continually seen growth and now consists of approximately 700 health clinics in the United States and abroad (Planned Parenthood, 2015c).

The mission of Planned Parenthood (2015b) is:

1. "to provide comprehensive reproductive and complementary health care services in settings which preserve and protect the essential privacy and rights of each individual

2. to advocate public policies which guarantee these rights and ensure access to such services

3. to provide educational programs which enhance understanding of individual and societal implications of human sexuality

4. to promote research and the advancement of technology in reproductive health care and encourage understanding of their inherent bioethical, behavioral, and social implications" (Mission, 2nd paragraph).

Planned Parenthood is the largest single provider of reproductive health services in the United States. According to the 2013–2014 Annual Report, PP saw 2.7 million patients in 4.6 million clinical visits. They have a revenue of $1.3 billion, which includes $530 million in government funding (Planned Parenthood, 2015a). Throughout its history, PP has experienced both support and controversy. Their clinics and offices face protests regularly, and violent attacks have also occurred.

In September 2015, the president of Planned Parenthood, Cecile Richards, testified before the House Oversight and Government Reform Committee. She was there to dispute accusations by Republicans that her organization profits from the sale of fetal tissue, telling Congress that the charges were incorrect.

The lawmakers were trying to strip Planned Parenthood's federal funding after videos, released by anti-abortion activists, supposedly showed officials from PP trying to sell fetal tissue. Richards said the videos had been edited to mislead. She also mentioned that Planned Parenthood facilitated the donation of only a small amount of fetal tissue.

While the funding fight is superficially about abortion and fetal tissue, the Republicans really view Planned Parenthood as a well-funded machine that promotes Democrat policies and politicians. Republican lawmakers charged the group as more a political advocacy organization that wastes federal money than a health-care group that deserves to receive taxpayer dollars.

Ms. Richards was also criticized over a video apology that she issued after the controversial video about fetal tissue emerged. Republicans insisted that she must have believed the contents of the video were true if she apologized for them. Ms. Richards said that she had apologized because she thought it was inappropriate that the physician in the video had a "clinical discussion in a nonconfidential, nonclinical setting" (Andrews, 2015).

Conclusion

We are at a crucial time in which to choose the future direction of the feminist movement. The consequences for women's lives are increasingly serious in light of the extreme political conservatism sweeping the nation and affecting reproductive and sexual health laws on all levels, from the U.S. President and the Supreme Court, all the way to state legislatures and local school boards. What's more, assaults upon the civil and human rights of under-represented members of our society continue to rise. Keeping all this in mind, it makes sense to incorporate a reproductive justice framework as a means to unite women and their communities. RJ can keep feminism relevant to society, and it links to activists from the nation's capitol to the California and everywhere in between to develop strategies to protect our lives and make our own choices. Keep all this information in mind as you look at the reading by Jennifer Baumgardner.

Suggested Readings

Boston Women's Health Book Collective. (2011). *Our bodies, ourselves.* New York: Simon & Schuster.

Dubriwny, T. (2012). *The vulnerable empowered woman: Feminism, postfeminism, and women's health.* New Brunswick, NJ: Rutgers University Press.

Ehrenreich, N., ed. (2008). *The reproductive rights reader: Law, medicine, and the construction of motherhood.* New York: NYU Press.

Oaks, L. (2015). *Giving up baby: Safe haven laws, motherhood, and reproductive justice.* New York: NYU Press.

Silliman, J. (2004). *Undivided rights: Women of color organize for reproductive justice.* Cambridge, Mass.: South End Press.

Sundstrom, B. (2015). *Reproductive justice and women's voices: Health communication across the lifespan.* Lanham, Maryland: Lexington Books.

References

Andrews, B. (2015). *Watch these dudes in congress tell Planned Parenthood how to protect women's health.* Retrieved December 15, 2015 from http://www.motherjones.com/mojo/2015/09/planned-parenthood-house-oversight

Beausman, C. (2014). *First woman arrested under law criminalizing drug use during pregnancy.* Retrieved December 15, 2015 from http://jezebel.com/first-woman-arrested-under-law-criminalizing-drug-use-d-1604675582

Beiser, V. (2000). *Fetal abuse.* Retrieved December 15, 2015 from http://www.motherjones.com/politics/2000/06/fetal-abuse

Capriccioso, R. (2010). *"Everyone was in awe of her": Wilma Pearl Mankiller, November 18, 1945–April 6, 2010.* Retrieved December 15, 2015 from http://www.thebluegrassspecial.com/archive/2010/may10/wilma-mankiller-news-notes.php

Cullen-DuPont, K. (1998). *Encyclopedia of women's history in America.* Boston: Da Capo Press.

Department of Justice. (2014). *Lacey Weld sentenced to 12 years in prison for conspiracy to manufacture methamphetamine.* Retrieved December 15, 2015 from http://www.justice.gov/usao-edtn/pr/lacey-weld-sentenced-more-12-years-prison-conspiracy-manufacture-methamphetamine

Disis, J. (2015). *The case of Purvi Patel: Should a pregnant woman be charged with feticide.* Retrieved December 15, 2015 from http://www.indystar.com/story/news/crime/2015/05/03/case-purvi-patel-pregnant-woman-charged-feticide/26825871/

Larris, A. (2010). *Utah bill criminalizes miscarriage.* Retrieved December 15, 2015 from http://rhrealitycheck.org/article/2010/02/20/utah-bill-criminalizes-miscarriage/

Obama, B. (2011). *Public papers of the presidents of the United States.* Washington, D.C.: Government Printing Office.

Paltrow, L. and Flavin, J. (2013, April). "Arrests of and forced interventions on pregnant women in the United States, 1973–2005: Implications for women's legal status and public health," *Journal of Health Politics, Policy & Law, 38*(2), 299–343.

Penner, D. (2013). *Woman freed after plea agreement in baby's death.* Retrieved December 15, 2015 from http://www.usatoday.com/story/news/nation/2013/08/02/woman-freed-after-plea-agreement-in-babys-death/2614301/

Planned Parenthood. (2015a). Annual report 2013–2014. Retrieved December 15, 2015 from http://issuu.com/actionfund/docs/annual_report_final_proof_12.16.14_/0

Planned Parenthood. (2015b). *Mission.* Retrieved December 15, 2015 from https://www.plannedparenthood.org/about-us/who-we-are/mission#sthash.8NHs1DMe.dpuf

Planned Parenthood (2015c). *Planned Parenthood at a glance.* Retrieved December 15, 2015 from https://www.plannedparenthood.org/about-us/who-we-are/planned-parenthood-at-a-glance

Tribe, L. (1992). *Abortion: The clash of the absolutes.* New York: W.W. Norton & Company.

Verhovek, S. (2010, April 6). Wilma Mankiller, Cherokee Chief and First Woman to Lead Major Tribe, Is Dead at 64. Retrieved December 15, 2015 from http://www.nytimes.com/2010/04/07/us/07mankiller.html?_r=0

Discussion Questions

1. Why is reproductive justice important, especially in today's world?

2. What are the consequences of loss of control for women over their own bodies & reproductive processes?

3. How does the fight against Planned Parenthood harm women?

4. Why is the legacy of Wilma Mankiller important in American history?

5. How do abortion laws help or harm women's overall health-care choices?

Why We Speak Out When We Speak Out

By Jennifer Baumgardner

In 1962, Sherri Finkbine, a star of TV's Romper Room and a mild-mannered, thirty-year-old mother of four, found herself at the center of a maelstrom around abortion. Her doctor told her, pregnant with her fifth child, that the baby would very likely be severely deformed because she had taken thalidomide during her pregnancy. He recommended a "therapeutic" abortion, then done quietly by many doctors and hospitals following this kind of diagnosis.

Hoping to warn women about the dangers of this drug and help others in her position, Finkbine went public with her story. That was her first mistake. The doctors could operate freely only under the cover of silence, so her abortion had to be a secret. Now, in the light of day, a media firestorm provoked death threats against her and her family. The hospital, fearing the controversy, canceled her procedure. On August 17, 1962, Sheri Finkbine traveled to Sweden; the next day, she underwent her therapeutic abortion.

Finkbine was one of the first significant instances of a woman's going on record to say, "I had an abortion." That simple declaration is one of the hardest, most vulnerable things a person can utter. Over time, women's speaking up and out about their own abortions has played a pivotal role in changing the law and the world as we know it today. For these women, the personal was political. I would one day find myself among them.

Abortion – legal or illegal, dirty or clean – has long magnetized women to feminism. In the early days of the women's liberation movement, ladies found each other and the movement by telling the truth about their abortions. Even Gloria Steinem didn't realize she was a feminist until she attended a hearing in a church basement where women were testifying about their own abortions. That historic event on March 21, 1969 was staged by the New York-based feminist group, Redstockings. To give you an idea of what they were up against in that era, a previous hearing the Redstockings had disrupted featured a panel of twelve men and one woman – a nun. These young feminists declared themselves the "real experts" on abortion because, as women, they were in danger of unwanted pregnancy and had actually experienced abortion.

Rosalyn Baxandall spoke first. She was terrified. When she got home, her grandmother called, having seen Ros on the news, and said, "You've had an abortion?" As Ros confirmed the information and braced herself to be scolded, her grandmother said, "Well, I have had six!" By April 1970, New York State passed the most liberal abortion laws in the country, beating Roe v. Wade by nearly three years.

On April 5, 1971, the French weekly newsmagazine Le Nouvel Observateur published the "Manifesto of the 343," a petition of 343 French women, including Simone de Beauvoir, Catherine Deneuve, Jeanne Moreau, and Monique Wittig, declaring that they had all had abortions. A year later, Ms. Magazine's debut issue featured a similar "I Had an Abortion" petition, signed by 53 well-known women, including Gloria Steinem and Billie Jean King.

Less than a year after the Ms. petition, on January 22, 1973, Roe v. Wade was handed down, legalizing abortion through the first trimester (and with restrictions in the second) in all states. On January 22,

2003, the thirtieth anniversary of Roe v. Wade, Patricia Beninato was so frustrated that every time she turned on the television, she saw anti-choicers claiming that having an abortion leads directly to clinical depression that she decided to create ImNotSorry.net – a space for women to say that they've had abortions and aren't going to apologize for it.

In the fall of 2003, I found Beninato and Baxandall – and all the women before them who had the courage to share their abortion experience – very inspiring. I'd never even been pregnant, but on January 22, 2004, feeling emboldened, I launched the I Had an Abortion Project. The first step was distributing T-shirts printed with the words I HAD AN ABORTION. At an event at the feminist bookstore Bluestock-ings, I invited women and men to come out about their abortion experiences. My friend, the filmmaker Gillian Aldrich, and I began interviewing women who'd had abortions for a film called I Had an Abortion. I wanted to destigmatize the experience, to point out that women who've had abortions aren't awful women we don't know; they are our mothers, sisters, aunts, friends, wives, and selves.

The next month, I was pregnant with my first son, and by the time Rush Limbaugh and Matt Drudge publicized the fact that Planned Parenthood was selling the T-shirt, I was seven months along. The pub-licity (Limbaugh and Drudge led to Fox, CNN, and dozens of other outlets) provoked both a run on the shirts (hundreds sold overnight) and a painful debate over whether the shirt was brave and important or callous and cheap. (I think the shirt is potentially quite brave and important; certainly I advocate using casual "everyday" spaces to discuss critical and silenced issues.)

I was inundated with stories from women about their abortions and their lives. I heard mainly from people who were grateful to have something to honor an experience they were told they had to keep secret. Women on Waves, Dutch doctor Rebecca Gomperts' radical project to provide abortions in international waters, created its own I HAD AN ABORTION T-shirts and bulletproof dresses as part of a larger art project about abortion. The project's mission statement declared its hope that by "making the reality of abortion visible, change will be catalyzed."

Our I Had an Abortion film debuted on the Roe v. Wade anniversary in 2005. The film featured ten women and ten funny, sad, frank, and complex stories of having a reproductive system and being female. I learned how diverse women's experiences of abortion are – depending on many factors, including where they are in their lives when the pregnancy occurs. In 2007, two other documentaries, Silent Choices (Faith Pennick's film about black women's abortion experiences) and The Abortion Diaries (Penny Lane's short centering on her own abortion as a teenager), began screening around the country, to great acclaim and gratitude from women and men.

And then the political became personal for me.

On March 22, 2010, three months after Angie Jackson, a twenty-seven-year-old mother in Florida, live-tweeted her abortion with RU-486 (causing another media firestorm), I bought a pregnancy test. My son Magnus was almost eight months; Skuli was five and a half. I would be forty in two months and was just getting my brain back and a handle on my responsibilities since I'd gotten knocked up seventeen months earlier.

I felt trepidacious. My period, which normally came about every three weeks, was late. I was a little edgy. My sense of smell was extra strong. I felt dizzy sitting on the couch watching the Tiger Woods South Park with my boyfriend. I wasn't sure when the right time was to take a test, given that I knew I probably would not want to continue with the pregnancy. It was really the pregnancy more than any-thing else, I realized, that weighed on me. I could pretty happily imagine a little daughter named

Effie gamboling around at age two in a ruffled dress, but I couldn't imagine spending the next eight months feeling alternatingly nauseous and like a whale, followed by the rigors of birth, and then sleep deprivation as we got to know our newborn.

Maybe I'm just late, I thought to myself as I bought the test. And it's better to know so I can be relieved and marvel at how paranoid I am – or figure this out. So, around 6:00 PM on a Sunday, while my boyfriend, BD, made bratwursts and salad and I showered Skuli and got Magpie into his PJs, I found time to pee on the stick. "Is that a tampon?" asked Skuli, in the bathroom with me, as always. "Gross."

Within seconds, the little boxes began showing their Polaroid news: a little +. Positive. Pregnant. Normally, I considered that positive. This time, it felt wrong – not devastatingly sad or tragic, just something I couldn't bear doing right then in my life.

The conversation with BD was wistful; he'd like more children. I was already having trouble meeting my obligations at work and with Skuli and Magnus. I didn't want to offer my body to that process again.

I called my OB's office at 9:00 AM, Monday. The nurse, Sally, called back to tell me "no one in the practice performs abortions." This surprised me. Had I never inquired whether my doctor was pro-choice? Then Dr. G, my actual doctor, called back to say that actually Dr. K, who delivered Magnus and who was in their practice, did do abortions. Suddenly, I remembered a conversation I'd had with Dr. K right after Magnus came out. She had asked me what I did, and I'd said I mainly wrote about abortion; she'd said she did them and was really committed to providing them.

I made an appointment with Dr. K for Friday, March 26. That day, I went to her office at 1:00 PM and filled out paperwork. The receptionist was warm. I went into the examining room, was weighed, and had my blood pressure taken. Dr. K examined my uterus and did a pap culture and an internal sonogram. Back in her office, surrounded by drawings by her daughters, she gave me Mifeprex, otherwise known as RU-486 -the "abortion pill." I swallowed the pill and felt ... totally fine. Dr. K told me I would be good to go all night – no need to change my plans. "Really?" I asked, assuming I should lie in bed and read Play It as It Lays. "You'll feel how you feel right now," she said. "Tomorrow's the bad part."

I went to the pharmacy to get Vicodin, an antibiotic, and misoprostol, which, taken the next day, would start the contractions that would expel the contents of my uterus. The pharmacist – I don't think I imagined this – glared at me and dropped the misoprostol on the counter. "That's for that woman in trouble," she muttered to her colleague. "What?" I said, feeling like I almost wanted to fight with her.

That night, I went out to dinner with friends and to a Spoon concert at Radio City. The next morning, I took the misoprostol. My plan had been to go hear Susan Faludi and Jack Halberstam speak at The New School and then take the pills, but I decided to get it over with earlier in the day. Until early 2006, women could take this drug vaginally, but due to increased instances of infection, it was now administered buccally. I dissolved the six pills in my cheeks for an hour and then swallowed the mess down with water. I took a Vicodin and got in bed.

Then came hours of contractions muted by painkillers, lots of blood and tissue, and the sweetness of getting to sleep during the day. By dinnertime, I was up and showered. A few days later, most of the blood had passed, though the bleeding lingered for nearly two weeks, like an extra-long period. After many years of connecting to complex emotions around ending a pregnancy, I wondered if I might have regret. I was surprised and relieved by how simple – emotionally and physically – the abortion had been.

"We have to give women healthy spaces to talk about their abortions," Steph Herold, a twenty-something reproductive justice activist, told me in the fall of 2010. She had just launched the hashtag #ihadanabortion on Twitter, and the media was once again fanning the flames of controversy. Was Twitter an appropriate medium in which to talk about something so serious? Wasn't this need to talk about one's abortion simply a sign of a generation devoted to oversharing? Herold answered no, and smartly placed her own decision to speak out within a history of speaking out.

Today, women and men who share their abortion experiences do so in a different environment. Abortion is legal, so it doesn't have the same historic impact that Sherri Finkbine's or the Redstockings' speak-outs had. Yet after several decades of speak-outs and attempts to come out about abortion, the stigma remains, proving that the high emotions around this issue aren't neutralized so easily. Despite this difficulty, a profound purpose remains in speaking out. When each of us does so, abortion history transforms into a beautiful and rich collective memoir.

"I had an abortion" is important for me to say because I stand shoulder to shoulder with other women, people who believe in the right of all human beings to make decisions about their bodies and lives. Most important, I say I had an abortion out loud because my life is no shameful secret.

CHAPTER 7

Family

Feminist theorists have investigated how an expectation of the stereotypical nuclear family affects society's roles for women. Feminist writers have studied the nuclear family's effect on women. Books such as *The Second Sex* by Simone de Beauvoir and *The Feminine Mystique* by Betty Friedan are well known for covering these issues, among others.

The term ***nuclear family*** became more common during the first half of the twentieth century. Historically, households have often consisted of groups of extended family members. In a more mobile, post-industrial revolution society, the emphasis became more on the nuclear family.

Smaller family units could move more easily, which was helpful for finding job opportunities in other cities or states. More people could afford to buy houses in new, urban areas. The larger households became less of a norm.

In feminism and women's and gender studies, we analyze and think about the division of labor in families and the roles women are expected to fill. There were women in the twentieth century who were discouraged from working outside the home and instead expected to maintain their homes and raise their children.

The industrial jobs of the time required one worker, usually the man, to leave the home for work outside the home. Since people were expected to have nuclear families, it meant that each woman was then encouraged to stay at home and take care of the children. This chapter is focused on why family and household arrangements are seen as less than perfect, unequal, or even abnormal if they aren't exactly the nuclear family model. Let's examine some definitions of other types of families.

Definitions

"Families mean support and an audience to men. To women, they just mean more work."—Gloria Steinem, 1983, pg. 131

Family structure has changed dramatically over the last 100 years. The traditional family is no longer the norm. There are several variations on the term family that have been created. We are going to discuss some different types of families that exist today, but keep in mind that some families naturally fall into multiple categories. The definitions aren't clear cut labels we just slap on, but they are guidelines that we can use for policies and other work. Or we can use them just to get a better understanding of how people live together.

Nuclear Family

The nuclear family is the traditional type of family structure. This family type consists of two parents and children. The nuclear family has long been held as being the ideal in which to raise children. Children in nuclear families receive strength and stability from the two-parent structure and generally have more opportunities due to the financial ease of two adults. Only 46% of U.S. kids younger than 18 years of age are living in a home with two married heterosexual parents in their first marriage (Livingston, 2014).

Single Parent Family

The single parent family is made up of one parent raising one or more children on their own. The single parent family is the biggest change society has seen in terms of family structures. According to Livingston (2014), 34% of children today are living with an unmarried parent, the majority of which are single. Single parent families are typically emotionally close. They will work together to find ways to solve problems, such as splitting up chores. There are obvious struggles in this family type. With only one parent, it may be a struggle to find and most certainly pay for childcare. Since there is only one parent income, this limits pay and opportunities sometimes. Many single parent families have help from relatives and friends, just as nuclear families usually do.

Extended Family

The extended family structure consists of two or more related adults living in the same house. This family includes many relatives helping each other out, with raising the children and taking care of the chores. Many extended families include cousins, aunts/uncles and grandparents living together. Extended families are becoming increasingly common all over the world because of the need to combine finances or care for elderly family members.

Childless Family

There are many couples who either cannot or choose not to have children. The childless family is often the forgotten family because it isn't seen as fitting in with the traditional family ideal set by some societies. Childless families consist of two partners, living and working together. Many of these families are pet owners or have extensive contact with their nieces and nephews as adult role models for those children.

Stepfamily

There are plenty of relationships that end in divorce, and in turn, many people then choose to get remarried. This is how stepfamilies are created, which involves two families creating one new family. Think of the Brady Bunch as an old school example. Stepfamilies are just as common as nuclear families, although they sometimes have more baggage. Transition time periods and discipline issues sometimes occur. Stepfamilies have to learn to work together and with other family members to ensure good cooperation.

Grandparent Family

Many grandparents also raise their grandchildren for a variety of reasons. This could be due to parent death, addiction, abandonment or being unfit. Many grandparents then have a need to find additional resources, particularly funds, to help raise their grandchildren.

There is no best type of family structure. When love and support are present every day, families tend to be successful and thrive. Families need to do what is best for all involved and that can be achieved in any family structure.

Families are also known as kinship systems. Those can be defined as patterns of relationships that define family forms. Kinship systems vary widely around the world and determine matters such as family descent or ancestry. Examples of this include *patrilineal* (the line of the father), *matrilineal* (line of the mother), *bilateral* (both parents), or *unilateral* (either parent).

Kinship rules are also deciding norms about marriage and the number of partners that are allowed in any one marriage. *Monogamy* involves two people only in a relationship with each other. *Polygamy* is the term for multiple spouses. *Polygyny* is specific to multiple wives where *polyandry* is multiple husbands. *Cenogamy* is the phrase for group marriage. If you choose to label your relationships, there are plenty of terms available for use.

All of these definitions for family structures are important, specifically as we consider the status and role of women in these families. A woman's perceived status is often dependent on a woman's access to power in society and availability of economic resources.

Traditional myths about family norms blur the lines of reality. There is a wide diversity of family life here in the United States. There has been a significant drop in the number of legally married heterosexual couples in the last few years. Reasons for that drop include more cohabiting, delaying marriage, divorcing/remarrying, living alone and/or single parent households, and lesbian partnerships, just to list a few. The list of reasons is not all encompassing.

Diverse families, like those defined above, represent all social classes, sexualities, as well as racial and ethnic groups. Currently, 22% of children in the United States speak a language other than English in their homes (Kids Count Data Center, 2014). Globally, family structure is affected by the consequences of the international economy as well as other factors.

The term *family values* is frequently used, especially in U.S. politics. There are ongoing political debates concerning family values that illustrate how supporters of the *status quo* (existing power structures) in society have made the term family values synonymous with traditional societal definitions of the family. This includes seeing women defined in terms of their reproductive roles, men as the powerful heads of the family, and married heterosexual families as the only legitimate family structure in our society.

This narrow view on what constitutes a family and its affiliation with the repressive political agenda is sometimes seen as offensive, especially to those who don't fit in such a narrow viewpoint. Determining what kinds of families get to be counted as real families and determining whose family values are used as standards for judging others are challenging topics currently up for discussion in the United States.

For many of us, our best memories of growing up come from times spent with our families. Nostalgia for better times or times gone past is popular in our society. As economic forces affect how families function, we yearn for a return to the traditional family and our fond memories. It helps us to escape from our problems and reality for a short time.

The issue with this nostalgia is that it is often accompanied by ideologies that glorify the patriarchal roles for women in families. It can also cover up conflict and violence. And, depending on the family, these ideologies also often show a clear, defined split between the public and private spheres. Poor and minority families have rarely been able to access the security and privacy assumed in the split between family and society. For example, as discussed in the last chapter, the social welfare policies and criminal justice statutes have a more direct impact and harsher consequences on poor families.

Power & Institutions

Power dynamics within families are important in order to understand how families function. There are dynamics in how families make decisions about money, housing, careers, education, and parenting, to name a few. Power can be defined by who is able to influence others or block others from getting their way. The rules of power within a family can change over time as children age, as relationships mature, or as family circumstances become better or worse. And even though it changes, power can be pretty predictable. This could be comforting to some in the family, but then also dangerous to others, especially for those who are dominated by other family members.

French and Raven (1959) took a ***microsystemic*** view of family power. They found six bases of family power, as they researched power from inside the family. ***Legitimate power*** is given by the belief system within the family, such as the religious belief that the husband should be the head of the household. For example, in the United States, aunts and uncles who try to influence their nieces and nephews might be seen as meddling, which would be ***illegitimate power***. In other countries, extended family members are given legitimate power with their nieces and nephews. They would be appreciated for sharing guidance.

Informational power is about specific knowledge that might only be known to one person. It could also be the persuasive way that a person shares the information they have. So one person may be seen as knowledgeable about money, so then they might be the one to make decisions about money for the family. On the other hand, the other partner can research the information for a new car, and then share that with the person who is typically in charge of finances for the family.

Referential power is based on affection within the family. Positivity can be an impactful force in making alliances with others. Positive feelings can also help when people want to make those they care about happy or they want to try hard not to disappoint them. Parents trying to please their children, partners trying to please their spouses, and/or children pleasing their grandparents are good examples of referential power.

Coercive power requires the use of some kind of force to get one's way in a family. Some impose their way on others with discipline, threats, conflict, and competition. Those deep-rooted examples are types of coercive power because getting one's way usually happens at the expense of others.

Expert power comes from relevant education, training, or experience. For example, a person may be knowledgeable about the area they grew up in, so this might influence where the family lives. Expert power can also be derived from the specific knowledge and experience of one individual in dealing with a specific issue. For example, a child might do research on a certain area of the world, including learning the language. They then might exert expert power to convince the rest of the family to take a trip there.

Reward power is the ability to influence others by providing benefits or bribery. With small children, parents often reward them for good behavior with candy or treats. With older kids, the benefits might be more expensive, such as money or video games. Adults in families often strike bargains with others to get their way.

The power bases discussed by French and Raven can sometimes be unclear. Family members often use coercion discreetly, so it might not be seen by others outside the family. Also, some family members have learned to keep their opinions to themselves in order to keep peace in the family. Much of these interactions wouldn't be obvious to outsiders, so the coercion continues even though there isn't any visible resistance.

Blood and Wolfe (1960) took a *macrosystemic* view with their ***resource theory of family power***. They examined connections between power inside the family and power outside the family. They argued that power was relatively equal between marriage partners based on the resources that each contributes. Blood and Wolfe specifically focused on income, occupation, and education. Based on interviews with hundreds of white, middle-class wives in Detroit, Michigan, the data showed that the greater the men's resources, the greater the men's recognized power within the family.

The resource theory was significant because the research indicated that men do not become heads of households by divine right or standard biological reasons, but because they have a lot more access to educational, financial, and occupational resources. Ultimately, it was suggested that women should have more access to resources outside the family, which could better balance the distribution of power within the family.

The resource theory of family power comes with criticism. For example, income, career, and education are only three types of resources that influence family power. There are many other resources that could also influence. Foa and Foa (1980) indicated that intangible resources like intelligence, attractiveness, likeability, and love also influence family power. Family resources can be anything that is valued by others that is then exchanged for power.

Most research on family power follows the ***macrosystemic*** view. Constantina Safilios-Rothschild (1976) wrote that family power is a manifestation of cultural gender ideologies and resources in society. This typically means that males have more power in families because of patriarchal beliefs about male authority. For example, men and women are often perceived to have specific personality traits. Women are often seen as more emotional and talkative, and men are perceived as more aggressive and ambitious (Borkenau, McCrae, Terracciano, 2012). These perceptions have been proven as stereotypes, but they still exert a strong influence on our society and others.

Breakout: Amy Richards

Courtesy of Amy Richards

Amy Richards is a prominent third-wave feminist author, speaker, and all-around badass. A feminist from the start, Amy would sing Helen Reddy's "I am Woman" in place of the national anthem. Her mother had convinced her that Reddy's song was the U.S. national anthem (Richards 2015). Amy graduated from Barnard College in 1992 and is a resident of New York City.

In feminist circles, Richards might be best known for her longtime friendship with Jennifer Baumgardner. Amy and Jennifer created the Third Wave Foundation after they met while working together at Ms. Magazine. They also co-wrote several books about Third Wave feminism.

Richard's writings can be found in various sources including NPR, *The New York Times, Bitch* magazine, and Feminist.com. In 2008, Amy authored a book about feminist parenting. Titled *Opting In: Having a Child Without Losing Yourself*, the book discusses the anxiety over parenting that women face today. Showing how feminism has addressed parenting historically, Richards ultimately tells readers to parent how best they see fit and forge their own paths.

Her leadership and groundbreaking work has allowed her space to be a spokesperson for current feminist issues. Amy continues to lecture frequently about the state of feminism both with

(*Continued*)

Baumgardner and solo. She is also often traveling the world representing U.S. feminism. She has had numerous television appearances and also won several activist awards.

Amy Richards has an impressive resume, and she still continues to do amazing work. She recently produced a project called Makers, which was featured on PBS. It was an extraordinary three-part documentary that highlights the history of feminism in the United States from the women that created the history. Besides the documentary, Makers.org continues to compile video interviews with women breaking barriers and supporting each other. Those videos are posted by theme frequently on their website.

Last but certainly not least, Amy Richards is also the president of Soapbox: Speakers Who Speak Out. Soapbox is the greatest feminist lecture agency in the United States. Soapbox also created the Feminist Camp, where feminists attend workshops in NYC about current issues. Amy hosts the campers and they visit several other sites, occasionally including *Ms. Magazine*, feminist bookstores, theater productions, and Gloria Steinem, to name a few awesome examples. Consider going and learning more information at:

http://www.soapboxinc.com/feminist-camp/.

Feminist Parenting

Amy Richards is not the only author that writes about the topic of feminist parenting. There are a plethora of books and even more blogs and websites that discuss this topic (Mills, 2007; O'Reilly, 2008; Valenti, 2012). This section of the chapter will define feminist parenting. It will also describe some basic goals and ideas that revolve around this topic.

So what is *feminist parenting* exactly? And how does it differ from the standard version of parenting? Feminist parenting is a set of skills for parents that choose to raise children that support equality and social justice. The problems like violence, discrimination, communication, and fear are issues that feminism addresses. They can best be conquered by raising the next generation to respect all people. When you have a basic understanding of differences, you will be less likely to participate in violence, fear people that are different than you, or discriminate against them.

Feminist parenting recognizes that caregivers have the most significant influence on self-identity in the formative years of growing up. Teaching and modeling self-respect and respect for others in all aspects of childhood is the best foundation for compassion, respect, and equality.

Respect for self is one of the goals of feminist parenting. The foundation of feminism focuses on the value of each person. To value others, you must first value yourself, but we aren't born with respect for self. We don't genetically know that we are valuable. We hopefully learn it from those around us. From an early age, we learn the value of our bodies and our thoughts from those who raise us.

Another goal is respect of *bodily autonomy*. This includes the basic understanding of your right to control your own body and what happens to it. It's one of the first lessons that we provide our kids. Depending on the age of the child, we can give kids ultimate responsibility over their bodies, such as when they eat or sleep. We can tell them that they have a right not to be hurt and to say *stop* when they feel uncomfortable, regardless of who the person is. We can tell them and then have them use real names for their body parts. We can trust their abilities in age-appropriate ways. The goal is to teach children to respect their own bodies and stand up for themselves when they're experiencing physical violations.

Feminist parenting also teaches kids about **_respecting feelings_**. Kids should understand the validation of their own thoughts and recognize that feelings are important. We should give children strategies to understand their emotions in a healthy way.

You might be surprised at how little we respect kids' voices. We too frequently dismiss them if we don't understand what they want to say. We need to give them time and space to let them share and name their emotions. Kids who can recognize and verbalize how they're feeling are less likely to resort to tantrums. Encourage all emotions as acceptable while still being responsible for their behavior. Model empathy toward themselves and others so that children value their own voices and emotions.

Respect for choices, gender, and sexuality is also a goal for feminist parenting, albeit a challenging one. Ultimately, though, respecting those topics is just branching out from respecting bodily autonomy and emotions. Allowing children to express themselves with clothing and hairstyles is beneficial for them to learn decision-making skills.

Exposing kids to a variety of gender expressions will allow them to honor their own preferences. Respect sexual body parts and sexual expression and try not to ignore, downplay, or forbid talk about sexuality. If you don't feel comfortable talking about sexuality, educate yourself or ask someone you trust who is educated on the topic. Feminist parenting wants to teach children to discover their own expression and to respect their own identity.

When children respect themselves, they will have an awareness of their body, feelings, and how they affect others. This knowledge translates into respect for others easily. By birth, humans are hardwired to pay attention to facial expressions (and they try to imitate those with toothless smiles). Empathizing with children's feelings will help build their emotional intelligence. Emotional intelligence is the ability to recognize, assess, and control your emotions and those of others.

There are ways to help build emotional intelligence. Describe your feelings to children so they know what you are feeling. Apologize if you make a mistake. It gives the child the benefit of knowing that everyone makes mistakes and that all mistakes can be fixed. Practice a perspective switch. When an opportunity presents itself, ask the child how they think the other kid is feeling or how they would feel if in the same situation.

Another goal of feminist parenting is **_respect for diversity_**. Adults can easily relate to people who are like them, but it can be more difficult to relate to someone that isn't like them. The interesting thing is that to small children (under ages 3–5) everyone is the same, and they usually don't treat those with differences in different ways.

Unfortunately, this is quickly replaced by labeling and stereotyping of people. Often, kids (ages 5–8) will adamantly reject ideas that are different so they might only play with "boy" toys or other boys. This is a natural stage of development, but we should challenge and discuss them so they continue to develop further.

We should expose kids to as many types of people as possible, and also to media that features diverse people. When they are exposed to media that perpetuates stereotypes, then identify them. Spark conversation about differences along with the positives and negatives of media.

Finally, no matter what occupation they choose as adults, these skills will help children live according to their values and principles. They need critical thinking, a direct method for problem solving. They should be able to brainstorm and be open-minded. They need to be able to identify core issues and interpret data. All these skills not only will help with careers, but even college before that. College is an excellent place to work on these skills if they haven't before.

Kids also need to know how to practice non-violent communication. Non-violent communication is a method for respectful problem solving. Kids can learn habits that increase resiliency and contentment. They can also learn to identify happiness as a choice instead of a condition. Ultimately, feminist parenting wants children to gain the skills to live a meaningful, authentic life.

Conclusion

In this day and age, American families are increasingly diverse. They are also forms of social organizations that directly connect to many other institutions in society. Families are basic social units around how much of our society is constructed. Families, no matter what the type, are fundamental to meeting individual and societal needs. The importance of families in U.S. society gives us a way to consider how families reproduce and/or resist gender norms. This space also allows us to examine what families mean to us in our own lives and also how we might construct our own families if we haven't already done so. Check out the reading "Who wants to Marry a Feminist?" by Lisa Miya-Jervis, to continue thinking about diverse family structures.

Suggested Readings

Berry, C. 2004. *Rise up singing: Black women writers on motherhood.* New York: Random House.

Coontz, S. (2006). *Marriage, a history: How love conquered marriage.* New York: Penguin Books.

Hertz, R. (2008). *Single by chance, mothers by choice: How women are choosing parenthood without marriage and creating the new American family.* New York: Oxford University Press.

O'Reilly, A. (2004). *Mother outlaws: Theories and practices of empowered mothering.* Toronto, Ontario: Women's Press.

Richards, A. (2008). *Opting in: Having a child without losing yourself.* New York: Farrar, Straus, and Giroux.

Wolf, N. (2003). *Misconceptions: Truth, lies, and the unexpected journey to motherhood.* New York: Anchor Books.

References

Blood, R. and Wolfe, D. (1960). *Husbands and wives: The dynamics of married living.* New York: Macmillan.

Borkenau P., McCrae R., & Terracciano A. (2012). "Do men vary more than women in personality? A study in 51 cultures." *Journal of Research in Personality, 47,* pp. 135–144.

Foa, E. and Foa, U. (1980). "Resource theory: Interpersonal behavior as exchange." In Gergen, K., Greenberg, M. and Willis, R., (Eds.). *Social exchange: Advances in theory and research,* pp 77–94, New York: Plenum Press.

French, J. and Raven, B. (1959). "The bases of social power." In Cartwright, D., (Ed.). *Studies in social power,* pp. 150–167. Ann Arbor, MI: Institute for Social Research.

Kids Count Data Center. (2014). *Children who speak a language other than English at home.* Retrieved December 15, 2015 from http://datacenter.kidscount.org/data/tables/81-children-who-speak-a-language-other-than-english-at-home#detailed/1/any/false/869,36,868,867,133/any/396,397

Livingston, G. (2014). *Less than half of U.S. kids today live in a "traditional" family.* Retrieved December 15, 2015 from http://www.pewresearch.org/fact-tank/2014/12/22/less-than-half-of-u-s-kids-today-live-in-a-traditional-family/

Mills, J. (2007). *My mother wears combat boots: A parenting guide for the rest of us.* Oakland, CA: AK Press.

O'Reilly, A. (2008). *Feminist mothering.* Albany: SUNY Press.

Richards, A. (2015). *Makers Profile.* Retrieved December 15, 2015 from http://www.makers.com/amy-richards

Safilios-Rothschild, C. (1976). "A macro- and micro-examination of family power and love: An exchange model." *Journal of Marriage and Family, 38*(2), 355–362. http://doi.org/10.2307/350394

Steinem, G. (1983). *Outrageous acts and everyday rebellions.* New York: Henry Holt & Company.
Valenti, J. (2012). *Why have kids?: A new mom explores the truth about parenting and happiness.* New York: New Harvest.

Discussion Questions

1. Do you think feminism and marriage work together?

2. Would you try feminist parenting tips if you have or plan to have children?

3. What are some myths/stereotypes that come with family?

4. How does society reinforce power relations in the family?

5. What tasks do members of your family do at home? Do those tasks reflect societal norms?

Who Wants to Marry A Feminist?

By Lisa Miya-Jervis

The winter I got engaged, a college friend was using some of my essays as course material for a Rhetoric 101 class she was teaching at a large Midwestern university. She couldn't wait to alert her students to my impending marriage. "They all think you're a lesbian," she told me. "One of them even asked if you hate men." I was blown over by the cliché of it all—how had we come to the end of the twentieth century with such ridiculous, outmoded notions even partially intact? But I was, at least, pleased that my friend was able to use my story to banish the stereotype once and (I hoped) for all in the minds of 30 corn-fed first-years. "To a man?" they reportedly gasped when told the news.

I'd been married less than a year when a customer at the bookstore where my husband works approached the counter to buy a copy of the feminist magazine I edit. "You know," a staffer told her while ringing up the purchase, "the woman who does this magazine is married to a guy who works here." The customer, supposedly a longtime reader, was outraged at the news—I believe the phrase "betrayal of feminism" was uttered—and vowed never to buy the magazine again.

These two incidents may be extreme, but they are nonetheless indicative. Although we are far from rare, young married feminists are still, for some, something of a novelty—like a dressed-up dog. We can cause a surprised "Oh, would you look at that" or a disappointed "Take that damned hat off the dog, it's just not right."

Let's take the disappointment first. Marriage's bad reputation among feminists is certainly not without reason. We all know the institution's tarnished history: women as property passed from father to husband; monogamy as the simplest way to assure paternity and thus produce "legitimate" children; a husband's legal entitlement to his wife's domestic and sexual services. With marriage rates falling and social sanctions against cohabitation falling away, why would a feminist choose to take part in such a retro, potentially oppressive, bigotedly exclusive institution?

Well, there are a lot of reasons, actually. Foremost are the emotional ones: love, companionship, the pure joy that meeting your match brings with it. But, because I'm wary of the kind of muddled romanticizing that has ill-served women in their heterosexual dealings for most of recorded history, I have plenty of other reasons. To reject marriage simply because of its history is to give in to that history; to argue against marriage by saying that a wife's identity is necessarily subsumed by her husband's is to do nothing more than second the notion.

And wasn't it feminists who fought so hard to procure the basic rights that used to be obliterated by marriage? Because of the women's rights movement, we can maintain our own bank accounts; we can make our own health care choices; we can refuse sex with our husbands and prosecute them if they don't comply. In the feminist imagination, "wife" can still conjure up images of cookie-baking, cookie-cutter Donna Reeds whose own desires have been forced to take a backseat to their stultifying helpmate duties. But it's neither 1750 nor 1950, and Donna Reed was a mythical figure even in her own time. Marriage, now, is potentially what we make it.

Lisa Miya-Jervis is the editor of "Bitch: Feminist Response to Pop Culture" and coeditor of "Young Wives' Tales," an upcoming anthology of feminist writings on partnership (Seal Press 2001).

Which brings me to the "surprise" portion of our program. As long as the yeti of the antifeminist world—the hairy-legged man-hater (everyone claims to have seen her but actual evidence is sparse)— roams the earth, we need to counteract her image. And as long as wives are assumed—by anyone—to be obedient little women with no lives of their own, those of us who give the lie to this straw bride need to make ourselves as conspicuous as possible.

I want to take the good from marriage and leave the rest. I know it's not for everyone, but the "for as long as we both shall live" love and support thang really works for me. Sure, I didn't need the wedding to get that love and support, but neither does the fact of marriage automatically consign me and my man to traditional man-and-wife roles. Like so many relationships, married and un-, ours is a complex weave of support, independence, and sex. We achieve this privately—from the mundanities of you-have-to-cook-tonight-because-I-have-this-deadline-tomorrow to sleepy late-night discussions on more profound matters, like the meaning of life or how many steps it takes to link Kevin Bacon to John Gielgud by way of at least one vampire movie. But also publicly—with our name change, for example (explaining to folks like the Social Security Administration and whoever hands out passports that, yes, we both need new papers, because we each have added the other's name was, and I mean this quite seriously, a thrill). And it's this public nature of marriage that appeals. It's what allows me to take a stab at all this change I've been yammering about.

I won't pretend I meet with success all the time. Disrupting other people's expectations is hard, and sometimes it's neither possible nor desirable to wear the workings of one's relationship on one's sleeve. An appropriate cocktail party introduction is not, "This is my husband, Christopher, who knows how to truss a turkey, which I don't, and who, by the way, doesn't mind at all that I make more money than him. Oh, and did I mention that the last time our toilet got scrubbed, it wasn't by me?"

Plus, some people's perceptions can only change so much. My 90-year-old grandfather, who has been nothing but open-minded and incredibly supportive of my feminist work, persists in asking what my husband is going to do for food whenever I leave town on my own. Each time, I say the same thing: "Christopher knows perfectly well how to feed himself. In fact, he's cooking dinner for me right now." And then my grandfather gives a little surprised chuckle: those crazy kids, what will they think of next? And my accountant, who's been doing my taxes for years and knows my husband only as a Social Security number, automatically assigned Christopher the status of "taxpayer" and put me down as "spouse" on our first joint return. Yeah, it was a tad annoying, but so far it's the sum total of the eclipse of my identity by his. Not so bad, really.

By and large I do believe that we're culturally ready to accept changes in the way marriages are viewed. Increasing rates of cohabitation and the growing visibility of long-term same-sex partnerships are changing popular notions of relationships. Even trash TV holds promise: Fox's Who Wants to Marry a Multi-Millionaire? debacle laid bare many ugly things about American capitalism and media spectacle, but there was one fairly unexpected result. The show was presented as a display, however crass, of old-fashioned marital values—a trade of youth, beauty, and fecundity for wealth, security, and caretaking, complete with the groom's friends and family on hand for that lovely arranged-marriage feel. But it turned out to be nothing of the kind. The bride, as it happened, just wanted the lark of a free trip to Vegas, and the groom, a boost to his moribund show-biz career. That the concept saw the outside of a Fox conference room proves that modern marriage is in dire need of feminist attention. But the widely expressed outrage and disgust that followed the show are evidence that the general public is more than ready to discard the notion that a woman's ultimate goal is the altar.

It's true that the most important parts, the actual warp and weft of Christopher's and my relationship, could be achieved without a legal marriage (and I could have kept my third-wave street cred). In the end, though, the decision to marry or not to marry is—no matter how political the personal—an emotional one. I wanted to link my life to Christopher's, and, yes, I admit to taking advantage of the universally understood straight-shot-to-relationship-legitimacy that marriage offers. But it is a testament to the feminists who came before me, who offered up all those arguments about marriage's oppressive roots and worked tirelessly to ensure that my husband owns neither my body nor my paycheck, that I can indulge my emotion without fear of being caught in those roots. Instead, I can carry on their struggle and help forge a new vision of what marriage is.

CHAPTER 8

Women & Work

No matter where you are, work, whether paid or unpaid and both in and out of the home, is a gendered thing. Certain types of work are considered masculine and some feminine. Some tasks are valued more than others.

Take housework. It doesn't matter who does it; it is a task that is not valued in American society. It's often tedious, hard work, and not many people enjoy doing it. Women are more often than not the ones doing work that is not valued in our society, whether it is housework or something else. They do the work and then are also paid less than men for doing it.

A majority of women are working outside the home, while also doing the housework. Women are working hard because they have to, paid or unpaid. When they get paid, women typically earn lower wages compared to men and less control of what they do and the wages they get. Let's take a look at how we got to this point.

During the Great Depression, there were many states that had laws barring married women from gaining employment. The idea behind the laws was that a married woman had a husband to provide for her, so she didn't need to take a job from a man. Single women could try to find jobs, but often they were in the category of *women's work*, which obviously paid a lot less. White single women were able to find jobs as salespeople, hairstylists, teachers, secretaries, and nurses. African American women at the time struggled even more. Those who did find work did so as maids or cooks.

Then World War II happened and everything changed. Sixteen million men served in the armed forces during the war and left their jobs to do so (World War II Foundation, 2015). Factories did not stop production, instead working 24/7 to supply the American war effort. This created a perfect storm that resulted in a labor shortage. All at once it was patriotic for women to work. By 1943, approximately 17 million women workers made up one-third of the total U.S. workforce. About five million of these women worked in defense factories (Stanley, 2005).

The U.S. government worked with a variety of media sources to convince women to take jobs outside the home. A fictional character named Rosie the Riveter was created and used for this purpose. There were posters and songs designed specifically for Rosie the Riveter to promote work as patriotism for women. Rosie was usually depicted as a temporary worker, a middle-class housewife who left the comforts of her own home to serve her country. She was also depicted as a woman who was eager to return to housework and domesticity when the war ended.

Rosie the Riveter had a very specific back story that didn't ring true for all women. Many of the women who held wartime industrial jobs had already been employed before the war. They worked in the low-wage women's work that was discussed earlier. These women were glad for higher-paying jobs in wartime factories. The women enjoyed more income, freedom, and self-esteem. While working, the women developed a new sense of purpose. The women felt pride in being referred to as the "Hidden Army" that was helping to win the war (Cushing, 1987).

Not everything was perfect. Men were almost always still filling the supervisor jobs and the gender pay gap existed even then. When the war ended, women workers were expected to relinquish their jobs to veterans that returned home. Women were forced go back home and then expected to have and raise children. In 1946, 4 million women were fired from the jobs they had during wartime. Many of the women couldn't just go back home; they had to work. It was a necessity, and so they went back to the kinds of women's work they had before the war.

After the war, the media that had once encouraged women to work during the war was now emphasizing that women's place was in the home. All kinds of popular culture told women of the times that they should be cooking, cleaning, and raising children. The women on TV and in movies and ads were portrayed at home, typically with an apron on in the kitchen. Women were also deterred from going to college. A smaller percentage of women attended college in the 1950s than in the 1920s (Ana, 2015).

But as the media gave one image of women, it was actually a much different reality for lots of women. There were more and more women entering the workforce at this time. They weren't employed in the fields they worked in during the war. Instead, they worked in clerical, teaching, and health-related jobs.

During the second wave of feminism, work was still an important topic. Betty Friedan and Gloria Steinem are two prominent women from the second wave whose writings discussed women and work. There are familiar similarities from earlier times to what they had to say in the second wave.

In 1957, **Betty Friedan** conducted a survey of graduates from Smith, her alma mater. She asked them specifically about their education, life after college, and contentment with their current lives. She started publishing articles about what she called "the problem that has no name." Friedan got passionate responses from many housewives grateful that they were not alone in experiencing this problem (Spender, 1985).

Friedan then made her work into a book, *The Feminine Mystique*. Published in 1963, it showed the roles of women in first-world societies, especially the housewife role that Friedan said was stifling. In her book, she spoke of her own "terror" at being alone, wrote that she had never once in her life seen a positive female role-model who worked outside the home and also kept a family, and cited numerous cases of housewives who felt similarly trapped (Friedan, 1963).

Friedan argued that women are as capable as men for any type of work or any career path against arguments to the contrary by the mass media, educators, and psychologists (Fox, 2006). Her work and the constraints of the time period influenced American women who began to attend consciousness-raising groups. They also lobbied for the modification of restrictive laws and social views that oppressed women.

Early in her career, **Gloria Steinem** worked as a Playboy Bunny at the New York Playboy Club. She published an article entitled "A Bunny's Tale," which described her experiences at the club (Steinem, 1963). The story also featured a photo of Steinem in Bunny uniform. Steinem has upheld that she is pleased with the work she did broadcasting the exploitative working environment of the bunnies. She particularly highlighted the sexual demands made of them, which was very sketchy from a legal viewpoint (Steinem, 1995). It wasn't all a positive experience for Steinem. She was not able to find another job for a time after the article came out. She was seen as a Playboy bunny instead of a journalist. Steinem eventually landed a job at *New York* magazine in 1968 (Steinem, 1995).

The ***third wave of feminism*** focuses on race, social class, transgender rights, and sexual liberation as the main issues. This wave also pays attention to workplace matters such as the glass ceiling, sexual harassment, and family leave policies. Motherhood is also an important issue for the third wave, including support for single mothers (financial and child care), respect for working mothers and no judgement of mothers who decide to stay at home to raise their children. These issues might have been pushed to the forefront in the 1990s, but they are still very relevant topics today. In the next section, we look at unpaid labor.

Unpaid Labor

Unpaid labor is work done without any wages for the worker. The workers could be family, forced labor, volunteer, and/or students who intern. Unpaid labor is sometimes a controversial topic within feminist economics, since it is an area that is notably affected by traditional family values (Phillips, 2008). Unpaid workers are often women who don't work outside the home, but work in the home and do domestic labor instead. There are several factors behind employment decisions that women make. These factors include, but are not limited to, spousal support, gender roles, and duty to their family.

The term ***unofficial employment*** typically refers to self-employment, a position within self-started enterprises and unpaid domestic labor. For a lot of women in the United States, such work is known more as part-time. In contrast, in many other parts of the world unofficial employment typically refers to unpaid domestic labor, as an extension of a pre-existing family role. The working position is placed within the framework of the family, and the laborer is required to both see to family matters as well as the occupation.

Employment demographics indicate that the employment of married women is affected greatly by marriage and childbirth. Women can sometimes be pushed into the role of an unpaid domestic worker through both traditional and economic pressure. Even when women work full-time outside the home, they may still take care of a majority of the household chores and childcare (Sirianni & Negrey, 2000). The gender wage gap, discussed later in this chapter, contributes to this happening. Women face lower wages, fewer opportunities for promotion, and become less ambitious along the way (Covert, 2015). Women also adjust their time in the labor market to respond to demands at home (Sirianni & Negrey, 2000).

The stereotypical traditional view of family involves women in unpaid labor positions maintaining the household. With more and more dual earning couples and a steadily aging population, the commercialization of housework and care has become unavoidable. Questions arise with this issue: What is the value of unpaid labor? Are unpaid workers exploited? Should unpaid labor be seen as legitimate employment?

The issue of unpaid workers is closely tied to concepts within feminism and gender equality. Some women are choosing to stay at home and raise their families. They usually have a husband or partner that can support them financially. The women are making choices that they believe will benefit themselves and their families, while still encouraging their children to be whatever they want to be. The women may also volunteer with local schools and organizations for the betterment of the community. The women self-identify as feminists and promote equality in everything they do.

Finally, students who work as ***unpaid interns*** fit into this category. From a survey of college grads in 2014, 61% had had an internship during college, and 53.5% of those internships were unpaid (Venator & Reeves, 2015). Internships should provide training for students, not to be used by employers to save costs according to labor law. Recently, the Second Circuit's U.S. Court of Appeals gave some good news to companies that utilize interns, declaring that private companies could use unpaid interns as long as the intern receives more value from the arrangement than the employer (Venator & Reeves, 2015).

Paid Labor

Women who have received wages for their employment have been challenged by inequality in the workforce. Women's lack of access to higher education basically excluded them from many well-paid occupations. Women's admission into professions like law and medicine was slowed due to women being denied entry to universities. Women were mainly limited to low-paid and poor status jobs for most of history and earning less pay than men for doing the same work.

Later on, cultural perceptions of ***paid work*** shifted as the workforce changed into less manufacturing positions and more office jobs. Women were then increasingly able to obtain the higher education they needed that led to better pay and careers. Women continue to be at a disadvantage compared to men simply because of motherhood. Women are still currently viewed as the primary caregiver to children, so their pay is lowered when they have children because companies do not expect them to continue to work after their family leave ends.

Restrictions on paid labor for women include the gender wage gap, the glass ceiling, so-called equal opportunity laws, and legal and cultural restrictions on job access. Women are frequently barred from reaching complete gender equality in the workplace because of the ***ideal worker norm,*** which "defines the committed worker as someone who works full-time and full force for forty years straight," a situation designed for men (Williams, 2009, pg. 100). On the contrary, women are still expected to be the family caretaker and take time off for domestic needs such as pregnancy and/or ill family members. These parts of their lives prevent them from being the ideal worker norm. With the current norm in place, women are forced to juggle full-time jobs and family care at home.

Access to paid labor continues to be unequal in many occupations and places around the world. There is often a clear differentiation between unpaid and paid labor when data about this topic is gathered. The researchers do this to provide analysis to a wide-ranging continuum of labor, including unpaid household work, childcare, eldercare, and internships, just to name a few.

Breakout: Lilly Ledbetter

© Carolyn Kaster/AP/Corbis

Lilly Ledbetter was the plaintiff in the American employment discrimination case entitled Ledbetter v. Goodyear Tire & Rubber Co. That case threw her into the spotlight, especially on the topic of the gender wage gap. She is now a celebrated feminist activist.

Lilly Ledbetter worked as a supervisor at Goodyear Tire and Rubber's plant in Gadsden, Alabama. For most of the years from 1979 to 1998, she worked as an area manager, a job mostly held by men. Ledbetter's income was originally in line with the wages of her male counterparts. Ultimately, though, over the course of her time with the company, her pay did not rise in comparison with her male co-workers. By 1997, Ledbetter was the only woman working as an area manager. The pay discrepancy between Ledbetter and her 15 male counterparts was blatant: Ledbetter was paid $3,727 per month and the lowest paid male area manager received $4,286 per month. The highest male area manager was paid $5,236 per month (LEDBETTER V. GOODYEAR TIRE & RUBBER CO., INC., 2007).

In 1998, she retired from Goodyear and then sued the company for paying her significantly less than her male counterparts (Pickert, 2009). Her lawsuit made it to the Supreme Court, where her claim was denied because she did not file suit 180 days from her first paycheck. Ledbetter said she didn't know at the time that she made less. She wasn't notified until close to her retirement (Pickert, 2009).

Consequently, Congress passed the Lilly Ledbetter Fair Pay Act in 2009 to relax the time requirements for filing of a discrimination lawsuit. The requirements are relaxed as long as the discrimination, including the paycheck as a past act of discrimination, occurs within the 180-day period of limitations (Brown, 2009). In 2012, Ledbetter released her autobiography, "Grace and Grit: My Fight for Equal Pay and Fairness at Goodyear and Beyond." She has appeared on numerous TV shows and spoken at many events, including two Democratic National Conventions.

Gender Wage Gap

As mentioned earlier, women make less than men do in the United States. This is called the ***gender wage gap***. In 2014, women working full time in the United States were typically paid 79% of what men were paid. Women's progress in education and workforce participation has narrowed the gap over time, but at a slow rate. The gender wage gap does not appear to be solved any time soon.

President John F. Kennedy signed the Equal Pay Act of 1963, but the gender wage gap still remains so many years later. And, as hard as many people try, the gap can't just be described as a statistical glitch. It is also because women prefer lower-paying industries or choose to take time off for their families.

Claudia Goldin has crunched the numbers and found that the gap persists for identical jobs, even after controlling for hours, education, race, and age. For example, female physicians and surgeons earn 71% of what their male colleagues make. Females who work as financial specialists are paid just 66% as much as men who do the same work (Miller, 2014).

Other researchers have calculated that women one year out of college earn 6.6 percent less than men after controlling for occupation and hours (Corbett & Hill, 2012). The gap doesn't close the higher women go. In 2014, the median weekly earnings for women in full-time management, professional, and related occupations was $981 compared to $1,346 for men (Bureau of Labor Statistics, 2015).

Most men are not deliberately discriminating against women. A majority of men are open-minded people who want women to be successful. They are certain that they don't have a gender problem themselves, but don't exactly know where the problem lies, or how to solve it. What they need to remember is that they are often leaders of companies that pay men more than women for the same jobs, so they could instill change and support success from there.

Women are making a tremendous effort to close the gender wage gap by themselves. Women are starting to be more assertive and ask for raises and promotions on their own. Women are told to lean in and to demand to be paid what they are worth. It is great advice, but it is not enough. It doesn't change the overall culture.

There are changes that can be made to close the gender wage gap. Some companies have publicly voiced their commitment to pay workers equitably, but women can't wait for change to trickle down from the top. Companies should conduct wage assessments to continually observe and address gender-based pay inconsistencies; then they should publish their findings for the public to see. It is good business practice to institute.

Women can learn strategies to better negotiate for equal pay. They can work on salary negotiation to help empower themselves to better self-advocate when it comes to salary, benefits, and promotions. One can never have enough education on this topic. There are books, articles, webinars, and workshops that women can use to better themselves with this issue.

The ***Paycheck Fairness Act*** would improve the scope of the Equal Pay Act, which hasn't been updated since 1963. The Paycheck Fairness Act has better incentives for employers to obey the law. It also improves federal implementation endeavors and forbids retaliation against workers asking about wage assessments. Contacting politicians to encourage them to support the Paycheck Fairness Act is important. Learn more about other actions you can take at fightforfairpay.org.

Conclusion

We can celebrate the advancement of women in work and the strides that have been made historically. Still, though, the harsh reality is that too many of us continue to struggle when we shouldn't have to. Sheryl Sandberg (2013) asked us to "lean in," but most working women are leaning in so much that we fall over. And we don't have a lot of resources to help us stand back up. We are forced to scrape by and make do.

Women serve as physicians, lawyers, soldiers, and astronauts. Women run big corporations such as Yahoo! and Pepsi. Today women are police chiefs and umpires and professional coaches. These are all jobs that were once for men only. We have made great strides and there's a pretty good chance a woman will be leading America in January 2017. No one can deny that progress has been made.

Women of color experience lower median weekly earnings, higher rates of poverty, and greater unemployment. The women's movement has been slow to address these issues. Feminism cannot stand by and let this happen. We cannot farm out this work to others. We must stand up for all working women, regardless of their race and class.

Feminists need to join together and speak out for good wages, benefits, fair scheduling, and equal pay for equal work. We must demand paid sick leave, family leave, and child care. We have to stand together to make these items accessible and available to everyone.

Recently, Congressman Paul Ryan made work/life balance a condition of his running for Speaker of the House. That had to have taken some guts, particularly for a man who has voted against EVERY proposal for workers to have more time and flexibility. Everyone should support paid family leave for Paul Ryan, as long as we get it too.

Think about these topics as you examine the reading for this chapter. Look at what is considered women's work and how it is (or isn't) valued in our society.

Suggested Readings

Barber, E.J.W. (1994). *Women's work: The first 20,000 years: Women, cloth, and society in early times.* New York: Norton.

Harley, S. (2002). *Sister circle: Black women and work.* New Jersey: Rutgers University Press.

Sandberg, S. (2013). *Lean in: Women, work, and the will to lead.* New York: Knopf Doubleday Publishing Group.

Williams, C., Ed. (2012). *Indigenous women and work: From labor to activism.* Chicago: University of Illinois Press.

Williams, J. & Dempsey, R. (2014). *What works for women at work: Four patterns working women need to know.* New York: New York University Press.

References

Ana, F. (2015). *More women in college now than ever before.* Retrieved December 15, 2015 from http://www .collegeresourcenetwork.com/college-admissions/more-women-in-college-now-than-ever-before/

Brown, H. (2009). Equal payback for Lilly Ledbetter. Retrieved December 15, 2015 from http://www.forbes.com/2009/04/28/equal-pay-discrimination-forbes-woman-leadership-wages.html

Bureau of Labor Statistics. (2015). Current population survey, Table 39. Retrieved December 15, 2015 from http://www.bls.gov/cps/cpsaat39.htm

Corbett & Hill. (2012). *Graduating to a pay gap: The earnings of women and men one year after college graduation.* Retrieved December 15, 2015 from http://www.aauw.org/files/2013/02/graduating-to-a-pay-gap-the-earnings-of-women-and-men-one-year-after-college-graduation.pdf

Covert, B. (2015). *How companies make women less ambitious over time.* Retrieved December 15, 2015 from http://www.thenation.com/article/how-companies-make-women-less-ambitious-over-time/

Cushing, R. (1987). "'Rosie The Riveter' found her glory in a home-front war." *Orlando Sentinel.* Retrieved from: http://articles.orlandosentinel.com/1987-10-11/lifestyle/0150240010_1_shipyards-rosie-the-riveter-harassment

Friedan, B. (1963). *The feminine mystique.* New York: W. W. Norton & Company.

Fox, M. (2006). "Betty Friedan, who ignited cause in 'Feminine Mystique,' Dies at 85." *The New York Times.* Retrieved December 15, 2015 from http://www.nytimes.com/2006/02/05/national/05friedan.html?pagewanted=all&_r=0

LEDBETTER v. GOODYEAR TIRE & RUBBER CO., INC. (2007). Supreme Court of the United States. Retrieved November 1, 2015.

Ledbetter, L., & Isom, L. (2012). *Grace and grit: My fight for equal pay and fairness at Goodyear and beyond.* New York: Crown Archetype.

Miller, C. (2014). *Pay Gap is because of gender, not jobs.* Retrieved December 15, 2015 from http://www.nytimes.com/2014/04/24/upshot/the-pay-gap-is-because-of-gender-not-jobs.html?abt=0002&abg=0&_r=1

Philipps, Lisa (2008). "Silent partners: The role of unpaid market labor in families." *Feminist Economics* 14 (2): 37–57.

Pickert, Kate (Jan 29, 2009). "Lilly Ledbetter." *TIME.* Retrieved December 15, 2015 from http://content.time.com/time/nation/article/0,8599,1874954,00.html

Sandberg, S. (2013). *Lean in: Women, work, and the will to lead.* New York: Knopf Doubleday Publishing Group.

Sirianni, C. and Negrey, C. (2000). "Working time as gendered time." *Feminist Economics.* 6 (1), pp. 59–76.

Spender, D. (1985). *For the record: The making and meaning of feminist knowledge.* London: Women's Press.

Stanley, G. (2005). *The Great Depression and World War II, 1929–1949.* Milwaukee: World Almanac Library.

Steinem, G. (1963). "A Bunny's Tale" *Show.* Retrieved December 15, 2015 from http://dlib.nyu.edu/undercover/sites/dlib.nyu.edu.undercover/files/documents/uploads/editors/Show-A%20Bunny%27s%20Tale-Part%20One-May%201963.pdf

Steinem, Gloria (1995). "I was a Playboy Bunny." In *Outrageous acts and everyday rebellions.* New York: Holt Publishing.

Venator, J. & Reeves, R. (2015). *The implications of inequalities in contraception and abortion.* Retrieved December 15, 2015 from http://www.brookings.edu/blogs/social-mobility-memos/posts/2015/02/26-implications-inequalities-contraception-abortion-reeves

Williams, Joan (2009). "Reconstructive feminism: Changing the way we talk about gender and work thirty years after the PDA." *Yale J.L. & Feminism* 79 (21), pp. 79–111. Retrieved December 15, 2015 from http://repository.uchastings.edu/faculty_scholarship/802

World War II Foundation, (2015). *World War II facts and figures.* Retrieved December 15, 2015 from http://www.wwiifoundation.org/students/wwii-facts-figures/

Discussion Questions

1. How do racism and sexism affect women in the workplace?

2. How do we solve the gender pay gap in the United States?

3. Why do you think housework is so undervalued in our society?

4. What problems are there among women and issues of work?

5. What forms of oppression are still prevalent with women in the workplace?

The Politics of Other Women's Work

by Barbara Ehrenreich
April 1, 2000

In line with growing class polarization, the classic posture of submission is making a stealthy comeback. "We scrub your floors the old-fashioned way," boasts the brochure from Merry Maids, the largest of the residential-cleaning services that have sprung up in the last two decades, "on our hands and knees." This is not a posture that independent "cleaning ladies" willingly assume—preferring, like most people who clean their own homes, the sponge mop wielded from a standing position. In her comprehensive 1999 guide to homemaking, *Home Comforts*, Cheryl Mendelson warns: "Never ask hired housecleaners to clean your floors on their hands and knees; the request is likely to be regarded as degrading." But in a society in which 40 percent of the wealth is owned by 1 percent of households while the bottom 20 percent reports negative assets, the degradation of others is readily purchased. Kneepads entered American political discourse as a tool of the sexually subservient, but employees of Merry Maids, The Maids International, and other corporate cleaning services spend hours every day on these kinky devices, wiping up the drippings of the affluent.

I spent three weeks in September 1999 as an employee of The Maids International in Portland, Maine, cleaning, along with my fellow team members, approximately sixty houses containing a total of about 250 scrubbable floors—bathrooms, kitchens, and entryways requiring the hands-and-knees treatment. It's a different world down there below knee level, one that few adults voluntarily enter. Here you find elaborate dust structures held together by a scaffolding of dog hair; dried bits of pasta glued to the floor by their sauce; the congealed remains of gravies, jellies, contraceptive creams, vomit, and urine. Sometimes, too, you encounter some fragment of a human being: a child's legs, stamping by in disgust because the maids are still present when he gets home from school; more commonly, the Joan & David-clad feet and electrolyzed calves of the female homeowner. Look up and you may find this person staring at you, arms folded, in anticipation of an overlooked stain. In rare instances she may try to help in some vague, symbolic way, by moving the cockatoo's cage, for example, or apologizing for the leaves shed by a miniature indoor tree. Mostly, though, she will not see you at all and may even sit down with her mail at a table in the very room you are cleaning, where she would remain completely unaware of your existence unless you were to crawl under that table and start gnawing away at her ankles.

Housework, as you may recall from the feminist theories of the Sixties and Seventies, was supposed to be the great equalizer of women. Whatever else women did—jobs, school, child care—we also did housework, and if there were some women who hired others to do it for them, they seemed too privileged and rare to include in the theoretical calculus. All women were workers, and the home was their workplace—unpaid and unsupervised, to be sure, but a workplace no less than the offices and factories men repaired to every morning. If men thought of the home as a site of leisure and recreation—a "haven in a heartless world"—this was to ignore the invisible female proletariat that kept it cozy and humming. We were on the march now, or so we imagined, united against a society that devalued our labor even as it waxed mawkish over "the family" and "the home." Shoulder to shoulder and arm in arm, women were finally getting up off the floor.

In the most eye-catching elaboration of the home-as-workplace theme, Marxist feminists Maria Rosa Dallacosta and Selma James proposed in 1972 that the home was in fact an economically productive and significant workplace, an extension of the actual factory, since housework served to "reproduce the labor power" of others, particularly men. The male worker would hardly be in shape to punch in for his shift, after all, if some woman had not fed him, laundered his clothes, and cared for the children who were his contribution to the next generation of workers. If the home was a quasi-industrial workplace staffed by women for the ultimate benefit of the capitalists, then it followed that "wages for housework" was the obvious demand.

But when most American feminists, Marxist or otherwise, asked the Marxist question cui bono? they tended to come up with a far simpler answer—men. If women were the domestic proletariat, then men made up the class of domestic exploiters, free to lounge while their mates scrubbed. In consciousness-raising groups, we railed against husbands and boyfriends who refused to pick up after themselves, who were unaware of housework at all, unless of course it hadn't been done. The "dropped socks," left by a man for a woman to gather up and launder, joined lipstick and spike heels as emblems of gender oppression. And if, somewhere, a man had actually dropped a sock in the calm expectation that his wife would retrieve it, it was a sock heard round the world. Wherever second-wave feminism took root, battles broke out between lovers and spouses over sticky countertops, piled-up laundry, and whose turn it was to do the dishes.

The radical new idea was that housework was not only a relationship between a woman and a dust bunny or an unmade bed; it also defined a relationship between human beings, typically husbands and wives. This represented a marked departure from the more conservative Betty Friedan, who, in The Feminine Mystique, had never thought to enter the male sex into the equation, as either part of the housework problem or part of an eventual solution. She raged against a society that consigned its educated women to what she saw as essentially janitorial chores, beneath "the abilities of a woman of average or normal human intelligence," and, according to unidentified studies she cited, "peculiarly suited to the capacities of feeble-minded girls." But men are virtually exempt from housework in The Feminine Mystique—why drag them down too? At one point she even disparages a "Mrs. G.," who "somehow couldn't get her housework done before her husband came home at night and was so tired then that he had to do it." Educated women would just have to become more efficient so that housework could no longer "expand to fill the time available."

Or they could hire other women to do it—an option approved by Friedan in The Feminine Mystique as well as by the National Organization for Women, which she had helped launch. At the 1973 congressional hearings on whether to extend the Fair Labor Standards Act to household workers, NOW testified on the affirmative side, arguing that improved wages and working conditions would attract more women to the field, and offering the seemingly self-contradictory prediction that "the demand for household help inside the home will continue to increase as more women seek occupations outside the home." One NOW member added, on a personal note: "Like many young women today, I am in school in order to develop a rewarding career for myself. I also have a home to run and can fully conceive of the need for household help as my free time at home becomes more and more restricted. Women know [that] housework is dirty, tedious work, and they are willing to pay to have it done . . . " On the aspirations of the women paid to do it, assuming that at least some of them were bright enough to entertain a few, neither Friedan nor these members of NOW had, at the time, a word to say.

So the insight that distinguished the more radical, post-Friedan cohort of feminists was that when we talk about housework, we are really talking, yet again, about power. Housework was not degrading because it was manual labor, as Friedan thought, but because it was embedded in degrading relationships and inevitably served to reinforce them. To make a mess that another person will have to deal with—the dropped socks, the toothpaste sprayed on the bathroom mirror, the dirty dishes left from a late-night snack—is to exert domination in one of its more silent and intimate forms. One person's arrogance—or indifference, or hurry—becomes another person's occasion for toil. And when the person who is cleaned up after is consistently male, while the person who cleans up is consistently female, you have a formula for reproducing male domination from one generation to the next.

Hence the feminist perception of housework as one more way by which men exploit women or, more neutrally stated, as "a symbolic enactment of gender relations." An early German women's liberation cartoon depicted a woman scrubbing on her hands and knees while her husband, apparently excited by this pose, approaches from behind, unzipping his fly. Hence, too, the second-wave feminists' revulsion at the hiring of maids, especially when they were women of color: At a feminist conference I attended in 1980, poet Audre Lorde chose to insult the all too-white audience by accusing them of being present only because they had black housekeepers to look after their children at home. She had the wrong crowd; most of the assembled radical feminists would no sooner have employed a black maid than they would have attached Confederate flag stickers to the rear windows of their cars. But accusations like hers, repeated in countless conferences and meetings, reinforced our rejection of the servant option. There already were at least two able-bodied adults in the average home—a man and a woman—and the hope was that, after a few initial skirmishes, they would learn to share the housework graciously.

A couple of decades later, however, the average household still falls far short of that goal. True, women do less housework than they did before the feminist revolution and the rise of the two-income family: down from an average of 30 hours per week in 1965 to 17.5 hours in 1995, according to a July 1999 study by the University of Maryland. Some of that decline reflects a relaxation of standards rather than a redistribution of chores; women still do two thirds of whatever housework—including bill paying, pet care, tidying, and lawn care—gets done. The inequity is sharpest for the most despised of household chores, cleaning: in the thirty years between 1965 and 1995, men increased the time they spent scrubbing, vacuuming, and sweeping by 240 percent—all the way up to 1.7 hours per week—while women decreased their cleaning time by only 7 percent, to 6.7 hours per week. The averages conceal a variety of arrangements, of course, from minutely negotiated sharing to the most clichéd division of labor, as described by one woman to the Washington Post: "I take care of the inside, he takes care of the outside." But perhaps the most disturbing finding is that almost the entire increase in male participation took place between the 1970s and the mid-1980s. Fifteen years after the apparent cessation of hostilities, it is probably not too soon to announce the score: in the "chore wars" of the Seventies and Eighties, women gained a little ground, but overall, and after a few strategic concessions, men won.

Enter then, the cleaning lady as dea ex machina, restoring tranquility as well as order to the home. Marriage counselors recommend her as an alternative to squabbling, as do many within the cleaning industry itself. A Chicago cleaning woman quotes one of her clients as saying that if she gives up the service, "my husband and I will be divorced in six months." When the trend toward hiring out was just beginning to take off, in 1988, the owner of a Merry Maids franchise in Arlington, Massachusetts, told the *Christian Science Monitor*, "I kid some women. I say, 'We even save marriages. In this new eighties period you expect more from the male partner, but very often you don't get the cooperation you would like to have. The alternative is to pay somebody to come in. . . . '" Another Merry Maids franchise owner has learned to capitalize more directly on housework-related spats; he closes between 30 and 35 percent of his sales by making follow-up calls Saturday mornings, which is "prime time for arguing over the fact that the house is a mess." The micro-defeat of feminism in the household opened a new door for women, only this time it was the servants' entrance.

In 1999, somewhere between 14 and 18 percent of households employed an outsider to do the cleaning, and the numbers have been rising dramatically. Mediamark Research reports a 53 percent increase, between 1995 and 1999, in the number of households using a hired cleaner or service once a month or more, and Maritz Marketing finds that 30 percent of the people who hired help in 1999 did so for the first time that year. Among my middle-class, professional women friends and acquaintances, including some who made important contributions to the early feminist analysis of housework, the employment of a maid is now nearly universal. This sudden emergence of a servant class is consistent with what some economists have called the "Brazilianization" of the American economy: We are dividing along the lines of traditional Latin American societies—into a tiny overclass and a huge underclass, with the latter available to perform intimate household services for the former. Or, to put it another way, the home, or at least the affluent home, is finally becoming what radical feminists in the Seventies only imagined it was—a true "workplace" for women and a tiny, though increasingly visible, part of the capitalist economy. And the question is: As the home becomes a workplace for someone else, is it still a place where you would want to live?

Strangely, or perhaps not so strangely at all, no one talks about the "politics of housework" anymore. The demand for "wages for housework" has sunk to the status of a curio, along with the consciousness-raising groups in which women once rallied support in their struggles with messy men. In the academy, according to the feminist sociologists I interviewed, housework has lost much of its former cachet—in part, I suspect, because fewer sociologists actually do it. Most Americans, over 80 percent, still clean their homes, but the minority who do not include a sizable fraction of the nation's opinion-makers and culture-producers—professors, writers, editors, politicians, talking heads, and celebrities of all sorts. In their homes, the politics of housework is becoming a politics not only of gender but of race and class— and these are subjects that the opinion-making elite, if not most Americans, generally prefer to avoid.

Even the number of paid houseworkers is hard to pin down. The Census Bureau reports that there were 549,000 domestic workers in 1998, up 9 percent since 1996, but this may be a considerable underestimate, since so much of the servant economy is still underground. In 1995, two years after Zoe Baird lost her chance to be attorney general for paying her undocumented nanny off the books, the Los Angeles Times reported that fewer than 10 percent of those Americans who paid a housecleaner reported those payments to the IRS. Sociologist Mary Romero, one of the few academics who retain an active interest in housework and the women who do it for pay, offers an example of how severe the undercounting can be: the 1980 Census found only 1,063 "private household workers" in El Paso, Texas, though the city estimated their numbers at 13,400 and local bus drivers estimated that half of the 28,300 daily bus trips were taken by maids going to and from work. The honesty of employers has increased since the Baird scandal, but most experts believe that household workers remain, in large part, uncounted and invisible to the larger economy.

One thing you can say with certainty about the population of household workers is that they are disproportionately women of color: "lower" kinds of people for a "lower" kind of work. Of the "private household cleaners and servants" it managed to locate in 1998, the Bureau of Labor Statistics reports that 36.8 percent were Hispanic, 15.8 percent black, and 2.7 percent "other." Certainly the association between housecleaning and minority status is well established in the psyches of the white employing class. When my daughter, Rosa, was introduced to the wealthy father of a Harvard classmate, he ventured that she must have been named for a favorite maid. And Audre Lorde can perhaps be forgiven for her intemperate accusation at the feminist conference mentioned above when we consider an experience she had in 1967: "I wheel my two-year-old daughter in a shopping cart through a supermarket . . . and a little white girl riding past in her mother's cart calls out excitedly, 'Oh look, Mommy, a baby maid.'" But the composition of the household workforce is hardly fixed and has changed with the life chances of the different ethnic groups. In the late nineteenth century, Irish and German immigrants served the northern upper and middle classes, then left for the factories as soon as they could. Black women replaced them, accounting for 60 percent of all domestics in the 1940s, and dominated the field until other occupations began to open up to them. Similarly, West Coast maids were disproportionately Japanese American until that group, too, found more congenial options. Today, the color of the hand that pushes the sponge varies from region to region: Chicanas in the Southwest, Caribbeans in New York, native Hawaiians in Hawaii, whites, many of recent rural extraction, in Maine.

The great majority—though again, no one knows exact numbers—of paid housekeepers are freelancers, or "independents," who find their clients through agencies or networks of already employed friends and relatives. To my acquaintances in the employing class, the freelance housekeeper seems to be a fairly privileged and prosperous type of worker, a veritable aristocrat of labor—sometimes paid $15 an hour or more and usually said to be viewed as a friend or even treated as "one of the family." But the shifting ethnic composition of the workforce tells another story: this is a kind of work that many have been trapped in—by racism, imperfect English skills, immigration status, or lack of education—but few have happily chosen. Interviews with independent maids collected by Romero and by sociologist Judith Rollins, who herself worked as a maid in the Boston area in the early Eighties, confirm that the work is undesirable to those who perform it. Even when the pay is deemed acceptable, the hours may be long and unpredictable; there are usually no health benefits, no job security, and, if the employer has failed to pay Social Security taxes (in some cases because the maid herself prefers to be paid off the books), no retirement benefits. And the pay is often far from acceptable. The BLS found full-time "private household cleaners and servants" earning a median annual income of $12,220 in 1998, which is $1,092 below the poverty level for a family of three. Recall that in 1993 Zoe Baird paid her undocumented household workers about $5 an hour out of her earnings of $507,000 a year.

At the most lurid extreme there is slavery. A few cases of forced labor pop up in the press every year, most recently—in some nightmare version of globalization—of undocumented women held in servitude by high-ranking staff members of the United Nations, the World Bank, and the International Monetary Fund. Consider the suit brought by Elizabeth Senghor, a Senegalese woman who alleged that she was forced to work fourteen-hour days for her employers in Manhattan, without any regular pay, and was given no accommodations beyond a pull-out bed in her employers' living room. Hers is not a particularly startling instance of domestic slavery; no beatings or sexual assaults were charged, and Ms. Senghor was apparently fed. What gives this case a certain rueful poignancy is that her employer, former U.N. employee Marie Angelique Savane, is one of Senegal's leading women's rights advocates and had told *The Christian Science Monitor* in 1986 about her efforts to get the Senegalese to "realize that being a woman can mean other things than simply having children, taking care of the house."

Mostly, though, independent maids—and sometimes the women who employ them—complain about the peculiar intimacy of the employer-employee relationship. Domestic service is an occupation that predates the refreshing impersonality of capitalism by several thousand years, conditions of work being still largely defined by the idiosyncrasies of the employers. Some of them seek friendship and even what their maids describe as "therapy," though they are usually quick to redraw the lines once the maid is perceived as overstepping. Others demand deference bordering on servility, while a growing fraction of the nouveau riche is simply out of control. In August 1999, the *New York* Times reported on the growing problem of dinner parties being disrupted by hostesses screaming at their help. To the verbal abuse add published reports of sexual and physical assaults—a young teenage boy, for example, kicking a live-in nanny for refusing to make sandwiches for him and his friends after school.

But for better or worse, capitalist rationality is finally making some headway into this weird preindustrial backwater. Corporate cleaning services now control 25 to 30 percent of the $1.4 billion housecleaning business, and perhaps their greatest innovation has been to abolish the mistress-maid relationship, with all its quirks and dependencies. The customer hires the service, not the maid, who has been replaced anyway by a team of two to four uniformed people, only one of whom—the team leader—is usually authorized to speak to the customer about the work at hand. The maids' wages, their Social Security taxes, their green cards, backaches, and child-care problems—all these are the sole concern of the company, meaning the local franchise owner. If there are complaints on either side, they are addressed to the franchise owner; the customer and the actual workers need never interact. Since the franchise owner is usually a middle-class white person, cleaning services are the ideal solution for anyone still sensitive enough to find the traditional employer-maid relationship morally vexing.

In a 1997 article about Merry Maids, *Franchise Times* reported tersely that the "category is booming, [the] niche is hot, too, as Americans look to outsource work even at home." Not all cleaning services do well, and there is a high rate of failure among informal, mom-and-pop services. The "boom" is concentrated among the national and international chains—outfits like Merry Maids, Molly Maids, Mini Maids, Maid Brigade, and The Maids International—all named, curiously enough, to highlight the more antique aspects of the industry, though the "maid" may occasionally be male. Merry Maids claimed to be growing at 15 to 20 percent a year in 1996, and spokesmen for both Molly Maids and The Maids International told me that their firms' sales are growing by 25 percent a year; local franchisers are equally bullish. Dan Libby, my boss at The Maids, confided to me that he could double his business overnight if only he could find enough reliable employees. To this end, The Maids offers a week's paid vacation, health insurance after ninety days, and a free breakfast every morning consisting—at least where I worked—of coffee, doughnuts, bagels, and bananas. Some franchises have dealt with the tight labor market by participating in welfare-to-work projects that not only funnel employees to them but often subsidize their paychecks with public money, at least for the first few months of work (which doesn't mean the newly minted maid earns more, only that the company has to pay her less). The Merry Maids franchise in the city where I worked is conveniently located a block away from the city's welfare office.

Among the women I worked with at The Maids, only one said she had previously worked as an independent, and she professed to be pleased with her new status as a cleaning-service employee. She no longer needed a car to get her from house to house and could take a day off—unpaid of course—to stay home with a sick child without risking the loss of a customer. I myself could see the advantage of not having to deal directly with the customers, who were sometimes at home while we worked and eager to make use of their supervisory skills: criticisms of our methods, and demands that we perform unscheduled tasks, could simply be referred to the franchise owner.

But there are inevitable losses for the workers as any industry moves from the entrepreneurial to the industrial phase, probably most strikingly, in this case, in the matter of pay. At Merry Maids, I was promised $200 for a forty-hour week, the manager hastening to add that "you can't calculate it in dollars per hour" since the forty hours include all the time spent traveling from house to house—up to five houses a day—which is unpaid. The Maids International, with its straightforward starting rate of $6.63 an hour, seemed preferable, though this rate was conditional on perfect attendance. Miss one day and your wage dropped to $6 an hour for two weeks, a rule that weighed particularly heavily on those who had young children. In addition, I soon learned that management had ways of shaving off nearly an hour's worth of wages a day. We were told to arrive at 7:30 in the morning, but our billable hours began only after we had been teamed up, given our list of houses for the day, and packed off in the company car at about 8:00 A.M. At the end of the day, we were no longer paid from the moment we left the car, though as much as fifteen minutes of work—refilling cleaning-fluid bottles, etc.—remained to be done. So for a standard nine-hour day, the actual pay amounted to about $6.10 an hour, unless you were still being punished for an absence, in which case it came out to $5.50 an hour.

Nor are cleaning-service employees likely to receive any of the perks or tips familiar to independents—free lunches and coffee, cast-off clothing, or a Christmas gift of cash. When I asked, only one of my coworkers could recall ever receiving a tip, and that was a voucher for a free meal at a downtown restaurant owned by a customer. The customers of cleaning services are probably no stingier than the employers of independents; they just don't know their cleaning people and probably wouldn't even recognize them on the street. Plus, customers probably assume that the fee they pay the service—$25 per person-hour in the case of The Maids franchise I worked for—goes largely to the workers who do the actual cleaning.

But the most interesting feature of the cleaning-service chains, at least from an abstract, historical perspective, is that they are finally transforming the home into a fully capitalist-style workplace, and in ways that the old wages-for-housework advocates could never have imagined. A house is an innately difficult workplace to control, especially a house with ten or more rooms like so many of those we cleaned; workers may remain out of one another's sight for as much as an hour at a time. For independents, the ungovernable nature of the home-as-workplace means a certain amount of autonomy. They can take breaks (though this is probably ill-advised if the homeowner is on the premises); they can ease the monotony by listening to the radio or TV while they work. But cleaning services lay down rules meant to enforce a factorylike—or even conventlike—discipline on their far-flung employees. At The Maids, there were no breaks except for a daily ten-minute stop at a convenience store for coffee or "lunch"—meaning something like a slice of pizza. Otherwise, the time spent driving between houses was considered our "break" and the only chance to eat, drink, or (although this was also officially forbidden) smoke a cigarette. When the houses were spaced well apart, I could eat my sandwich in one sitting; otherwise it would have to be divided into as many as three separate, hasty snacks.

Within a customer's house, nothing was to touch our lips at all, not even water—a rule that, on hot days, I sometimes broke by drinking from a bathroom faucet. TVs and radios were off-limits, and we were never, ever, to curse out loud, even in an ostensibly deserted house. There might be a homeowner secreted in some locked room, we were told, ear pressed to the door, or, more likely, a tape recorder or video camera running. At the time, I dismissed this as a scare story, but I have since come across ads for devices like the Tech-7 "incredible coin-sized camera" designed to "get a visual record of your babysitter's actions" and "watch employees to prevent theft." It was the threat or rumor of hidden recording devices that provided the final capitalist-industrial touch—supervision.

What makes the work most factorylike, though, is the intense Taylorization imposed by the companies. An independent, or a person cleaning his or her own home, chooses where she will start and, within each room, probably tackles the most egregious dirt first. Or she may plan her work more or less ergonomically, first doing whatever can be done from a standing position and then squatting or crouching to reach the lower levels. But with the special "systems" devised by the cleaning services and imparted to employees via training videos, there are no such decisions to make. In The Maids' "healthy touch" system, which is similar to what I saw of the Merry Maids' system on the training tape I was shown during my interview, all cleaning is divided into four task areas—dusting, vacuuming, kitchens, and bathrooms—which are in turn divided among the team members. For each task area other than vacuuming, there is a bucket containing rags and the appropriate cleaning fluids, so the biggest decision an employee has to make is which fluid and scrubbing instrument to deploy on which kind of surface; almost everything else has been choreographed in advance. When vacuuming, you begin with the master bedroom; when dusting, with the first room off of the kitchen; then you move through the rooms going left to right. When entering each room, you proceed from left to right and top to bottom, and the same with each surface—top to bottom, left to right. Deviations are subject to rebuke, as I discovered when a team leader caught me moving my arm from right to left, then left to right, while wiping Windex over a French door.

It's not easy for anyone with extensive cleaning experience—and I include myself in this category—to accept this loss of autonomy. But I came to love the system: First, because if you hadn't always been traveling rigorously from left to right it would have been easy to lose your way in some of the larger houses and omit or redo a room. Second, some of the houses were already clean when we started, at least by any normal standards, thanks probably to a housekeeper who kept things up between our visits; but the absence of visible dirt did not mean there was less work to do, for no surface could ever be neglected, so it was important to have "the system" to remind you of where you had been and what you had already "cleaned." No doubt the biggest advantage of the system, though, is that it helps you achieve the speed demanded by the company, which allots only so many minutes per house. After a week or two on the job, I found myself moving robotlike from surface to surface, grateful to have been relieved of the thinking process.

The irony, which I was often exhausted enough to derive a certain malicious satisfaction from, is that "the system" is not very sanitary. When I saw the training videos on "Kitchens" and "Bathrooms," I was at first baffled, and it took me several minutes to realize why: There is no water, or almost no water, involved. I had been taught to clean by my mother, a compulsive housekeeper who employed water so hot you needed rubber gloves to get into it and in such Niagaralike quantities that most microbes were probably crushed by the force of it before the soap suds had a chance to rupture their cell walls. But germs are never mentioned in the videos provided by The Maids. Our antagonists existed entirely in the visible world soap scum, dust, counter crud, dog hair, stains, and smears—and were attacked by damp rag or, in hardcore cases, by a scouring pad. We scrubbed only to remove impurities that might be detectable to a customer by hand or by eye; otherwise our only job was to wipe. Nothing was ever said, in the videos or in person, about the possibility of transporting bacteria, by rag or by hand, from bathroom to kitchen or even from one house to the next. Instead, it is the "cosmetic touches" that the videos emphasize and to which my trainer continually directed my eye. Fluff out all throw pillows and arrange them symmetrically. Brighten up stainless steel sinks with baby oil. Leave all spice jars, shampoos, etc., with their labels facing outward. Comb out the fringes of Persian carpets with a pick. Use the vacuum to create a special, fernlike pattern in the carpets. The loose ends of toilet paper and paper towel rolls have to be given a special fold. Finally, the house is sprayed with the service's signature air freshener—a cloying floral scent in our case, "baby fresh" in the case of the Mini Maids.

When I described the "methods" employed to housecleaning expert Cheryl Mendelson, she was incredulous. A rag moistened with disinfectant will not get a countertop clean, she told me, because most disinfectants are inactivated by contact with organic matter—i.e., dirt—so their effectiveness declines with each swipe of the rag. What you need is a detergent and hot water, followed by a rinse. As for floors, she judged the amount of water we used—one half of a small bucket—to be grossly inadequate, and, in fact, the water I wiped around on floors was often an unsavory gray. I also ran The Maids' cleaning methods by Don Aslett, author of numerous books on cleaning techniques and self-styled "number one cleaner in America." He was hesitant to criticize The Maids directly, perhaps because he is, or told me he is, a frequent speaker at conventions of cleaning-service franchise holders, but he did tell me how he would clean a countertop: first, spray it thoroughly with an all-purpose cleaner, then let it sit for three to four minutes of "kill time," and finally wipe it dry with a clean cloth. Merely wiping the surface with a damp cloth, he said, just spreads the dirt around. But the point at The Maids, apparently, is not to clean so much as it is to create the appearance of having been cleaned, not to sanitize but to create a kind of stage setting for family life. And the stage setting Americans seem to prefer is sterile only in the metaphorical sense, like a motel room or the fake interiors in which soap operas and sitcoms take place.

But even ritual work takes its toll on those assigned to perform it. Turnover is dizzyingly high in the cleaning-service industry, and not only because of the usual challenges that confront the working poor—child-care problems, unreliable transportation, evictions, and prior health problems. As my long-winded interviewer at Merry Maids warned me, and my coworkers at The Maids confirmed, this is a physically punishing occupation, something to tide you over for a few months, not year after year. The hands-and-knees posture damages knees, with or without pads; vacuuming strains the back; constant wiping and scrubbing invite repetitive stress injuries even in the very young. In my three weeks as a maid, I suffered nothing more than a persistent muscle spasm in the right forearm, but the damage would have been far worse if I'd had to go home every day to my own housework and children, as most of my coworkers did, instead of returning to my motel and indulging in a daily after-work regimen of ice packs and stretches. Chores that seem effortless at home, even almost recreational when undertaken at will for twenty minutes or so at a time, quickly turn nasty when performed hour after hour, with few or no breaks and under relentless time pressure.

So far, the independent, entrepreneurial housecleaner is holding her own, but there are reasons to think that corporate cleaning services will eventually dominate the industry. New users often prefer the impersonal, standardized service offered by the chains, and, in a fast-growing industry, new users make up a sizable chunk of the total clientele. Government regulation also favors the corporate chains, whose spokesmen speak gratefully of the "Zoe Baird effect," referring to customers' worries about being caught paying an independent off the books. But the future of housecleaning may depend on the entry of even bigger players into the industry. Merry Maids, the largest of the chains, has the advantage of being a unit within the $6.4 billion ServiceMaster conglomerate, which includes such related businesses as TruGreen-ChemLawn, Terminix, Rescue Rooter, and Furniture Medic. Swisher International, best known as an industrial toilet-cleaning service, operates Swisher Maids in Georgia and North Carolina, and Sears may be feeling its way into the business. If large multinational firms establish a foothold in the industry, mobile professionals will be able to find the same branded and standardized product wherever they relocate. For the actual workers, the change will, in all likelihood, mean a more standardized and speeded-up approach to the work—less freedom of motion and fewer chances to pause.

The trend toward outsourcing the work of the home seems, at the moment, unstoppable. Two hundred years ago women often manufactured soap, candles, cloth, and clothing in their own homes, and the complaints of some women at the turn of the twentieth century that they had been "robbed by the removal of creative work" from the home sound pointlessly reactionary today. Not only have the skilled crafts, like sewing and cooking from scratch, left the home but many of the "white collar" tasks are on their way out, too. For a fee, new firms such as the San Francisco-based Les Concierges and Cross It Off Your List in Manhattan will pick up dry cleaning, baby-sit pets, buy groceries, deliver dinner, even do the Christmas shopping. With other firms and individuals offering to buy your clothes, organize your financial files, straighten out your closets, and wait around in your home for the plumber to show up, why would anyone want to hold on to the toilet cleaning?

Absent a major souring of the economy, there is every reason to think that Americans will become increasingly reliant on paid housekeepers and that this reliance will extend ever further down into the middle class. For one thing, the "time bind" on working parents shows no sign of loosening; people are willing to work longer hours at the office to pay for the people—housecleaners and baby-sitters—who are filling in for them at home. Children, once a handy source of household help, are now off at soccer practice or SAT prep classes; grandmother has relocated to a warmer climate or taken up a second career. Furthermore, despite the fact that people spend less time at home than ever, the square footage of new homes swelled by 33 percent between 1975 and 1998, to include "family rooms," home entertainment rooms, home offices, bedrooms, and often bathrooms for each family member. By the third quarter of 1999, 17 percent of new homes were larger than 3,000 square feet, which is usually considered the size threshold for household help, or the point at which a house becomes unmanageable to the people who live in it.

One more trend impels people to hire outside help, according to cleaning experts such as Aslett and Mendelson: fewer Americans know how to clean or even to "straighten up." I hear this from professional women defending their decision to hire a maid: "I'm just not very good at it myself" or "I wouldn't really know where to begin." Since most of us learn to clean from our parents (usually our mothers), any diminution of cleaning skills is transmitted from one generation to another, like a gene that can, in the appropriate environment, turn out to be disabling or lethal. Upper-middle-class children raised in the servant economy of the Nineties are bound to grow up as domestically incompetent as their parents and no less dependent on people to clean up after them. Mendelson sees this as a metaphysical loss, a "matter of no longer being physically centered in your environment." Having cleaned the rooms of many overly privileged teenagers in my stint with The Maids, I think the problem is a little more urgent than that. The American overclass is raising a generation of young people who will, without constant assistance, suffocate in their own detritus.

If there are moral losses, too, as Americans increasingly rely on paid household help, no one has been tactless enough to raise them. Almost everything we buy, after all, is the product of some other person's suffering and miserably underpaid labor. I clean my own house (though—full disclosure—I recently hired someone else to ready it for a short-term tenant), but I can hardly claim purity in any other area of consumption. I buy my jeans at The Gap, which is reputed to subcontract to sweatshops. I tend to favor decorative objects no doubt ripped off, by their purveyors, from scantily paid Third World craftspersons. Like everyone else, I eat salad greens just picked by migrant farm workers, some of them possibly children. And so on. We can try to minimize the pain that goes into feeding, clothing, and otherwise provisioning ourselves—by observing boycotts, checking for a union label, etc.—but there is no way to avoid it altogether without living in the wilderness on berries. Why should housework, among all the goods and services we consume, arouse any special angst?

And it does, as I have found in conversations with liberal-minded employers of maids, perhaps because we all sense that there are ways in which housework is different from other products and services. First, in its inevitable proximity to the activities that compose "private" life. The home that becomes a workplace for other people remains a home, even when that workplace has been minutely regulated by the corporate cleaning chains. Someone who has no qualms about purchasing rugs woven by child slaves in India or coffee picked by impoverished peasants in Guatemala might still hesitate to tell dinner guests that, surprisingly enough, his or her lovely home doubles as a sweatshop during the day. You can eschew the chain cleaning services of course, hire an independent cleaner at a generous hourly wage, and even encourage, at least in spirit, the unionization of the housecleaning industry. But this does not change the fact that someone is working in your home at a job she would almost certainly never have chosen for herself—if she'd had a college education, for example, or a little better luck along the way—and the place where she works, however enthusiastically or resentfully, is the same as the place where you sleep.

It is also the place where your children are raised, and what they learn pretty quickly is that some people are less worthy than others. Even better wages and working conditions won't erase the hierarchy between an employer and his or her domestic help, because the help is usually there only because the employer has "something better" to do with her time, as one report on the growth of cleaning services puts it, not noticing the obvious implication that the cleaning person herself has nothing better to do with her time. In a merely middle-class home, the message may be reinforced by a warning to the children that that's what they'll end up doing if they don't try harder in school. Housework, as radical feminists once proposed, defines a human relationship and, when unequally divided among social groups, reinforces preexisting inequalities. Dirt, in other words, tends to attach to the people who remove it—"garbagemen" and "cleaning ladies." Or, as cleaning entrepreneur Don Aslett told me with some bitterness—and this is a successful man, chairman of the board of an industrial cleaning service and frequent television guest—"The whole mentality out there is that if you clean, you're a scumball."

One of the "better" things employers of maids often want to do with their time is, of course, spend it with their children. But an underlying problem with post-nineteenth-century child-raising, as Deirdre English and I argued in our book For Her Own Good years ago, is precisely that it is unmoored in any kind of purposeful pursuit. Once "parenting" meant instructing the children in necessary chores; today it's more likely to center on one-sided conversations beginning with "So how was school today?" No one wants to put the kids to work again weeding and stitching; but in the void that is the modern home, relationships with children are often strained. A little "low-quality time" spent washing dishes or folding clothes together can provide a comfortable space for confidences—and give a child the dignity of knowing that he or she is a participant in, and not just the product of, the work of the home.

There is another lesson the servant economy teaches its beneficiaries and, most troublingly, the children among them. To be cleaned up after is to achieve a certain magical weightlessness and immateriality. Almost everyone complains about violent video games, but paid housecleaning has the same consequence-abolishing effect: you blast the villain into a mist of blood droplets and move right along; you drop the socks knowing they will eventually levitate, laundered and folded, back to their normal dwelling place. The result is a kind of virtual existence, in which the trail of litter that follows you seems to evaporate all by itself. Spill syrup on the floor and the cleaning person will scrub it off when she comes on Wednesday. Leave *The Wall Street Journal* scattered around your airplane seat and the flight attendants will deal with it after you've deplaned. Spray toxins into the atmosphere from your factory's smokestacks and they will be filtered out eventually by the lungs of the breathing public. A servant economy breeds callousness and solipsism in the served, and it does so all the more effectively when the service is performed close up and routinely in the place where they live and reproduce.

Individual situations vary, of course, in ways that elude blanket judgment. Some people—the elderly and disabled, parents of new babies, asthmatics who require an allergen-free environment—may well need help performing what nursing-home staff call the "ADLs," or activities of daily living, and no shame should be attached to their dependency. In a more generous social order, housekeeping services would be subsidized for those who have health-related reasons to need them—a measure that would generate a surfeit of new jobs for the low-skilled people who now clean the homes of the affluent. And in a less gender-divided social order, husbands and boyfriends would more readily do their share of the chores.

However we resolve the issue in our individual homes, the moral challenge is, put simply, to make work visible again: not only the scrubbing and vacuuming but all the hoeing, stacking, hammering, drilling, bending, and lifting that goes into creating and maintaining a livable habitat. In an ever more economically unequal culture, where so many of the affluent devote their lives to such ghostly pursuits as stock-trading, image-making, and opinion-polling, real work—in the old-fashioned sense of labor that engages hand as well as eye, that tires the body and directly alters the physical world—tends to vanish from sight. The feminists of my generation tried to bring some of it into the light of day, but, like busy professional women fleeing the house in the morning, they left the project unfinished, the debate broken off in midsentence, the noble intentions unfulfilled. Sooner or later, someone else will have to finish the job.

CHAPTER 9

Religion & Spirituality

It can sometimes be difficult to discuss religion. Many people have different, often strong opinions about the topic. Even though it's difficult to talk about, religion is still a complicated and intricate part of many women's lives. Some women feel empowered by religion because they feel like they belong and are comfortable in the gatherings and practices. They also feel acceptance, friendship, and encouragement within their chosen religion. There are others who feel oppressed by religion because it can often be excluding and degrading, especially for women or those who don't fit stereotypical norms. Religion is also an important force in women's lives. It plays a pivotal role in many current issues, such as abortion, marriage equality, sex education, racial violence, domestic violence, to name a few.

Most major religions are founded on a groundwork of masculine god language. Masculine iconography is often seen in major religions as both all-knowing and all-powerful. Many major religions are focused on male prophets and gods. There are also stringent rules for male and female behavior, predominantly regarding sexuality, reproduction, and marriage. Masculine god language that discusses deities as "He" and/or "Our Heavenly Father" emphasize the appearance of an omnipotent male leader. Religious texts also often share repressive ideas about gender roles and relationships. Here are some examples from the Bible:

"Let the woman learn in silence with all subjection. But I suffer not a woman to teach, nor to usurp authority over the man, but to be in silence" (1 Tim. 2:11–15).

"Wives, submit yourselves unto your own husbands, as it is fit in the Lord" (Col. 3:18).

"Women should keep silence in churches. For they are not permitted to speak, but should be subordinate, as even the law says" (1 Cor. 14:34).

"I would have you know that the head of every man is Christ; and the head of the woman is the man; and the head of Christ is God" (1 Cor. 11:3).

In several religions, women are excluded from religious practices. Hindu women carry out rituals such as fasting to produce positive energy and influence for their husbands. The self-sacrifice of a woman for her husband is an implicit religious offering. Men do not perform such rituals for their wives. Women are also habitually excluded from leadership roles. Female ministers, bishops, priests, rabbis, mullahs, or gurus continue to be fairly rare or missing in countless religious traditions. Children who go to worship services observe and learn the roles played by both men and women in those places. They also acquire clear and obvious lessons about their proper gender roles.

This chapter will go into more detail about women and religion. It will discuss oppression and empowerment, along with ideas for reinterpreting traditions in religion. The next section focuses on oppression.

Oppression

Christianity is not the only world religion that operates as an oppressive force to women. There are several ways that religion has assisted in ***subordinating women***. Fundamental to religion's oppressive purpose is the idea of a divine directive from creation where females are seen as inferior. Men then are not only deemed superior but also closer to God. As mentioned above, gendered language in religion supports the idea of male domination.

The perception of women's subordination is typically reinforced by creation myths that insert woman's lesser status in the religion's description of identity. These are the tales told in a religion to describe itself. As Elizabeth Cady Stanton (1972) indicated in *The Woman's Bible*, the Bible has specifically been used to uphold the oppression of women by keeping them out of certain positions in the church family and society.

Misogyny is also a factor in the religious oppression of sexual minorities. For the most part, religious exclusions of same-sex relationships are all about preserving gender roles that reinforce male domination. Same-sex relationships confront these differences by rebuffing the idea that there is an essential male or female role at home or in sexuality.

This is particularly troubling for homosexual male relationships because of the shame that the patriarchy links with men being "treated" like women. The same holds true for men who might be taking on stereotypically female roles in relationships. To put it in another way, the problem in some religions is the so-called idea that gay male sex feminizing the men involved. To be a gay male is to be like a woman, and that's the absolute worst thing that a man could possibly be.

When women are excluded from rituals, their status is lowered even further. There are many religions all over the world that allow women to pray in public, hear confession, baptize, read sacred scriptures aloud publicly, preach, lead prayers, or teach men. However, for all the religions that include women, there are just as many that build female exclusion into their beliefs.

One argument for keeping women from becoming priests has been that a priest stands as a representative of God, so since a woman is female she cannot represent God. The basic assumption is that men are more Godlike than women. When participants see only men as agents of God, it fortifies the belief that men are more Godlike, which continues the exclusion of women.

Religions maintain the subordination of women directly with church laws that require wives to defer to their husbands. The laws also try to control women's sexuality and they produce extremely specific gender roles. These laws may make women feel forced to stay in abusive relationships or prevent them from having access to birth control and/or other reproduction resources, like abortion.

Women may be told by the church that their role in the home is to support their husband and to submit to his authority all the time. When abuse happens, a woman might be told that she should continue to submit because that is her role. She might be also told that it is God's will and he will change her husband because of her obedience to God. The husband's abusive behavior is then the wife's responsibility because his ability to change is dependent upon her obedience in the religion. The circumstances are aggravated by a ban on divorce in some denominations, precluding women from permanently leaving abusive or problematic marriages.

Historically, religions have also wielded power over women through church-sanctioned control. Early on, Christianity encouraged a spiritual accord that combined the oppressiveness of Roman laws and some status that was afforded to women in the church. Let's keep it straight though, because women were still considered inferior.

The lessons from Jesus Christ about equality did not always appear in the teachings and practices of the church. Some women found comfort in devotional space of the convent where they could live a religious life and be leaders. They were also able to circumvent the restrictions of old-fashioned femininity that involved marriage and childbearing.

A great example of this is ***Sor Juana Inés de la Cruz***. She lived in the late 1600s and was a self-taught scholar and poet, who also happened to be a nun. A resident of Mexico City, her intelligence became known during her teen years. When she was denied the opportunity to dress as a boy to learn more, she began her life as a nun so that she could study at will. After moving into the convent, Sor Juana read as much as she could and wrote plays and poetry. She is known for challenging societal values and becoming an early proponent of women's rights. She defended women's rights to educational access and is credited as the first published feminist of the New World (Sor Juana, n.d.).

Also during the 1600s, there were women who were convicted and hanged for being witches. For many of these women, **witchcraft** was merely the tradition of healing and spirituality along with the rejection of Christianity. For other women, witchcraft had nothing to do with religion and everything to do with accusations resulting from envy, avarice, and fear. During this time, defending oneself against a charge of witchcraft was virtually impossible and just being accused usually meant death.

Christian imperialism has also been disastrous for people of color, reinforcing racism, and ethnocentrism. The genocide of Native Americans was carried out with the fundamental idea that it was the God-given destiny of Europeans to vanquish the native peoples of the Americas. Without a basic understanding of any African cultures, Christian missionaries forced indigenous African peoples to adopt their Western ways.

The aftermath of Christian racism can also be found in the American South, where many Christians argued in favor of slavery based on their reading of scripture. Hate groups such as the Ku Klux Klan came into prominence, demanding continued power for white Christians. The KKK is still active today, even though Anonymous has been working to out members recently (BBC, 2015).

In Germany, thousands of Christians joined in to support Hitler. They directly contributed to the genocide of 6 million Jews. They put patriotism and nationalism before their religious beliefs, much to the detriment of Jews worldwide.

In the 1950s and 1960s, many Christians worked endlessly for the civil rights movement. African-American churches became places of resistance to racism. Many other Christians defended segregation and contributed to acts of racism and hatred. Some of that hatred continues today.

Bob Jones University, a fundamentalist school in South Carolina, did not repeal its rule against interracial dating until 2000. Despite the many advances in our society, problems of racism and intolerance continue by many who identify as Christians. The problems remain with collaboration between the executive branch of government and policies that provide a course for structured inequalities.

There are some Hindus that believe self-immolation is the most honorable type of wifely commitment. They also believe that it leads to the spiritual redemption of a deceased spouse. The wife who commits **sati** is honored as a goddess. *Sati* is the practice of a widow placing herself on the burning pyre with her husband's body. This custom was prohibited by British colonizers in the nineteenth century, but cases of sati have been documented since Indian independence. Indian feminists disagree with the practice. There are also still some others that support women's right to commit sati. It is a tricky topic.

The Religious Right is a group of religious conservatives in America that has garnered political support. It routinely aims to control women by exerting influence over the U.S. legal system.

Faith-based programs that give government funding to religious institutions are overtly blurring the line between church and state.

This programming also frequently serves to minimize women's choice and freedom. Abortion rulings are a prime example of this. Religious leverage on federal and state policies has managed to chip away at abortion rights. The Religious Right has been convincing lawmakers to put a myriad of restrictions on abortion into effect.

Sharia is the sacred law of Islam that has been interpreted and integrated into some societies. In places such as Iran and Saudi Arabia, sharia has been integrated into society as a way to control women's lives. Depending on the type and location of the Muslims, the scope and interpretations of sharia differ greatly. Sharia addresses many public concerns within secular law along with familial and community topics.

Choosing to wear (or not wear) the hijab is also a particularly complex topic. It is an important example of how religion can be simultaneously oppressive and empowering for women. For some, wearing a veil is often automatically viewed as oppressing. There are many Muslim women that are critical of veiling. There are women who also see choosing to wear the hijab as an empowering practice of ethnic and cultural identity. This is especially important in our society where everyone is influenced from other cultures.

Some Muslim women describe how they feel safer when veiled in public. The hijab signifies that a woman is righteous and pure. It also means that Muslim men will not objectify and sexualize the veiled woman. They claim that the hijab protects them from sexual assault and allows them more freedom to be in public without fear, unlike other American women who don't veil. In some instances, they use the hijab to claim their identity and take a stand against international imperialism.

Ultimately, it is important to recognize the differences between what the Quran says and how it is interpreted. In some Muslim societies, the goal is keeping women subordinate to men. Islam is not an inflexible religion. Conservative and progressive Muslims interpret the Quran in different ways. More progressive Muslims interpret the Quran to advocate for women's worth and equality.

Empowerment

Religion has a long history of oppression, but women have also experienced profound support and encouragement in different types of religion. There are a variety of aspects of **empowerment**. For many women, religion presents a place where they can experience a real sense of community with other women.

Women who stay at home mothers and/or work from home might only find a social outlet within their religion. They create relationships and friendships with other women. They also get involved in the religious community and create their own meaningful experiences.

Religion can also assist women with developing their **leadership** skills. Again, for women who spend a majority of their time at home, religious activities, and events help women develop skills they might not have otherwise. They can learn these on their own or learn from other women.

Leadership within religious organizations could then create pathways for women to have power in other areas. It could be within their local or regional communities. Women could also use these skills to participate in social activism.

There are many examples of women who intersected religion with social activism. A great example is **Jesse Daniel Ames**. She helped organize the anti-lynching movement in the 1930s and 1940s. She worked through women's organizations in Methodist and Baptist churches in the South (Dickson,

1995). Black churches were at the heart of the civil rights movement in America. Lots of early leaders of the second wave of feminism got their start with political organizing in the civil rights movement (King, 1987).

Social justice is also a key component of Judaism. Jewish women have been active and very much involved in anti-racist and anti-sexist work. They have been doing this work for a long time and they have been doing it well.

Additionally, feminist Mormon women have taken their activism online and worked for social change there. They have gone on the Internet as activists calling for social change. They have created websites like **Feminist Mormon Housewives** (feministmormonhousewives.org) and **Young Mormon Feminists** (youngmormonfeminists.org). These women seek to challenge the church's stances on feminist issues through their activism. They want to reclaim the power they believe women held in early Mormon history.

Besides these specific examples, religion generally can provide a space where women can find a sense of worth as a person. Many women have become empowered through the feminine-centered spirituality or witchcraft. This is also known as Wicca.

Wicca is a nature-oriented religion that has origins before both Judaism and Christianity. Wiccan ceremonies involve celebrating the feminine and connecting with nature. According to Starhawk:

"The Goddess falls in love with Herself, drawing forth her own emanation, which takes on a life of its own. Love of self for self is the creative force of the universe. Desire is the primal energy, and that energy is erotic: the attraction of lover to beloved, of planet to star, the lust of electron for proton. Love is the glue that holds the world together" (Rowan, 1997, pg. 96).

Checkout the Breakout box to learn more about Starhawk and Wicca.

Breakout: Starhawk

Nic Neish/Shutterstock.com

Starhawk is a writer and activist, most well-known for her theories of feminist Neopaganism and ecofeminism. She believes that the Earth is a living entity. She also believes that faith-based activism can reconnect oneself to basic needs. Starhawk asserts that the principal religious ideas of community and self-sacrifice are also important to paganism and ecofeminism.

Starhawk urges the combination of social justice issues with a nature-based spirituality. Her activism is extremely rooted in the anti-war movement. She writes broadly about activism, examining white privilege within activist communities. Starhawk (n.d.) asks for an intersectionality of fighting oppression that includes spirituality, eco-consciousness, and sexual and gender liberation.

Starhawk's feminism and spirituality are closely interconnected, and her belief that feminism should challenge power structures denotes her intersectional approach (Christ and Plaskow, 1979). Her ecofeminism links Mother Nature with women giving birth. She also links ecological carnage and cultural oppression with patriarchal first-world economies.

Reinterpreting Traditions

Plenty of feminist women have decided to participate in a variety of religious traditions. In those traditions, the women have tried to rewrite the oppressive parts. Theology was created with men's experience as the norm. It has not considered the experiences of women for the most part. Feminist theologians have been rethinking traditional theological ideas, using women's experiences.

An example of this is the idea of sin from Genesis comes from pride and selfishness. Redemption then happens with sacrificial love. However, that isn't the typical experience for most women, since they are typically unselfish, particularly when it comes to their families. A story encouraging women to be self-sacrificing to be redeemed redemption simply puts women in their place.

Alicia Ostriker (1986) describes feminist theology as bringing women's experiences to the forefront. A feminist viewpoint reconstructs theological concepts using women's lived experiences. Since Christianity is so prevalent in America, the Bible plays a large role in shaping women's lives. Feminist reinterpretations of religion often include reconstruction and re-examination of main ideas.

Reinterpretation is identifying passages that are especially troublesome for women. It also includes highlighting the passages that laud equality between women and men. Supporters of this reinterpretation include feminists that hold a positive view of scripture as guidelines for their lives. The ultimate goal of reconstruction is to recognize the patriarchal underpinnings and discuss the ways they have oppressed women.

Feminist theologians have also created feminine images of deity. Some, like Virginia Mollenkott (1977), have pointed out the existence of feminine images within scripture. Others, like Sallie McFague (1959), challenged people to develop new forms of God such as God as mother, lover, and/or companion. And other theorists have returned to the image of the Goddess herself (Christ & Plaskow, 1979; Parsons, 2002).

Judith Plaskow (1991) is a Jewish feminist scholar who writes about reconceptualizing the idea of God and other Jewish traditions that should be inclusive of women. There are also "womanist" biblical interpretations of women of color (Junior, 2015). Womanism analyzes the Bible in frames of both sexism and racism. The Bible is scrutinized in terms of justice and injustice. Using this perspective, readers can focus on the moral and ethical issues of justice contained in the Bible, highlighting the struggle for liberation for women of color.

Women are not just challenging scripture, but they are also reconfiguring *religious traditions*. This includes the ordination of women. Historians have used archival information to show a long tradition of women as rabbis, priests, pastors, and bishops. Many denominations still do not ordain women, only a few do.

Quakers have a long and special history of women's equality. Quakers don't ordain anyone, but some Quakers do record ministers. Women have always been in the records in Quaker meetings. Women and men are treated equally and assumed to be able to give and take the word from God.

Men are still the larger percentage of senior pastors in almost every denomination. Several churches ordain openly gay and lesbian clergy, but that has not been without problems. Some denominations still struggle with the idea of gay or female or both types of clergy.

Islamic feminists seek to recover the tradition of gender equality that originates from the Quran. They believe that patriarchy is not inherent in Islam. They argue that it is a result of the patriarchal context and history from interpretation, which, until recently, was only done by men. Islamic feminists want to recover gender equality from the text's foundational principles.

Conclusion

Although some feminists believe in the reinterpretation of scriptures and choose to work within existing religions, there are others that choose to create their own empowering spiritual texts and organizations. Some believe that traditional religious scriptures are so male-centered, that they can only continue to support the patriarchy. They believe that even reinterpreting biblical texts cannot change the patriarchal center of the Bible and other texts.

Feminist philosopher Mary Daly (1978) maintained that patriarchal language is an essential element of the Bible. She said that this fact rendered the Bible useless in the liberation of women. Women such as Daly look beyond traditional religious texts for spiritual understanding. Wiccan groups and theories relate to this too.

Many women express their spirituality within standard religious traditions. Others create new forms of spiritual expression outside the traditional methods. Spirituality is an empowering force for women that takes various forms. These include social action, music, meditation, poetry, art, and prayer. Spirituality allows women to connect with creation, with other humans, and with the divine. To each their own with religious choices and practices.

Spirituality is also a central force in feminist politics. The interconnectivity of everything motivates action toward justice and peace. It encourages feminists to work together across differences. Nature-based spirituality and religious practices reaffirm the connections among all things. Feminist spirituality values and supports the diversity that makes up creation. Finally, it also challenges women to reclaim and redefine the systems of power that create injustice. Religion and spirituality can work within feminism to create equality for all.

Suggested Readings

Coleman, M. (2013). *Ain't I a womanist, too?: Third wave womanist religious thought*. Minneapolis: Fortress Press.

Hayes, D. (2010). *Standing in the shoes my mother made: A womanist theology*. Minneapolis: Fortress Press.

Joyce, K. (2010). *Quiverfull: Inside the Christian patriarchy movement*. Boston: Beacon Press.

Kidd, S. (2006). *The dance of the dissident daughter: A woman's journey from Christian tradition to the sacred feminine*. New York: Harper One.

Stuckey, J. (2010). *Women's spirituality: Contemporary feminist approaches to Judaism, Christianity, Islam, and Goddess worship*. Toronto: Inanna Publications.

References

BBC. (2015). *Anonymous posts Ku Klux Klan alleged sympathizers list*. Retrieved December 15, 2015 from http://www.bbc.com/news/technology-34736941

Christ, C., & Plaskow, J. (1979). *Womanspirit rising: A feminist reader in religion*. New York: HarperOne.

Daly, M. (1978). *Gyn/Ecology: The metaethics of radical feminism*. Boston: Beacon Press.

Junior, N. (2015). *An introduction to womanist biblical interpretation*. Louisville, KY: Westminster John Knox Press.

Dickson, B. (1995). "Antilynching campaign" In Davidson, C., & Wagner-Martin, L. (Eds.). *The Oxford companion to women's writing in the United States*. New York: Oxford University Press.

King, M. (1987). *Freedom song: A personal story of the civil rights movement*. New York: Morrow.

McFague, S. (1959). *Metaphorical theology: Models of God in religious language.* Minneapolis, MN: Augsburg Fortress.

Mollenkott, V. (1977). *Women, men, and the Bible.* Nashville, TN: Abingdon Press.

Ostriker, A. (1986). "Everywoman her own theology." In *The Imaginary Lover.* Pittsburgh, PA: University of Pittsburgh Press.

Parsons, S. (2002). *The Cambridge companion to feminist theology.* Cambridge, UK: Cambridge University Press.

Plaskow, J. (1991). *Standing again at Sinai.* New York: HarperOne.

Rowan, J. (1997). *Healing the male psyche: Therapy as initiation.* New York: Routledge.

Sor Juana Inés de la Cruz. (n.d.). Retrieved November 1, 2015 from https://www.poets.org/poetsorg/poet/sor-juana-in%C3%A9s-de-la-cruz

Stanton, E. (1972). *The woman's Bible.* New York: Arno Press.

Starhawk. (n.d.). *Biography.* Retrieved December 15, 2015 from http://starhawk.org/about/biography

Discussion Questions

1. How, in your opinion, has religion been oppressive to women?

2. How has religion been empowering to women?

3. How have stereotypes of witchcraft harmed women?

4. How can religion be reformed to be more inclusive?

5. Why might some women feel the need to leave religious practices altogether?

Religion and Spirituality

by Rachael D. Smith, M.A.

Introduction

America's religious landscape has evolved more in the last 75 years, than it has in its entire 229 year history. During the first 154 years of American religious history, Christianity was the primary religious tradition. Even though other faiths still prevailed in the United States, they were smaller in number than Christians. However, in the previous 75 years, more Americans have opened their religious minds to incorporate other traditions and practices, than ever before. This is not to say that Christianity is not the predominant religion practiced in the United States, because it still is. Yet, as more Americans have "rebelled" against religious tradition, different faiths and beliefs have been introduced and adopted by American citizens. It has also been recently founded that many Christians are losing members in the new millennium, while Jews, Muslims, and Hindus are making gains in membership.[1] It should also be stated that many Americans are finding themselves content with identifying as atheist, agnostic, or simply, without any religious faith and those individuals are on the rise in the United States.[2]

The one constant throughout America's religious landscape is the fact that more women are involved with religion than men. More women are members of specific religious organizations than men, and women, more than men are oppressed by religious traditions. This does not mean that religion does not empower women, because it most certainly does. But, before women feel that empowerment, they have historically been forced to deal with significant trials at the hands of males and perhaps even left the faith they were born and raised into for another organization that was much more accepting of them as women.

The United States has not been the role model for equality and that is especially true when it comes to women and religion. In recent American history, women have been told to stay out of the pulpit, since they are not worthy enough to teach in many Judeo-Christian traditions. Within the last seven decades, American women have experienced the full range of belonging in American religious traditions. Many women have faced a great sense of acceptance for who they are as women to shunning for simply having breasts and a vagina. In pre-historical traditions, this was not the case.

Patriarchal Takeover

Archeologists and Anthropologists have discovered that ancient religious traditions were goddess centered and women were revered in those societies for their ability to give life.[3] The feminine was sacred, and most clans were matrilineal, as well as matrilocal. These goddess-centered religions focused on survival. The objective of the clan was to gather and/or plant enough crops to feed the entire group, and to hunt animals for other sources of food. These people did not have material possessions, as we have them now. Any possessions served a purpose and had some type of function for the group as a whole.

Once metals were introduced into society, they were used for the betterment of the group. Males made new hunting spears and women made jewelry to honor the goddess, as an honored goddess bestowed blessings on the group. As time passed, more weapons were fashioned and less jewelry was manufactured. This will allow for the rise of the patriarchal religious traditions and the demise of the goddess traditions. Males will begin to take over by force and for the sake of their children, women will comply.[4]

This demonstration of religious life in antiquity shows that the patriarchal structure that is enforced in today's society has not always been. The archaic clichés that "women are the weaker sex", "women do not belong as religious leaders", and "religion has always been dominated by men" does not hold true. According to some feminist theologians, it took 2,500 for the patriarchal systems to take over religious organization and force women to comply through violence.[5] That violence is still being systematically used on women in the current century.

As the years became centuries and centuries became millennia, the patriarchal takeover of religion was felt in every part of the globe. As Western Europeans began to explore the world and take control of the "new world", they noticed that many Native Americans lived in matrilineal and matrilocal societies and they felt that it was their duty to educated the Native males on the ways in which their society was wrong. Europeans believed these Native men "needed" white males to "help" them become more European or civilized. Of course, it would not be long until whites had decimated the Native American population and worked arduously to destroy any part of their savage culture. Many Native languages, religious rituals, and traditions have been lost. Some Native groups are still trying to recover the culture that was lost to assimilation.

America: Land of the Free (Unless you are a Minority)

Over the years of creating a new nation, most Americans held on to their European religious practices and while many of the initial settlers of the new world were escaping religious persecution, they were not accepting of other religious traditions or most people outside of those religious teachings. In America's 229 year history, Christianity has been the prevailing religious tradition. Unfortunately, many of the gendered atrocities that have taken place in this country have been due to religious belief and personal interpretation of scripture.

Many Americans look to their faith and scripture for comfort in a time of crisis or to help them make an important decision. (WWJD?) The problem that occurs when looking to sacred texts in a time of confusion is these texts do not account for change. These texts were written so long ago, they do not consider that humans do not live in the 21st century as people lived in the 1st century. Values, social norms, and religious belief changes over time and social change must occur in societies in order for people to live better lives and to maintain order.

There are countless scenarios in which religious teaching advocated, and still advocates, discrimination and prejudice. For example, some used Biblical scripture to advocate for slavery. Most Americans have realized this advocacy is wrong and no human should be kept in bondage. However, it would appear that while an entire group of people have been freed from physical slavery based on race, many others are physically or emotionally religiously confined based on their sex or gender.

While women were revered in pre-historic societies as the givers of life, today women are still viewed by many as the weaker sex and religious teachings are used to control women. Numerous examples of this can be found in religious scripture. In Hinduism, women need to be controlled by their male counterparts due to the "fact" that women are too emotional and if they do not have a male to control them, they could allow their emotions to take over and destroy the world. Hinduism also endorses the caste system and in order for an individual to escape the cycle of life and death, a human needs to live a virtuous life as a male. This means that women are taught that their cycle of life and death is not over. They must first be reincarnated as a male to achieve *moksha*.[6]

The Quran actually advocates equality among the sexes, but it is the Hadith within Islam that makes room for sexism. The Hadith is a book of supposed quotes the Prophet Muhammad was to have said to various narrators. In one such quote, Abu Huraira, one of Allah's Apostles, narrated that Muhammad said, "If a man invites his wife to sleep with him and she refuses to come to him, then the angels send their curses on her till morning."[7] This instills fear in women to perform sexual acts on demand or else they will be punished.

Within Judaism and Christianity, scripture dictates that if a man sexually violates an unmarried woman, he is punished by marrying her. Deuteronomy 22:28-29 states, "If a man happens to meet a virgin who is not pledged to be married and rapes her and they are discovered, he shall pay the girl's father fifty shekels of silver. He must marry the girl, for he has violated her. He can never divorce her as long as he lives."[8] This does not take into account the woman's feelings of being violated, nor does it consider that most likely, she does not want to marry the man who raped her. Her feelings about the situation is of no concern. She is property and it is her virginity that is sacred, so she may produce her rapist's heirs.

Buddhism is another religious tradition that began as a patriarchal religious tradition. The Buddha did not initially believe that women should be nuns or instructors of his teachings. This was in large part due to Buddhism originating in India and his upbringing in the caste system. Fortunately, he did change his mind and women were trained as teachers of enlightenment. Regardless, they were only allowed to teach other women and usually their monasteries were not given the financial support their fellow monks received. Buddhist monks viewed women as sexual temptation, and did not encourage women to follow a spiritual life.[9]

Of course, this is only one example from the most popular religious traditions. Unfortunately, there are many more examples that can be used to validate the argument of feminine restraints being placed on women in religion. Along with the scriptural statements of men's treatment of women, there is more to consider when analyzing how women are viewed by their own faiths. For the most part, women are to blame for separating humans from their deity or deities. There are examples in tribal African religions, as well as the most popular separation; Adam and Eve in the Garden of Eden. Eve was tempted by the serpent and she convinced Adam to eat the fruit from the tree of knowledge. Both were expelled from the garden, never to be reunited with their god again, and nor were any other followers able to be in the presence of the deity.

Women are also responsible for unleashing evil upon the world, according to various religious texts. One of the most recognizable stories is Pandora's Box. According to Greek mythology, Pandora was created as the most beautiful woman and Zeus gave her a jar (later story telling will turn the jar into a box) and told her to never open it. Because Pandora was a woman and could not control her feminine curiosity, she opened the jar and unleashed every form of evil upon humanity. Both Eve and Pandora have been vilified in religious tradition for stories that have been impressed upon every student since the faiths began and neither, will ever be known for anything else. Women today will look to Pandora and Eve with contempt. This in turn, will become contempt for other women who possess the traits of Eve or Pandora and do not follow the patriarchal rules set for women in religion.

When faith dictates that women are to behave in a certain fashion and some of those women choose not to obey, other women oftentimes will be the first to judge those actions. It causes a separation among females. It is actually a well-used military tactic, divide and conquer. If religious women are judging, blaming, and shaming other religious or even non-religious women for their actions, they are not focused on what the faith is teaching males. They are not paying attention to the fact that their religious teachers are promoting male dominance, while subjugating all women, including those who are passing judgement.

Within the Judeo-Christian-Islamic belief structures, the divine is male. The most important teachers and followers are male. Women play a supporting role in these traditions and are viewed as secondary. Humans are made in the deity's image, which is a male image. Rules for women are much more strict than for men within these faiths. Yet, women are the force that drive the family to attend religious services. Ironically, women make up the majority of religious attendees and yet, they are being told by their faith that they are to blame, for everything gone wrong.

So, how are women to relate to their deity? How are they to overcome the blatant sexism within religious traditions? Some women have changed the rules. When women are told they are not allowed to attend services because they are menstruating, they hold services in their homes and become the teachers of the faith. Some women have even left their churches and synagogues to create their own places of worship. In extreme cases, women have even changed scripture. For example, Elizabeth Cady Stanton published in 1898 *The Woman's Bible*, in which she challenges the sexist language.[10] The challenging of the language is where the next change needs to be resurrected. Stanton was most certainly ahead of her time and it is unfortunate that 117 years later, the changes she made are still not part of religious teachings. But, they should be.

America's Religious Future

Some religious institutions and communities are finally realizing that the patriarchal religious structures are in jeopardy. In May 2015, the Pew Research Center released a demographic study on America's religious landscape. The study revealed a significant increase in religious "nones" in the United States. These "nones" are people who did not identify with any religious group and the majority of these individuals were Millennials. This suggests that the current religious trends of those 18-30 years old appear to not adhere to any religion tradition or its teachings. What happens to a country when religion is removed from the family and its youth? The results are interesting.

According to Phil Zuckerman, a professor of sociology and secular studies, secular people are more empathic, more independent, possess rational problem solving skills, and a great sense of personal autonomy. They are also far less likely to end up in the prison system and are less likely to be racist and are more tolerant of others than their religious counterparts.[11] If this is the case in "godless" individuals, why is religion still a part of so many lives?

Religion is important for a variety of reasons. Primarily, most humans want to know that there something greater than themselves and there is some type of afterlife. Religion is also very comforting for many, especially in times of personal turmoil. Regardless, patriarchal religious structures will be a thing of the past unless changes are made to be more inclusive and less exclusive.

Religious institutions need to start practicing the love and acceptance they are teaching and preaching. Religious language need to be changed to bring women closer to the divine. Pronouns should be eliminated when referring to a monotheistic deity to ensure that both sexes can relate to that deity. Understanding that religious text may not be adaptable to the 21st century is important to the survival of religion in the United States. Citing specific passages in scripture will not bring the masses to the faith, teaching the messages of understanding and compassion that many religious figures are known for, would be more appealing to an individual.

Restricting another person's rights to live as they see fit due to one's own personal religious beliefs is damaging to the survival of religion. Passing legislation that seeks to attach religious doctrine of one group to the masses, will eventually lead to the demise of that religious group. Teaching discrimination, in any form, will most likely lead to the extinction of many religious groups. As the number of religious "nones" continue to rise, the only hope for religious groups to survive is to change. Change must happen.

Endnotes

1   "America's Changing Religious Landscape,"
2   Ibid.
3   Marianne Ferguson, *Women and Religion*. (Upper Saddle River: Prentice-Hall, 1995), 1–2.
4   Ibid, 28-29.
5   Ibid.
6   Denise Lardner Carmody, *Women & World Religions* (Upper Saddle River: Prentice-Hall, 1989), 41.
7   "Wedlock, Marriage (Nikaah)," accessed September 21, 2015, Sunnah.com/bukhari/67.
8   *Holy Bible*, New International Version, Deuteronomy 22:28-29.
9   Carmody, 68-71.
10 Elizabeth Cady Stanton, *The Woman's Bible*. (Boston: Northeastern University Press, 1993).
11 Phil Zuckerman, "How Secular Family Values Stack Up," Los Angeles Times, January 14, 2015, accessed September 21, 2015, http://www.latimes.com/opinion/op-ed/la-oe-0115-zuckerman-secular-parenting-20150115-story.html.

Bibliography

"America's Changing Religious Landscape," Last modified May 12, 2015, http://www.pewforum.org/2015/05/12/americas-changing-religious-landscape/

Carmody, Denise Lardner. *Women & World Religions*. Upper Saddle River: Prentice-Hall, 1989.

Ferguson, Marianne. *Women and Religion*. Upper Saddle River: Prentice-Hall, 1995.

Holy Bible. New International Version. Deuteronomy 22:28-29.

Stanton, Elizabeth Cady. *The Woman's Bible*. Boston: Northern University Press, 1993.

Sunnah.com. "Wedlock, Marriage (Nikaah)." accessed September 21, 2015. Sunnah.com/bukhari/67.

Zuckerman, Phil. "How Secular Family Values Stack Up." Los Angeles Times, January 14, 2015. Accessed September 21, 2015. http://www.latimes.com/opinion/op-ed/la-oe-0115-zuckerman-secular-parenting-20150115-story.html.

CHAPTER 10
Feminism in the Future

Think back to the beginning of the book where we discussed women's and gender studies (WGS) as a discipline. As a WGS student, hopefully you are gaining an understanding of the social construction of gender, particularly the ways gender identities are physically demonstrated. You should also be able to analyze the intersectionality of feminism with other systems of inequality. Students in WGS classes should also have a familiarity with the status of women and others who are marginalized, and then know how they as individuals can work independently or collectively with others to be agents of change.

Hopefully this book has also helped you will begin to think about patterns of privilege and discrimination in your own life. Think critically about how pop culture and society affect lives daily, including your own. Ultimately, I hope that this book has provided you with new insights about feminism and the empowering confidence to continue on in WGS or work feminism into your daily life and future pursuits.

Feminist educators at all levels try to give their students more inclusive and active social justice models of learners. They also aim to support teachers who make their classrooms non-exploitive environments. WGS as a field typically involves non-hierarchical classrooms where teachers respect students and learn from them as much as they teach them. The focus is on giving importance to the student voice and experience. WGS faculty also encourage both personal and social change.

Most WGS classes are housed in colleges and universities that do not necessarily share the same ideas and goals. Many feminist educators work within the constraints of institutions that see counter-hegemonic education as problematic or unnecessary. Counter-hegemonic education is a type of learning that challenges the status quo. Despite these potential issues, feminist education, whether in WGS courses or in other fields, is an important part of most college campuses.

For many students, the term feminism is still fraught with problems. The political biases that many people associate with feminist education is enough to scare anyone away. Many people think that knowledge should be objective and free from political values. I'm of the mindset that we all bring biases and opinions to the classroom, so we need to confront those and learn from them, instead of trying to stifle them.

It is critical to recognize that all knowledge is associated with power. All kinds of knowledge is created from communities with different understandings of the world. This means that all knowledge is associated with history and politics and so unbiased objectivity is impossible.

WGS is more outspoken than other disciplines when discussing power in society. This does not mean that WGS is more biased than other fields. It really just means that WGS confronts this issue head on. The field does not shy away from teaching students about controversial topics. Where else will students learn about them or have a safe space to discuss them?

Feminist Activism

You may remember another section at the beginning of this book with the same heading. Let's revisit that topic. We can see where we started with this topic and how far we've come over the course of the semester.

Women are making significant progress in many areas of society. Women are also integrated into most of the important cultural institutions in America. The overall big picture is far from perfect. Society as a whole has not changed and focused on equality as feminists have hoped. We have come a long way throughout history, but we still have a long way to go.

Violence is increasing on college campuses and in life in general. The balance of power is still skewed unequally. The power is also only in the hands of relatively few (old, white) men. Global climate change is also affecting everyone, no matter where they live. Capitalism and consumerism are also widening the gaps between the classes of people internationally. These are the issues that global feminist activism focus on. They, of course, are not the only feminist issues, but perhaps the largest and most well-known.

Some other issues addressed by feminism that are specific to college students include access to affordable higher education (re: student loans) and preparing for careers in a time of job uncertainty. Approximately a little more than half of all bachelor's degrees are earned by women. There are also more and more women in colleges and universities (Allen, Bracken, and Dean, 2008).

Many female college students are also thinking about ways to balance work and family. Women want to combine careers and motherhood. They want to choose when they combine those and they don't want their employers to try and influence them. Access to affordable childcare and equitable sharing of domestic responsibilities are also priorities. Access to affordable health care and reproductive services should also be at the top of the list, especially for students in college.

College students like yourself are talking about media and technology, specifically how both shape our society and culture. Students also question politicians and if they are making the best choices for them. These are the issues that many college students talk and write about, maybe you did the same thing this semester. These are also the issues that feminism is addressing, one way or another.

People may identify themselves feminists or not. (P.S. You should!) That identification may not be as important as collective action around these and other issues mentioned above. Issues such as: LGBQT issues and discrimination, sexual freedom, and safety from all kinds of abuse. Labels and identities are as important as the issues mentioned above. Discussion around claiming the term feminist continues to happen. When I'm in a discussion like that, I always refer back to one of my favorite quotes:

> *"Feminism has fought no wars. It has killed no opponents. It has set up no concentration camps, starved no enemies, practiced no cruelties. Its battles have been for education, for the vote, for better working conditions, for safety in the streets, for child care, for social welfare, for rape crisis centers, women's refuges, reforms in the law."* If someone says, *"Oh, I'm not a feminist,"* I ask, *"Why? What's your problem?"*
> — *Dale Spender (1980)*

Despite the belief that people in the United States have the ability to move out of poverty or into wealth, America and United Kingdom are the least mobile postindustrial societies. In 2011, about 1.46 million households lived in extreme poverty. Approximately 2.8 million children lived in extreme poverty during the same time (Shaefer & Edin, 2012).

Personal debt is also a major problem in the United States. Many people spend more than what they make each year. We need to use some feminist transformational politics with this issue. Encourage a consciousness shift about what is important in life. Practice generosity and compassion with each other. Use justice-based equality with a focus on love, dignity, and celebration of community.

As Audre Lorde (1984) so wisely said: "Your silence will not protect you (pg.41)." Lorde also wrote about the need to be part of social change efforts. During her lifetime, she encouraged feminists to speak out and address the problems in their lives and communities.

Feminist justice-based movements involve multi-issue and multi-strategic approaches to tackle important issues. Multi-issue means organizing on many fronts that include political, legal changes, educational reform, welfare rights, violence, and reproductive issues. Basically this text is comprised as a multi-issue approach to feminism.

Multi-strategic means working with coalitions that mobilize around shared issues toward a shared goal. Use this book after the class ends. Wave it in people's faces when they ask you to justify your feminist ideals. Check out the references and suggested readings. Tell your friends about feminism, WGS, and this class. Become active in your local feminist movement!

Liberal feminist activists work within the system and advocate for change from within. This kind of approach locates the source of inequality in society. The activists work to change women's lives through erasing the gender pay gap, sexual harassment policy, and parenting leaves. Legal attacks on abortion rights have been stopped by the work of liberal feminists. Civil rights legislation has also been the focus of scholars, activists, and politicians.

These liberal activist organizations tend to be hierarchical with a centralized governing structure and local chapters around the country. The National Organization of Women (NOW) and the American Association of University Women (AAUW) are good examples of this. They both are large national groups with active state and local chapters.

Other strategies take a radical approach. These groups want to change the system instead of adapting what we have now. Both liberal and radical feminists work together to advocate for justice-based equality. Current feminists use a variety of strategies to promote change.

Strategic differences can cause problems among feminists. However, different strategies can also strengthen the ability to work on multiple issues from multiple approaches. It makes sense that any given issue lends itself to both liberal and radical approaches. LGBTQ rights is something that can be challenged legally and politically. Organizations work through the official channels to fundraise and support the creation of laws for domestic partner rights or other civil protections. Consciousness-raising groups and grassroots events, like Pride days/parades, work locally. Working together, liberal and radical strategies can fight for equality. This is an example of a multi-strategic approach.

Just increasing women's participation and their active role in leadership does not automatically imply a more feminist future. There are plenty of women (and men) who don't support feminist values. Mixing up the people in charge, such as replacing men with women, doesn't mean that change will happen. The liberal feminist practice of considering females for leadership positions, simply because they are women, has been criticized for promoting women into positions of power and authority without examining their viewpoints on different aspects of feminism. However overall, encouraging women into leadership is important to feminist change.

Breakout: Feminist Visions

What does the future look like to you? How do you picture yourself using feminism in the future? Will technology help or hinder equality for everyone? Our visions of the future help us understand the present. We plan for the future based on how we think about the past and the present. We have to be mindful in the present so that we can see the likelihood for change.

We must also consider the issue of integrity. It is not only about the distinction between right and wrong, but also how we act out what we believe in our daily lives. What does feminist-inspired integrity look like? How does feminist integrity fit in your life and your future plans?

There are plenty of things to consider when planning your feminist future. Set feminist priorities and keep them. Priorities are essential, so decide what your truths are and base your priorities on your own values. Figure out which battles are worth fighting. Use your energy for things that really matter.

"Maria Alyokhina and Nadezhda Tolokonnikova are members of the band Pussy Riot. Pussy Riot is an internationally known Russian feminist punk rock protest group based primarily in Moscow."

Picture a feminist society that balances independence and individuality with collective responsibility. American culture values individualism in its utmost form. Our society often forgets that just because you have the right to do something, it doesn't mean that you can't be criticized about it. The Constitution exists to protect choices and rights, but it doesn't tell us which ones are best for us.

Technology is both liberating and limiting, but necessary for both the present and the future. Sustainability is also a concern as we need to figure out how to live now and save room for the future. We have to focus on sustainability, both ethically and efficiently.

We have to keep in mind that new technologies are not always the best solutions. They don't always work for the collective good. International capitalism is affecting both technological use and the sustainability of the Earth for the future.

There is only one world and we all live here. Global climate change is a huge issue and feminism needs to work on this issue. We can work on developing clean and sustainable energies to replace reliance on fossil fuels. As mentioned above, addressing international capitalism can also help with sustainability. What are the consequences for America's overall lack of sustainability? What happens if we continue to focus on fossil fuels? Environmental justice demands protection from nuclear testing and disposal of hazardous wastes that threaten our clean air, land, water, and food. Employees should also have the right to safe and healthy work environment. Workers shouldn't have to choose between employment and safety.

Intersectionality

What Is Intersectionality? Including everyone in feminism that wants to be included. Those with some kind of privilege typically have a harder time including oppressed people in their feminism. Sometimes people don't realize their privilege, so it's easier to focus on ways that people are oppressed. It can be easier to identify oppression than confronting people about their privilege.

We need intersectionality, because we can't be anti-oppressive without it. We have to use an intersectional framework to decipher the oppressions that people are experiencing. Women of color do not separate the racism they experience from the oppression related to their gender. Trans people with disabilities don't get to choose which part of their identity faces the most oppression. The issues they face are all a part of their larger experience.

Intersectionality isn't always easily defined. In my view, intersectionality is a framework that recognizes the multiple facets of identity that cultivate our experiences and that compounds different marginalizations. Multiple oppressions cannot be separated. They are experienced and executed within an intersectional framework. So the title of Flavia Dzodan's 2011 piece rings true: "My feminism will be intersectional or it will be bullshit."

To better understand the concept of intersectionality, let's look at one of the most cited pieces of evidence for the oppression of women: violence targeting women and girls. According to the CDC (n.d. B), 20 people per minute are victims of intimate partner violence in America. That's more than 10 million women and men yearly. Approximately 2 million women are raped in a year. Over 7 million women and men are stalking victims of stalking each year. This information is shocking, but also contributes to oppression by not breaking down the data by specific identities.

Women of color are more likely to experience these forms of violence than white women. The privilege of wealth can sometimes protect some women from forms of violence. Bisexual women experience more sexual violence than other groups of women (CDC, n.d. A). By breaking down the numbers we can pinpoint the oppression and work on ways to overcome it. That's a part of intersectional feminism.

All women are at risk for violence in America, but some women are more at risk. If we only talk generally about violence against women (or other issues), then we don't address all of the important issues. Without the main issues, we cannot create solutions that rid us of the oppressions at work in our lives.

Intersectionality is not only about breaking down the obvious problems like violence and inequality. It is also about letting people live full lives. It also lets them have a voice in the feminist movement.

Some critics think that intersectionality fosters separation and exclusion in the feminist movement. Other critics think that including race, class, sexuality, and other identities in feminist analysis spreads the movement too thin. They think it can't be unified with that many issues.

The trouble with a one-size-fits-all feminist movement is that the focus is only on the common ground between women. It will erase differences and focus on similarities. All women deal with sexism, but not all women deal with racial issues or trans issues or disability issues.

We shouldn't be glossing over the issues faced by particular groups of women, just to try to unify everyone into one central feminism. Those who decide what issues are considered feminist are often those who have the most privilege and visibility. Those people then take up a large amount of space in the movement and don't give up any space for others.

Intersectionality demands that we look within ourselves and identify where we feel challenged. We must take upon ourselves the desire to learn about issues and identities that do not impact us personally or that we don't easily understand. We need to challenge ourselves.

Identifying our own privilege is an important part of intersectional feminism. We need to have a basic theoretical understanding of feminism to start with. Then we can move beyond theory to consider how we treat people in our daily lives. We have to understand ourselves and our own problems, along with that of those close to us. If we don't consider those concerns, then our feminism will not be intersectional and productive.

We don't just have to use feminism to end sexism. We also have to end the systems of oppression that are all connected. Not only are they connected, but they affect different women in different ways.

For example, it might be challenging for a white middle-class woman to understand issues of poverty in the lives of Black people. Feminists can be knowledgeable about issues of race, but still need to listen to the stories of those different from our lived experiences. It's a similar situation for able bodied people, who might not easily recognize ableism. White people don't always easily recognize racism. Cis people don't always easily recognize transphobia.

Our privileges let us take a lot of things for granted. Recognizing the reasons behind our privilege is a prime example for the need for intersectional analysis. That analysis will allow us to do inclusive feminist work. We need to recognize our privilege and the issues around it so that we don't focus feminism just on those, but on issues that are often marginalized.

So you, as a WGS student, can identify your own privilege. Make an effort to seek out issues that you don't understand or know much about. Make space for your friends to share their different lived experiences and learn from them!

Be mindful of the space you are in. No matter what your privileges are or who you are, you can make a difference. Share your stories, but also know when to step back when things aren't about you. Educate yourself on things that don't affect you directly and broaden your perspective. Probably most important, listen to others when they share their own experiences.

Feminism is by no means perfect. Not by a long shot. Feminists must realize that everyone makes mistakes. We have to learn from the mistakes we make as you do feminist work. If you are reading this, then you might be learning about feminism for the first time. And that's great!

However, don't feel like you have to be an expert on all things of feminism. Take more classes; read more books. Pick a few issues within feminism that you are passionate about and focus on talking points for those. Listen and learn from other feminists. Join a feminist student group on campus!

Being an intersectional feminist is not easy. You have to seek out and try to understand things that are challenging for you. Empathize and support people who are not like you.

Don't speak over others. Give fellow feminists their space to speak, as they will do for you. Hold yourself accountable. Be prepared to not to know everything. Always continue to learn.

It is better to try and fail than it is to not try at all. Make an effort to be intersectional and don't dismiss other people's lived experiences. They are just as important as your own to the feminist movement.

You need to make mistakes and accept criticism. Be open to growing and self-correcting as part of your continuous learning process. You will mess up at one point or another and that's ok. You might be called out about a mistake, so think about how you would respond without being defensive. Your response to criticism matters.

Being called out is not an attack. It's about holding people accountable within the feminist movement. It's supporting the work being done and showing its value to the movement.

Instead of taking it personally, realize that being called out isn't about you as a person. You can have the best intentions and still do things that uphold repressive systems. Adjust your actions. Figure out how you make change in patriarchal oppression.

Intersectional feminism is hard. No one has ever said feminism is easy. Intersectional feminism is challenging and should make you uncomfortable.

Making people uncomfortable within feminism is another attempt to incite change. This involves critical thinking as feminists to challenge our privileges. We then work to create an intersectional lens for our feminism.

Working on intersectionality is a process. It's full of mistakes and that's fine. We all make mistakes. We have to learn from those and then move forward. That's the only way to be as intersectional as we can.

Conclusion

A feminist future is one that celebrates difference and diversity. A feminist future recognizes that diversity does not always equal equality. We can't just be tolerant of the differences among us. We must work toward equality for all. "Nothing About Us Without Us" is a popular chant and phrase used in the disability rights movement. It's a universal theme that can be applied to feminism as well.

Most importantly, it is important to have a sense of humor. We need to celebrate as much as we work. Amy Poehler (2014) says that if you can dance and be free and not embarrassed you can rule the world. So let's all take some time to dance so we can then go on to take over the world.

Feminism embraces equality for everyone. Our feminist future should improve the quality of our lives and our planet. A feminist future values all life. It works to share resources equally, using peaceful solutions for global problems. A feminist future will focus on justice and equality. We have nowhere to go but up and forward.

Suggested Readings

Aptheker, B. (2006). *Intimate politics: How I grew up red, fought for free speech, and became a feminist rebel.* Berkeley, CA: Seal Press.

Daly, M. (2006). *Amazon grace: Re-calling the courage to sin big.* New York: Palgrave Macmillan.

Finley, L., & Stringer, E. (2010). *Beyond burning bras: Feminist activist for everyone.* Santa Barbara, CA: Praeger.

Hewitt, N. (Ed.) (2010). *No permanent waves: Recasting histories of U.S. feminisms.* Piscataway, NJ: Rutgers University Press.

James, S., Foster, F., & Guy-Sheftall, B. (Eds.) (2009). *Still brave: The evolution of black women's studies.* New York: The Feminist Press.

References

Allen, J., Bracken, S., & Dean, D. (Eds.). (2008). *Most college students are women: Implications for teaching, learning, and policy.* Sterling, VA: Stylus.

CDC, (n.d. A). *NIPSVS Infographic.* Retrieved December 15, 2015 from http://www.cdc.gov/violenceprevention/nisvs/infographic.html

CDC, (n.d. B). *The national intimate partner and sexual violence survey.* Retrieved December 15, 2015 from http://www.cdc.gov/violenceprevention/nisvs/

Dzodan, F. (2011). *My feminism will be intersectional or it will be bullshit.* Retrieved December 15, 2015 from http://tigerbeatdown.com/2011/10/10/my-feminism-will-be-intersectional-or-it-will-be-bullshit/

Lorde, A. (1984). *Sister outsider: Essays and speeches.* Trumansburg, NY: Crossing Press.

Poehler, A. (2014). *Yes please.* New York: Dey Street Books.

Shaefer, H., & Edin, K. (2012). *Extreme poverty in the United States, 1996–2011.* Retrieved December 15, 2015 from http://www.npc.umich.edu/publications/policy_briefs/brief28/

Spender, D. (1980). *Man made language.* Ontario, Canada: Pandora Press.

Discussion Questions

1. How does a feminist classroom differ from a non-feminist classroom? What impact do these differences have on students?

2. What activist work must be done to build a truly inclusive, peaceful, healthy, and egalitarian community?

3. How can feminist activists build inclusive alliances and coalitions for social change?

4. How do you define intersectionality? What does it look like to you in the feminist movement?

5. How do you incorporate feminism into your future plans? Or in your current daily life?

The War on Women & Women's and Gender Studies

By Dr. Julee L. Rosser

"They prepare women psychologically for whatever role the society feels, at that particular point, they want her to play. After losing so many men, America wanted babies, and we wanted babies, its ok. But we gave up everything for that. We gave up everything."
(Lola Weixel, 1980, *The Life and Times of Rosie the Riveter*)

On April 5, 2012, the head of the Republican Party, compared women's reproductive rights with the concerns of caterpillars. In an interview with Al Hunt, Reince Priebus, Republican National Committee Chairman, was asked what he thought about the War on Women. He responded by saying:

> Well, for one thing, if the Democrats said we had a war on caterpillars, and mainstream media outlet talked about the fact that Republicans have a war on caterpillars, then we have problems with caterpillars. The fact of the matter is it's a fiction. (Political Capital with Al Hunt, 2012)

Does Priebus think we cannot recognize the difference between a War on Caterpillars (that is not happening) and the War on Women (that is happening)? In this interview, he used a tactic that has been used by many before him. He attempts to take the focus off of a very real problem and trivializes it. Minimizing women's concerns has become a hallmark the Republican Party.

The War on Women refers to the increase activity of political conservatives, who target women's bodies by attacking birth control and abortion availability. There are other ways the War on Women is manifesting itself. For instance, when House Republicans passed H.R. 4970, on May 16, 2012, they voted to exclude certain women from the Violence Against Women Act. The GOP version of the Violence Against Women Act, "leaves immigrant, Native American, and LGBT survivors inadequately protected" (Emily's List, 2012).

While this attack and other attacks on women's sexuality and equal pay are all incredibly important, for the scope of this paper, I will focus on the legislation about birth control and abortion availability. Then, I will discuss how women's studies offers the education to effectively offer resistance to the War on Women. At the end, I will apply a women's studies perspective to the current War on Women.

War on Women

"Last year, across the country, Republican lawmakers tried to turn over a thousand pieces of legislation into laws all aimed at restricting abortion or Reproductive Rights" (Fault Lines, 2012). In this section, I will report on attacks reproductive rights to birth control and access to abortion in the United States. Then, I will discuss how women's studies provides the education needed to respond to these attacks.

There are some who say the War on Women is a figment of the liberal imagination, like the War on Caterpillars, and others who say it's a lie. Montana Republican, Rep. Denny Rehberg, said, "It's all fabricated, this war on women. I don't get it," after he put "forward a budget that would eliminate funding for Title X and deny affordable care to 14,000 Montana women" (Women are Watching, 2012, p. 1). He "should consider his own legislative agenda before suggesting that the attacks on women's health don't exist" (Women are Watching, 2012, p.1).

The War on Women is not a figment of the liberal imagination, or a lie by the liberal media and the Democrats. It is an ongoing phenomenon of patriarchal control over women's bodies. "Among the litany of charges: Republicans are soft on domestic violence, they don't want women to be paid as much as men and they aren't willing to allow women to make their own decisions on contraception (Kim, 2012, p.1).

> Make no mistake about it—the Republican Party is attempting to cut off all access to abortion and to defund all family planning programs. Since 2011, the Republican controlled state legislatures have introduced over 1000 bills to cut off access to abortion and birth control or to humiliate women or girls through measures like transvaginal probe requirements for access to abortion services. (Feminist Majority Foundation, 2012)

The War on Women has dominated the Congressional calendar. "During the 46 weeks Congress was in session, from January 2011 through July 2012, the Republicans spent 38 of them attacking women's rights" (Emily's List, 2012).

Birth Control

Title X has "become a political whipping post for the GOP—despite the fact that none of the program's dollars are used to fund abortions" (Bassett, 2011, p. 1). Title X is being repeatedly attacked in the War on Women by House Republicans who seek to cut spending by targeted the Title X program.

Title X is "the federal family planning grant that funds birth control and preventative health services for more than five million low-income people annually" (Bassett, 2011, p. 1). It "was established under President Nixon in 1970 with bipartisan support and remained largely uncontroversial through the 1990s" (Bassett, 2011, p. 1). I was surprised to find out that "President George H. W. Bush and his family actually sat on the board of Planned Parenthood, and during his term in office he approved giving Planned Parenthood about $2.2 billion in federal funds" (Bassett, 2011, p. 1). Jacobson (2011) explains, "This was in the good ol' days" when Republicans were for Title X and before they were against it" (p. 1). "While women's rights have always been political, this was before it became fashionable and politically expedient to quite obviously sacrifice both evidence and women's bodies openly on the altar of electoral gains" (Bassett, 2011, states p. 1).

I will share two examples of attacks on Title X: one from Republican House Speaker John Boehner and the other from Montana Republican, Rep. Denny Rehberg. Boehner proposed a budget that would "eliminate funding for birth control and cancer screenings, defund Planned Parenthood, redirect funds for science-based teen-pregnancy-prevention initiatives into 'abstinence-only' programs" (Emily's List, 2011, p. 1). Rehberg, proposed a budget bill for fiscal year 2012 that "eliminates 79 wasteful programs" (Rehberg, 2012, p. 1). He considers Title X one of these "wasteful programs" (The United States House of Representatives Appropriations, 2012, pp. 81-82). "The budget would also defund Planned Parenthood, cut funding for teen pregnancy prevention initiatives and redirect it toward "abstinence only" education programs, and prevent abortions from being covered by insurance under the Affordable Care Act" (Bassett, 2011, p. 1).

Title X saves U.S. taxpayers money but "GOP lawmakers are trying to axe the program . . . in the in the name of slashing the deficit" (Bassett, 2011, p. 1).

Title X supporters argue that anti-abortion advocates should be the program's biggest supporters, since it helps more than a million low-income women to prevent unwanted pregnancies every year and thus reduces the overall number of abortions. Yet the latest wave of anti-Planned Parenthood sentiment among conservatives seems to have leaked over into all federally funded family planning programs. (Bassett, 2011, p. 1)

In this section, I shared two examples of attacks on Title X: one from Republican House Speaker John Boehner and the other from Montana Republican, Rep. Denny Rehberg. I cannot address all the attacks birth control availability with attacks on Title X in a short essay, so I focused on a few examples.

Abortion

In *The Abortion War*, a documentary about the repeated attacks on women's access to legal abortion, Elizabeth Nash, from the Guttmacher Institute, states:

Essentially, when you come to abortion, Americans go crazy. One side is trying to insure access so that women can have families when they want to and one side is trying to insure that every pregnancy ends in a baby.

Rep. Jim Buchy, a very active anti-choice Ohio Republican lawmaker, was asked why he thought a woman would want to have an abortion. He said, "It's a question I have never thought about" (Fault Lines, 2012). He has never thought about women's experiences with abortion, yet he supports legislative changes, like H.B. 125, The Heartbeat Bill, that would criminalize abortion if a heartbeat can be detected.

California Democratic Rep. Jackie Speier shared her experience with her abortion when she addressed the House of Representatives on Feb. 19, 2011, after the house voted to pass the Pence Amendment. A month earlier, Rep. Mike Pence, from Indiana, introduced H.R. 217, the "Title X Abortion Provider Prohibition Act". This Act, known as the Pence Amendment, "would prevent Planned Parenthood and 102 affiliated organizations from receiving any federal funds—including money for STD testing, pregnancy testing and cancer screenings (Bosch, 2011, p. 1).

Rep. Speier reflected on experience with abortion. She said:

When one of my colleagues on the House floor trivialized a woman's decision to have a second trimester abortion, I stood to correct his mischaracterization by giving my own account of a painful time in my life when the pregnancy my husband and I prayed for was unsuccessful . . . There was no guilt, only the pain of a pregnancy that did not work. The fetus had slipped from my uterus into my vagina and could not survive. To stave off a life-threatening infection and to keep the possibility of a future birth alive, I had what's called dilation and evacuation or "d & e." But for people, particularly my colleagues who don't want Planned Parenthood to be funded, I simply had an abortion. I am saddened and angered by how politicians misuse women's health. For some, describing a procedure like the one I endured is nothing more than talking points. But for millions of women like me, it's much more—it's something that will always be a part of us. (Speier, 2011, p. 1)

On February 18, 2011, the House passed H.R. 217 with a vote of 240 to 185. They did not value or appreciate a woman's experience with abortion and did not make their decisions based on women's actual experiences with abortion. The difference between Rep. Buchy and his lack of experience dealing with abortion and Rep. Jackie Speier and her very real experience with abortion should remind us how important it is for us to learn to understand and appreciate women's experiences with abortion.

Women's Studies Framework

Education in women's studies investigates women's experiences in detail and across racial, class, ability, and sexuality lines. Without education in women's studies, women's roles and women's experiences historically have been repeatedly marginalized and then controlled by men in positions of political power.

What is a women's studies framework? What is women's studies? "Women's studies is an important field of inquiry that arose from the effort to understand gender roles and women's historic struggle for justice throughout the world" (Berea, 2009, p. 1). In the United States, women's studies began following a decade of activism for equal human rights in the 1960s. The first women's studies department was created in 1970 . . . (at) San Diego State, "arriving on the heels of multiple social justice movements in which students and faculty were actively challenging the status quo of race and gender on their predominantly white male campuses" (Berger, 2012, p. 39). People concerned for women's rights came together with their belief that education was an important key in the struggle for equality.

Feminist activism in academia "forced new questions about academic study, and students and instructors brought such topics as domestic violence, the feminization of poverty, and women's health to the classroom" (Berger, 2012, p. 39). The movement spread and people went on to develop women's studies classes. "Courses about feminist theory and women's roles in history multiplied, and the first women's studies professors served as pioneers by mapping the readings and perspectives" (Berger, 2012, p. 39). Since then, there has been "an explosion of research and scholarship on women and gender issues, which helped give the new discipline academic legitimacy" (Reynolds, el al., 2007, p. 3).

Levin (2007) explains that an education in women's studies enables people to apply "cross-cultural and global awareness to 'big questions' about women and gender", consider "an issue from multiple perspectives", think critically, recognize "sexist / racist writing and thinking, and construct "arguments with evidence obtained from research" (p. 17). In addition to using gender as a category for analysis, an education in women's studies enables people to locate, evaluate, and interpret "diverse sources" of information "including statistics" (Levin, 2007, p. 17). An education in women's studies provides the opportunity "to connect knowledge and experience" and "theory and activism," and apply "knowledge for social transformation" and "citizenship" (Levin, 2007, p. 17). More than any other discipline, women's studies "values the interplay between scholarship, theory and activism, creating a new type of college student—and teacher—who is civically engaged, globally competent, self-reflective and dexterous in many disciplines. (Berger, 2012, p. 40)

Students and faculty in women's studies, "develop the ability to examine the cultural construction of gender, and exercise a feminist critique of dominant power relationships in the global community" including political, familial, social, and economic power relations (Berea, 2009, p. 1).

Using Education to Respond to the War on Women

Education can be used when responding to the recent trend of repeated attacks on women's rights by political conservatives who target women's bodies with attacks on birth control and abortion availability. Investigating the intersections of the roles and experiences of women and girls affected by the War on Women provides a richer understanding of the problems and more effective approaches to the solutions.

Today, one of the first things students learn in women's studies classes is how to look at women's lives through these multiple lenses. The concept of intersectionality has been a key factor in this transition. Intersectionality has brought the distinctive knowledge and perspectives of previously ignored groups of women into general discussion and awareness, and has shown how the experience of gender differs by race, class and other dimensions of inequality. (Dill, 2009, p. 1).

There is now more scholarly attention in women's studies to issues of race, class, ethnicity, sexuality, and ability as a way to understand the complexity of women's and men's lives—hence the inclusion of gender and sexuality in the titles of many departments and programs" (Berger, 2012, p. 40).

With women's studies, we investigate the trends and issues experienced by women and girls. Why is it important to bring awareness to the experiences of women and girls? It is important because we are living in a time of repeated attacks on reproductive rights. In a recent conversation about how birth control and abortion, Dr. Maude Jennings, activist and women's studies educator, said:

The men in the Congress have been insulting women for some time. From transvaginal examinations for abortions to cutting funds for women's health to retaining the lower wages for women and who knows when it will stop. Women have been under attack and we all seem to be letting it happen. Why is that? Why are all the rights we fought for so hard in the past being taken away and we aren't speaking out about it? Are times so hard that we are all living in fear?" (Personal Correspondence, Saturday August 11, 2012). Is it fear? If so, what are people afraid of? If not, what else might be happening?

Some people are living in fear while others are actively resisting patriarchal control of our lives. There are many ways to look at the War on Women. It is helpful to look at the trends that affect government control over women's bodies. We see one of these trends when looking at how governments tend to increase control over women's reproductive rights when service members are lost to war.

The United States started and fought two wars recently: Operation Enduring Freedom and Operation Iraqi Freedom. The Washington Post's *Faces of the Fallen* is "a collection of information about each U.S. service member who has died as a result of the wars in Iraq and Afghanistan" (2012, p. 1). According to *Faces of the Fallen*, 6,589 U.S. service members died in Operation Iraqi Freedom and Operation Enduring Freedom (Washington Post, 2012, p. 1). It is not uncommon for countries to become more pronatalist after war. "Pronatalist policies seek to increase birth rates and do this by reducing or banning contraception and abortion and providing government benefits based on family size" (Burn, 2011, p. 54).

Sometimes pronatalist policies are intended "to replace wartime casualties" (Burn, 2011, p. 54). For instance, "Following large casualties from war with Iran, in the 1980s Iraq banned contraceptives" (Burn, 2011, p. 54). Other times, it is meant to increase the workforce, like when "the Romanian government outlawed contraception in the 1970s and 1980s because it was feared that population growth was too low to keep up with projected labor needs" (Burn, 2011, p. 55). I contend the increase in pronatalist polices may be intended to replace wartime casualties. Is it possible that U.S. conservative Republican lawmakers are trying to establish more pronatalist policies to govern the girls and women because they want more children to be born to replace wartime casualties from Operation Enduring Freedom and Operation Iraqi Freedom?

Conclusion

In this essay, I described the War on Women, focusing on the legislation about birth control and abortion availability. I documented the attacks on Title X programs and abortion availability. Then I discussed how women's studies offers the education to effectively offer resistance to the War on Women by investigating the intersections of the roles and experiences of women and girls affected by the War on Women. In the end, I applied a women's studies perspective to the current War on Women, bringing up the issue of pronatalism as a cause for some of the attacks on women's reproductive rights.

Lola Weixel's insightful statement (at the beginning of the essay) comes from the documentary, *The Life and Times of Rosie the Riveter* (1980). Is it true that governments have such a strong hand in making women play whatever role society wants us to play?

War may not the only reason why conservative Republican lawmakers are attacking Title X programs and abortion access, but it certainly is one we should understand better. What do you think could be other contributing factors?

References

Bassett, L. (2011). *House GOP Targeting Title X In Push To Axe Family Planning Programs*. Found on September 20, 2012 at http://www.huffingtonpost.com/2011/10/04/title-x-republicans-planned-parenthood-family-planning_n_993957.html

Berea College (2009). *Women's & Gender Studies Program. Retrieved on 04-06-12 from http://www.berea.edu/womensstudies/default.asp.*

Berger, M. T. (2012). *So you want to change the world?* Ms. Magazine. Fall 2012 Vol. XXII, No. 3.

Bosch, T. (2011). *What Is the Pence Amendment, and What Does It Mean for Planned Parenthood?* Retrieved on September 3, 2012 at http://www.aolnews.com/2011/02/18/what-is-the-pence-amendment-and-what-does-it-mean-for-planned-p/.

Burn, S.M., (2011). *Women Across Cultures: A Global Perspective.* New York, NY: McGraw-Hill.

Clarity Films (1980). *The Life and Times of Rosie the Riveter.*

Dill, B. T. & Zamrana, R. (Eds.) (2009) *Emerging Intersections: Race, Class, and Gender in Theory, Policy, and Practice.*

Emily's List (2012). *War on women calendar.* Retrieved on September 1, 2012 at http://emilyslist.org/waronwomen.

Fault Lines (2012). *The Abortion War.*

Feminist Majority Foundation (2012). Mass e-mail received 8-23-2012.

Jacobson, J. (2011). *My how things change! President Bush praises family planning.* Retrieved on September 3, 2013 at http://www.rhrealitycheck.org/blog/2011/09/26/former-president-bush-praises-family-planning-ambassador-1972

Kim, S. M. (2012). *GOP lawmakers rebutting 'war on women'.* Retrieved on September 2, 2012 at http://www.politico.com/news/stories/0612/77043.html.

Levin, A. K. (2007). *Questions for a New Century: Women's Studies & Integrated Learning.* http://www.niu.edu/wstudies/staff/files/documentpretty.pdf

Political Capital with Al Hunt (April 5, 2012). *Republican Priebus Says Gender Battle Is Fictional* (Video). A Bloomberg Television production found at http://www.bloomberg.com/video/89986001-rnc-chairman-gop-gender-problem-a-media-fiction.html

Rehberg, D. (2011). *Chairman Rehberg statement on release of FY12 Labor, Health and Human Services, Education Appropriations Bill.* Retrieved on 9/20/2012 at http://rehberg.house.gov/index.cfm?sectionid=26&parentid=5&sectiontree=5,26&itemid=1758.

Reynolds, M., Shagle, S., & Venkataraman, L. (2007) *A National Census of Women's and Gender Studies Programs in U.S. Institutions of Higher Education.* Found on September 1, 2012 at http://082511c.membershipsoftware.org/files/NWSA_CensusonWSProgs.pdf

Speier, J. (2011). "Abortion" fuels intolerant thinking. Found on October 1, 2012 at http://www.huffingtonpost.com/rep-jackie-speier/abortion-fuels-intolerant_b_825783.html

The United States House of Representatives (2012). *Chairman Rehberg's FY12 Budget*. Found on 10-1-2012 at http://appropriations.house.gov/uploadedfiles/fy_2012_final_lhhse.pdf

Washington Post (2012). *Faces of the Fallen*. Found on October 5, 2012 at apps.washingtonpost.com/national/fallen

Women are Watching (2012). *Rep. Dennis Rehberg doesn't get it*. Found on October 5, 2012 at http://www.womenarewatching.org/article/rep-dennis-rehberg-doesnt-get-it.

CPSIA information can be obtained
at www.ICGtesting.com
Printed in the USA
LVOW02s1132270516
489329LV00001B/4/P

9 781465 278074